Italian
Grammar

Alwena Lamping
Author and Series Editor

talk

Published by BBC Active, an imprint of Educational Publishers LLP, part of the
Pearson Education Group, Edinburgh Gate, Harlow, Essex CM20 2JE, England.

© Educational Publishers LLP 2009

BBC logo © BBC 1996. BBC and BBC ACTIVE are trademarks of the British Broadcasting
Corporation.

First published 2009.

ISBN 978-1-4066-5235-2

Cover design: Johanna Gale
Cover photograph: © David Sutherland/Alamy
Insides design and layout: BBC Active design team
Illustrations © Mark Duffin
Publisher: Debbie Marshall
Development editor: Francesca Logi
Language consultant: Liviana Ferrari
Project editor: Emma Brown
Marketing: Fiona Griffiths
Senior production controller: Franco Forgione

Printed and bound in the UK by Ashford Colour Press Ltd.

The Publisher's policy is to use paper manufactured from sustainable forests.

Contents

introduction

Talk Italian Grammar is the essential handbook for anyone setting out to learn Italian, at home or in a class. With its straightforward approach and clear layout, it promotes a real understanding of how Italian works and how it relates to English.

It's much more than an ordinary grammar book. Using the tried-and-tested principles of the bestselling **Talk** series, it demystifies grammar and guides you through the key structures of Italian in a way that's really easy to follow even if you have no experience at all of grammar and its terminology.

Its parallel focus is on building a large vocabulary – fast – for you to combine with an understanding of grammar to say whatever you want in Italian, without having to rely on phrase books.

Among its special features you'll find:

- systematic references to **the most significant differences** in the way Italian and English work

- clear **jargon-free explanations** of Italian grammar, set out in units and illustrated by hundreds of **practical examples**

- **Word power** pages, tailored to individual units. Some of these focus on the fact that large numbers of Italian and English words are easy to convert from one language to the other if you know what to look out for. **False friends** are highlighted too: words which look as though they might mean one thing but in fact mean something different.

- great **learning tips and strategies**, positioned just where you need them

- **dictionary guidance**, with abbreviations and sample entries

- regular **Checkpoints** with practice activities to reinforce the language patterns and help you remember them. These are also useful as revision or to jog your memory.

- **verb tables**: full tables of widely used regular and irregular verbs

- a **glossary of grammar term**s with examples in English to make them crystal-clear

- a **comprehensive easy-to-use index**.

Talk Italian Grammar can be used successfully alongside any learning materials, and is the perfect companion for both levels of **Talk Italian**. The **Talk** series has online activities at www.bbc.co.uk/languages/italian, and if you'd like to practise your grammar online, try out the grammar section of the **Steps** course at the same address.

How to use Talk Italian Grammar

This book works on several levels – make it work for you!

New to language learning or forgotten everything you've learnt? Or perhaps you already know some Italian words but have no structure to use them in?
Go to **Getting started** on page 8 which gives you an overview of what grammar is about, introduces you to the keystones of grammar and offers a few short activities to help you recognise and remember them.

New to Italian but understand the meaning of basic terms such as noun, adjective, verb?
Go to page 10 which prepares you for learning Italian by highlighting the principal differences between Italian and English.

Learning Italian on your own or in a class and need extra support?
Choose the unit you want, work through it then complete the **Checkpoint** at the end to see how much you've understood and remembered. You can select the units in the order that suits you because they're free-standing and they cross-reference to each other so that you can easily check things out if you need to.

Need a clear and comprehensive Italian grammar reference book?
The index will show you where everything is. It uses key words in English and Italian as well as grammar terms, making it easy for you to find what you're looking for quickly.

Want to brush up on your Italian or do some revision?
The first page of each unit summarises the key points. Reading these and trying your hand at the **Checkpoint** activities will pinpoint any gaps in your knowledge so that you know what might be useful to spend some time on.

Just want to generally improve your Italian, deepen your understanding and boost your vocabulary?
Dip into the book at random, reminding yourself of the structures, reading the examples, checking out the **Word power** pages and using the **Checkpoints**.

getting started

What is grammar?

When we talk we do more than just say words randomly; we use them in a specific order and they relate to one another. Grammar is the explanation of how that works: it provides definitions of the structures of a language and how they're used.

Can I communicate without learning grammar?

Yes – if you're happy restricting yourself to phrases from a book or pidgin-type communication. You'll just about be able to make yourself understood but conversation will be a strain and communication hit-and-miss. With relatively little knowledge of grammar you can produce correct and unambiguous Italian instead. You'll sound more articulate and it will be a much more constructive and satisfying experience.

How do babies cope without knowing about grammar?

It's true that children learn to talk without ever having heard of a verb or a noun. But if you listen to a toddler you'll often hear words like *hided*, *eated*, *sheeps* or *mans*, showing that the child has in fact absorbed the regular patterns of English and is applying them quite unconsciously – albeit not always correctly. As time goes on, irregularities get ironed out and the child, with no apparent effort, starts saying *hid* and *ate*, *sheep* and *men*.

It takes many months of constant exposure to a language to learn in this way. By the time the average child is starting to form sentences, he will have been hearing his mother tongue for around 4,500 hours over a period of 20 months or so.

Most adults want results more quickly than that. By consciously learning how Italian is structured and how new words fit within sentences, you shortcut the process considerably. But you'll still experiment and make mistakes, just as children do, because that's part of the learning curve too.

How much grammar will I need?

At the start, you can get by comfortably with the basics. As you carry on with your Italian you'll gradually accumulate knowledge, and more pieces of the jigsaw will slot into place. There are some aspects of grammar that you might never need or want to know about – as with most things there's a level that's largely of interest only to the professional or the enthusiast.

Where do I start?

It pays to become familiar with some of the terms used to describe how a language works because it allows you to make sense of statements that you might come across in course books, such as: *The adjective usually goes after the noun* or *The definite article is not used when …*

Focus first on the six main building blocks of a sentence. Read these descriptions, then see if you can pick them out in sentences.

- **Nouns** are the words for living beings, things, places and abstract concepts: *woman, son, doctor, Oliver, dog, table, house, Scotland, time, joy, freedom.*
- **Pronouns** are words used to avoid repeating a noun: *I, me, we, us, you, he/she, him/her, it, they, them, these, ours.*
- **Articles** are *the, a/an* and *some.*
- **Adjectives** are words that describe nouns and pronouns: ***good*** *wine*; ***strong red*** *wine*; ***my*** *wine*; *I am* ***tired***; *it was* ***superb***.
- **Adverbs** add information to adjectives, verbs and other adverbs: ***very*** *good wine*; *you speak* ***clearly***; *you speak* ***really*** *clearly*.
- **Verbs** are words like *go, sleep, eat, like, have, be, can, live, do, die* that relate to doing and being.

---

1 Have a look at the underlined words and write N by the nouns, V by the verbs and ADJ by the adjectives.

  a <u>Sofia</u> works for a <u>glossy</u> <u>magazine</u>. She <u>organises</u> <u>interviews</u>, <u>hires</u> <u>professional</u> <u>models</u> and <u>photographers</u> and <u>travels</u> all over the <u>world</u>. Her <u>boyfriend</u> is a <u>well-known</u> <u>actor</u>.

  b <u>My</u> <u>father</u> <u>comes</u> from <u>Naples</u> although he <u>lives</u> in <u>Rome</u> because he <u>works</u> at the <u>central</u> <u>office</u> of a <u>large</u> <u>company</u>.

  c They <u>prepared</u> a <u>fantastic</u> <u>meal</u> for us. We <u>ate</u> <u>grilled</u> <u>fish</u>, <u>fresh</u> <u>asparagus</u> and <u>new</u> <u>potatoes</u>, <u>drank</u> a <u>superb</u> <u>Italian</u> <u>white</u> <u>wine</u> – and the <u>dessert</u> was absolutely <u>incredible</u>.

2 Now pick out the adjectives ADJ and the adverbs ADV.

  a The house was <u>very</u> <u>reasonable</u> but it was <u>rather</u> <u>dilapidated</u> … and the garden was <u>really</u> <u>small</u> and <u>overgrown</u>.

  b We played <u>superbly</u>. It wasn't our fault that the pitch was <u>terribly</u> <u>uneven</u> and the ref <u>deliberately</u> <u>unfair</u>.

How different are Italian and English?

On the whole, Italian grammar is very similar to English, but there are a few aspects which are rather different. If you're prepared for these, you'll find that you get used to them very quickly.

Gender: masculine and feminine

Every single Italian noun – not just the words for people and animals – is either masculine (m) or feminine (f). There's no sense of *it*, not even for things like cars, furniture, sport or days of the week – everything is *he* or *she*. Words linked to a noun, such as articles and adjectives, also have to be masculine or feminine.

The endings of nouns and adjectives

Nouns and adjectives end in a vowel, and that vowel is significant. It can show whether the word is masculine or feminine: generally speaking -**o** is masculine and -**a** is feminine – as you might expect from names like Antonio, Giorgio, Leonardo, Maria, Anna, Angela. Also, when there's more than one of something, instead of -**s** being added as in English, the end vowel changes.

Articles

There are seven versions of *the* in Italian. The one you use depends on whether the following noun is masculine or feminine, singular or plural; whether it begins with a vowel or a consonant. And there are four words for *a/an*.

Different versions of *you*

In English there's only one word for *you*; in Italian there are three, depending on who you're talking to. **Tu** and **lei** convey different degrees of familiarity, friendliness and respect when you're talking to one person. When there's more than one person, you use **voi**.

Verb endings; I, we, you, s/he, they

In English a verb stays pretty much the same no matter who's carrying it out: *I eat, we eat, you eat, the cats eat, Joe eats*.
In Italian, instead of using *I*, *you*, *she*, etc. you change the ending of the verb to show who's doing what.

Word order

On the whole, word order is similar to English. The most noticeable differences are adjectives which come after nouns, not before them as in English: **musica classica** *classical music*. Also, words like *it* and *them* often come before a verb not after it.

What about vocabulary?

Learning a new language is a several-pronged process. Knowledge of grammar has a key place, with even a few simple structures going a long way towards making sure you're understood. Knowing how to use verbs and when to include words like **ma** *but*, **perché** *because* or **altrimenti** *otherwise* take you a big step further, letting you express more complex thoughts.

But all these are of limited use without a good stock of words to slot into the structures – and the most obvious source of these is a dictionary.

What sort of dictionary is best?

When choosing your first English/Italian dictionary, go for a medium-sized one. Too small and it won't give you enough information; too big and it will confuse you with too much. There are also dictionaries online, many of them free.

Why are dictionaries so full of abbreviations?

Some words are straightforward, with just one meaning: **preferire** *prefer* can only be a verb, **possibile** *possible* can only be an adjective.

Others are more complex, with the same word belonging in more than one grammatical category. *Mind* can mean what you think with (noun) and to look after (verb). *Book* can mean something you read (noun) and it can mean to reserve a place (verb). *Calm* can mean peaceful (adjective), peace (noun) and to soothe (verb).

To make sure you find the right category of word, each has an abbreviation next to it. The most common are:

art article	*adj* adjective	*adv* adverb
f feminine	*m* masculine	*n* noun
pl plural	*prep* preposition	*pron* pronoun
sing singular	*v* verb	

You may find slight variations in some dictionaries so it's worth checking with the introduction.

How do I make sure I choose the right translation?

Some words have more than one meaning even within the same grammatical category: the adjective *hard* can mean *solid* and it can mean *difficult*. The noun *habit* can be something a nun wears or it can be something you do on a regular basis. The verb to *press* can mean to iron clothes or to push down on something.

There's often an explanation or a phrase to guide you, but if you've looked up an English word and are still not sure which of the Italian translations to use, look them all up and see what English translations are given.

hard *adj* **1.** duro, rigido: ~ *seat* sedia dura; ~ *surface* superficie rigida
2. difficile: ~ *problem* problema difficile **3.** severo, rigido: ~ *father* padre severo; ~ *winter* inverno rigido **4.** duro, vigoroso ~ *match* partita dura
5. ~ *shoulder* corsia d'emergenza; *to learn the hard way* imparare per esperienza

habit *n* **1.** abitudine *f*, usanza *f*: *force of* ~ forza dell'abitudine
2. vizio *m*: *bad* ~ brutto vizio; *drug* ~ vizio della droga, tossicodipendenza
3. (*relig*) abito *m*, tonaca *f*

press *v* **1.** premere: *to* ~ *the right key/button* premere il tasto/ pulsante giusto **2.** spremere: *to* ~ *oranges* spremere delle arance **3.** stirare: *to* ~ *a shirt* stirare una camicia **4.** comprimere *to* ~ *down* **5.** stringere *to squeeze*
6. denunciare *to* ~ *charges* **7.** insistere: *to* ~ *for an answer* insistere per una risposta

What if I can't find the word I'm looking for?

This is where your knowledge of grammar comes in. The two main points to remember are that:

- adjectives in a dictionary are in the masculine singular
- verbs are in the infinitive, so you have to replace any other endings with **-are**, **-ere** or **-ire** before you look up a verb.

If you still have a problem, it probably means that you've come across part of an irregular verb, the most common of which are written out in full on pages 191–241.

How else can I build up a wide vocabulary?
The most obvious source of Italian outside Italy is the internet, where you can find information in Italian on practically anything. Use a dictionary to find the key words relating to your interests then just browse. You'll be surprised at how much Italian you absorb when words are in a familiar context that interests you.

Don't forget that you already have a huge latent vocabulary simply because, for historical reasons, Italian and English have a lot of words in common. Some word groups are all but identical, others have moved apart slightly. These are the main focus of the **Word power** pages, which show you how to 'convert' from one language to the other. Not only will you find your vocabulary increasing dramatically but you'll also have the knowledge and the confidence to make an educated guess at the meaning of new words.

Is it true that many English words are used in Italian?
Over the years Italian and English have borrowed and absorbed many words from each other. Most of them have stayed unchanged but a few have adapted to their adopted language. For example, *stressed* is **stressato** and *to click* is **cliccare**, while **snobismo** has become an Italian noun from *snob*.

Similarly, the rules of English grammar are often applied to Italian imported words: when ordering more than one **cappuccino** people don't ask for **cappuccini** as an Italian would but add *-s* as if it were an English word. Some words have acquired a whole new meaning: in Italy **un golf** is a *sweater*, **footing** is used for *jogging* and **box** means *garage*.

Do these shared words sound the same?
Many of them are recognisable for speakers of the other language – but many more are pronounced with a 'local' accent, whether Italian or English. When you hear something like *hard drive* pronounced the Italian way, you'll be as surprised as an Italian is on hearing **bruschetta** pronounced *brooshetter* or the **g** sounded in **tagliatelle**.

The key to good pronunciation is to assume that even words you recognise on paper might sound different in Italian, and to approach **Sounds and Spelling** on page 15 with a completely open mind.

Here are just a few of the Italian words used in English:

scenario	*cappuccino*
manifesto	*espresso*
propaganda	*broccoli*
graffiti	*salame*
stiletto	*risotto*
casino	*pasta*
paparazzi	*villa*
incognito	*terracotta*
vendetta	*pergola*
diva	*studio*
impresario	*replica*
pronto	*lava*
bravo	*orchestra*
ghetto	*tempo*
idea	*prima donna*
zero	*solo*
fiasco	*piano*
motto	*cello*

… and some English words regularly used in Italian:

sport	weekend
tennis	shopping
squash	fashion
golf	relax
windsurf	stress
club	bar
computer	business
mouse	manager
default	leader
internet	marketing
network	meeting
spam/spamming	stop

Sounds and spelling

In English, letters sound different according to which word they're in.
a: c**a**rt, c**a**re, w**a**r, wom**a**n
ea: b**ea**rd, h**ea**rd, m**ea**t, gr**ea**t, thr**ea**t

This doesn't happen in Italian, where the connection between a letter and its sound doesn't vary from one word to the next.
a is always pronounced like *a* in *arm*: p**a**sta, Chi**a**nti,
ea is always pronounced like *e* in *end*, followed by *a*: id**ea**, Cor**ea**.

This means that once you're familiar with a few straightforward rules, you'll know how to pronounce any new words that you come across.

As well as knowing those rules, the key to success lies in remembering never to pronounce Italian words as if they were English, even when they look identical or have become accepted as English. For example:
olive *olives* is pronounced ol<u>ee</u>veh
per *for* is pronounced like *per* in *periscope*, not like *purr*
pane *bread* is pronounced <u>pah</u>neh
cinema is pronounced <u>chee</u>nehmah
automobile *car* is pronounced owtoh<u>moh</u>beeleh
bruschetta is pronounced broo<u>sket</u>ta
tagliatelle is pronounced talia<u>tel</u>leh

Finally, good pronunciation comes from listening at every available opportunity to native Italian speakers, and practising new words and phrases by saying them out loud. At first, exaggerate your pronunciation and **act** Italian: open your mouth more than you do for English and use the muscles of your face more.

pronunciation

vowels

Italian vowel sounds are pure and always pronounced distinctly, even when there are two or more next to each other. And they're never silent like the -e in English words like *make*, *some* or *file*.

They sound much as they do in these English words, with the vowel longer in some words than others but still essentially the same sound.

a	c**a**t/c**a**rt
e	p**e**n/p**ay**
i	m**ee**t
o	p**o**t/p**our**
u	c**oo**l

consonants

Most consonants sound very similar in Italian and English, and the only ones to look out for are **c**, **g**, **h**, **r**, **s** and **z**. A double consonant has the same sound as the single version but it's longer and stronger.

	English	
c + e/i	*ch*	**ci**occolato, cappu**cci**no, dol**ce**
c + h	*k*	**Chi**anti, **chi**lo
c + all other letters	*k*	**c**affè, **c**rema
g + e/i	*j*	**ge**lato, **gi**n
gn	*ny*	lasa**gne**, bolo**gne**se, **gn**occhi
gli	*lli*	tag**li**atelle, conchi**gli**e
g + other letters	*g*	spa**gh**etti, ra**gù**
h has no sound of its own – but it changes the sounds of **c** and **g**		
r is a strong sound as it is in Scotland		
s	*s*	pa**s**ta, pe**s**to
s between two vowels	*z*	ro**s**a, ba**s**e
s + ce/ci	*sh*	**sce**nario, pro**sci**utto
s + c + other letters	*sk*	bru**sc**hetta, Lambru**sc**o
z can either be	*dz* or *tz*	**z**ucchini, pi**zz**a

stress

Some words have a written accent indicating that the stress is on the final vowel: **difficoltà**, **caffè**, **tassì**. But as a general rule, Italian words have the stress on the last syllable but one: **animale**, **tradizione**, **cappuccino**, **professore**.*

*The final **e** is dropped from titles like **professore**, **signore** or **dottore** when they're followed by a name but the stress stays in the same place: **professor Rinaldi**, **signor Armani**, **dottor Agnello**.

However, there are exceptions to the normal stress patterns, and most of these have the stress on the third syllable from the end. In this book they're highlighted: **sabato**, **telefono**, **economico**. An important example of unusual stress is the third person plural of verbs in the present tense, where the stress is never on the **-ano/-ono** ending: **arrivano**, **telefonano**.

There are a handful of words where the position of the stress makes all the difference to the meaning:

panico panic	**panico** millet
subito straightaway	**subìto** suffered
capitano they happen	**capitano** captain

accents

A few identical words have a written accent to distinguish between them:

Papa Pope	**papà** daddy
ancora still, yet	**àncora** anchor
da from	**dà** gives
e and	**è** is
la the	**là** there
li them	**lì** there
ne of it/them	**né** neither/nor
si himself/herself/one	**sì** yes
te you	**tè** tea

Other words with accents include one-syllable words such as:
già already, **giù** down, **più** more, **può** he/she can

The accent used most is the grave accent (ˋ). The acute accent (ˊ) is mainly found in words ending in **ché** and **tré**, e.g. **perché** why/because, **trentatré** 33, showing that the **é** is pronounced ay not eh.

the Italian alphabet

Italian uses much the same alphabet as English, but doesn't include **j**, **k**, **w**, **x** and **y**. When spelling words out, the letters of the alphabet sound like the highlighted parts of the English words in the third column below. The towns listed in the right-hand column are used when clarification is needed, in the same way as the UK uses: *alpha*, *bravo*, *charlie* … *x-ray*, *yankee*, *zulu*.

a	a	**arm**	Ancona
b	bi	**bee**	Bologna
c	ci	**chea**p	Como
d	di	**dee**p	Domodossola
e	e	**e**nd	Empoli
f	effe	ref**eree**	Firenze
g	gi	**gi**raffe	Genova
h	acca	**j**ackal	Hotel
i	i	**eel**	Imola
l	elle	**ele**ment	Livorno
m	emme	**emmet**	Milano
n	enne	**ene**my	Napoli
o	o	**off**	Otranto
p	pi	**peep**	Padova
q	qu	**qu**estion	Quarto
r	erre	fe**rre**t	Roma
s	esse	**esse**ntial	Savona
t	ti	**tee**	Torino
u	u	p**u**t, f**oo**d	Udine
v	vu/vi	**voo**doo/**vee**	Venezia
z	zeta	**dzehta**	Zara

Although **j**, **k**, **w**, **x** and **y** don't feature in the Italian alphabet, they're needed when spelling out non-Italian names, email addresses, acronyms, website links and so on, and are said as follows:

j	**i lunga**
k	**cappa**
w	**doppia vu**
x	**ics**
y	**ipsilon** or **i greca**

spelling things out

Spelling out Brighton would sound like this:
bee, erre, ee, gee, acca, tee, oh, enne

Double is **doppia**, so Liverpool would be:
elle, ee, voo, eh, erre, pee, doppia oh, elle

When using **Ancona**, **Bologna**, etc. the link word is **come** *as/like*:
James: **i lunga, a come Ancona, emme come Milano, e come Empoli, esse come Savona**
Bond: **bi come Bologna, o come Otranto, enne come Napoli, di come Domodossola**

punctuation marks

* **asterisco**	@ **chiocciola, chiocciolina**
. **punto**	/ **barra**
, **virgola**	\ **barra inversa**
; **punto e virgola**	# **cancelletto**
: **due punti**	*ABC upper case* **maiuscola**
- **trattino**	*abc lower case* **minuscola**
_ **trattino basso**	*(in brackets)* **tra/fra parentesi**
space **spazio**	*"in inverted commas"* **tra/fra virgolette**

It's useful to know the Italian for punctuation marks and keyboard symbols for when you want to spell out, for example, your **indirizzo email** *email address*.

And when spelling out a **sito internet/sito web** *website* or a **pagina web** *web page*, you need *www* which is pronounced **vu vu vu**.
www.bbcactive.com would sound like this:
vu vu vu, punto, bee, bee, chee, ah, chee, tee, ee, vu, eh, punto, com

… and if you add */languages*:
barra, elle, ah, enne, gee, oo, ah, gee, eh, esse

Have a go at saying it out loud, then try spelling your own name and email address.

capital letters

Italian uses **lettere maiuscole** *capital letters* less than English. They're used at the beginning of a sentence but they're not used for:

- **io** *I* (unless it starts a sentence)
- titles followed by a surname:
  la signora Perrone *Mrs Perrone*; **il dottor Valletta** *Dr Valletta*
- names of days or months (see page 28):
  giovedì *Thursday*; **marzo** *March*
- languages, peoples or adjectives of nationality:
  Parlo inglese *I speak English*;
  gli italiani *the Italians*; **i gallesi** *the Welsh*;
  sono scozzese *I'm Scottish*; **un paese europeo** *a European country*

Capital letters ***are*** used:

- in very formal or legal correspondence for **Lei**, **Loro**, **Voi** *you*, and related words such as **Le**, **Vi**, **Vostro** *your*:
  La ringraziamo per la Sua lettera. *Thank you for your letter.*
  la Vostra gentile richiesta di ... *your valued enquiry concerning ...*
- for names of people and institutions:
  Giovanni e Marta abitano qui. *Giovanna and Marta live here.*
  Unione Europea *European Union*; **Stati Uniti** *United States*; **Croce Rossa** *Red Cross*
- for place names:
  continenti: Africa, America del Nord/Sud, Asia, Antartide *Antarctica*, **Europa**
  paesi: Australia, Canada, Finlandia, Francia, Galles, Germania, Inghilterra, Irlanda, Irlanda del Nord, Italia, Nuova Zelanda, Regno Unito *UK*, **Scozia, Spagna, Svezia** *Sweden*, **Svizzera** *Switzerland*
  città: Roma, Londra, Milano, Napoli, Torino, Palermo, Berlino, Parigi, Firenze, Edimburgo

If you see **Rispettare maiuscole e minuscole** on, for example, a login page or a form, it means that it's case sensitive; literally *Respect upper and lower case.*

word power

Look at the way these consonants correspond in English and Italian.

🇬🇧	🇮🇹	
bs	s/ss	*absolute* **assoluto**, *absurd* **assurdo**, *abstract* **astratto**, *observatory* **osservatorio**, *obstacle* **ostacolo**, *substance* **sostanza**
ct	tt	*active* **attivo**, *actual* **attuale**, *character* **carattere**, *correct* **corretto**, *direct* **diretto**, *October* **ottobre**, *sector* **settore** but not in the ending -*ction*: *action* **azione**, *section* **sezione**
dm	mm	*administration* **amministrazione**, *admire* **ammirare**, *admit* **ammettere**
dv	vv	*adverb* **avverbio**, *adversary* **avversario**, *advocate* **avvocato**
j	g	*jaguar* **giaguaro**, *Japan* **Giappone**, *Jordan* **Giordania**, *jewel* **gioiello**, *juvenile* **giovanile**, *Juliet* **Giulietta**, *jury* **giuria**
k	c /ch	*kangaroo* **canguro**, *kayak* **caiaco**, *kilo* **chilo**, *kilometre* **chilometro**, *Korea* **Corea**
h	-	*habitual* **abituale**, *heroism* **eroismo**, *horizontal* **orizzontale**, *horrible* **orribile**, *hospital* **ospedale**, *humid* **umido**, *alcoholic* **alcolico**, *prehistoric* **preistorico**, *vehement* **veemente**
ns	s	*construction* **costruzione**, *transfer* **trasferire**, *transmission* **trasmissione**, *transport* **trasporto** but not in words like **transatlantico**, **transalpino**, **transcontinentale**
ph	f	*pharmacy* **farmacia**, *philosophy* **filosofia**, *photograph* **fotografia**, *telephone* **telefono**, *Stephen* **Stefano**
pt	tt	*adopt* **adottare**, *Egypt* **Egitto**, *helicopter* **elicottero**
x	s	*exclude* **escludere**, *exercise* **esercizio**, *explosion* **esplosione**, *export* **esportare**, *taxi* **tassì** *excuse* **scusa**, *explain* **spiegare**, *extraordinary* **straordinario**

checkpoint 1

1   These names illustrate the contents of this unit and are useful
    pronunciation practice. Say them out loud – the position of
    stress is shown – and work out the English equivalents.

    Men: Vittorio, Matteo, Ugo, Ettore, Filippo, Enrico
    Women: Giulia, Giada, Elena, Ilaria, Alessandra, Giuseppina
    Countries: Cile, Turchia, Giamaica, Filippine, Cina

2   Now do the same with these random words:
    avventura, ossessivo, perfetto, fosforo, oscuro, fotocopia,
    trattore, ammirazione, ammiraglio, stravagante, orrendo

3   When spelling words out, what towns are used for the letters
    b, **f**, **n** and **r**?

4   How is *www* pronounced?

5   How do you say @ in an email address?

6   la tanzania è un paese africano Which of the words in this
    sentence need a capital letter?

7   Where does the stress go in most Italian words?

8   Is Papà or Papa the Italian for *Pope*?

9   Does te or tè mean *you*? And does da or dà mean *from*?

10 Without looking at page 20, name four western European
    countries in Italian.

> Once you're comfortable with spelling out your own details,
> have a go at spelling out the names and email addresses of
> friends and family.

Numbers, time and date

Numbers aren't difficult to learn in Italian.

- 1-10 have a flow and a rhythm to them, so that they're best learnt by repeating them out loud.
- 11-19 don't flow quite as smoothly because 17, 18 and 19 have a different pattern from 11-16.
- 20 and onwards are straightforward once you're familiar with 1-10, just as they are in English.

One difference from English is that there are no spaces between digits when larger numbers are written down in Italian:
centocinquantacinque *a hundred and fifty-five*

Don't be fazed by this thought – you actually see large numbers written as words very rarely.

A more crucial difference is the punctuation used with numbers.
In Italian:

- **punto** *full stop*, or a space, separates thousands:
  24.000   24 000
- **virgola** *comma* is used to indicate a decimal point:
  7,5 **sette virgola cinque**; 0,4 **zero virgola quattro**

Zero is **zero** in Italian. If you look it up in a dictionary, you'll find it has the following English translations:

zero 1. nought, zero: *sotto* ~ below zero; *sopra* ~ above zero;
ora ~ zero hour; *cominciare da* ~ start from scratch **2.** *[sport]* nil:
vincere per due a ~ to win 2-0 **3.** *[tennis]* love: *trenta a* ~ thirty-love.
4. *[telephone]* 0

The plural of **zero** is **zeri**: **due zeri** *two noughts*.

cardinal numbers 1-99

1	uno	11	undici
2	due	12	dodici
3	tre	13	tredici
4	quattro	14	quattordici
5	cinque	15	quindici
6	sei	16	sedici
7	sette	17	diciassette
8	otto	18	diciotto
9	nove	19	diciannove
10	dieci		

- uno changes to agree with its noun, like *a/an* (see page 44):
  un parco, un adulto, uno chef, una persona, un'idea

20	venti	30	trenta
21	ventuno	40	quaranta
22	ventidue	50	cinquanta
23	ventitré	60	sessanta
24	ventiquattro	70	settanta
25	venticinque	80	ottanta
26	ventisei	90	novanta
27	ventisette		
28	ventotto		
29	ventinove		

- The numbers 31–99 repeat the pattern 21–29:
  quarantotto *48*, **settantacinque** *75*, **novantanove** *99*
- **venti, trenta, quaranta,** etc. drop the final vowel before **uno** and **otto**:
  trentuno *31*, **cinquantotto** *58*
- **ventuno, trentuno,** etc. drop the final -o before a noun:
  ventun giorni *21 days*
- **tre** has a written accent when combined with another number:
  ottantatré *83*
- % is **per cento** and percentages start with **il**:
  il trenta per cento *30%*

100 +

100	cento	1 000	mille
101	centouno	1 100	millecento
102	centodue	1 500	millecinquecento
110	centodieci	2 000	duemila
150	centocinquanta	10 000	diecimila
200	duecento	100 000	centomila
500	cinquecento	500 000	cinquecentomila
		1 000 000	un milione
		2 000 000	due milioni
		1 000 000 000	un miliardo

In the plural:
- **cento** *a hundred* doesn't change:
  300 **trecento**, 500 **cinquecento**, 700 **settecento**
- **mille** *a thousand* changes to -mila:
  2 000 **duemila**, 5 000 **cinquemila**
- **un milione** *a million* and **un miliardo** *a billion* have the regular plurals **milioni** and **miliardi**. They're followed by **di** when used alone before a noun: **un milione di euro** *1,000,000 euro*
  cinque milioni di sterline *5,000,000 pounds*
  sette miliardi di dollari *7,000,000 dollars*
  … but **un milione cinquecentomila euro** *1,500,000 euro*

approximate numbers

- **una decina** *about 10* and **una dozzina** *a dozen* require **di** when followed by a noun:
  una decina di giorni *about 10 days*
  una dozzina di clienti *a dozen or so clients*
- **-ina** added to **venti**, **trenta** … **novanta** without their final vowel are used in the same way as **decina**:
  una trentina di pagine *about 30 pages*
  una cinquantina di pezzi *50 or so pieces*
- **centinaio** (m) *about a hundred* has the plural **centinaia** (f) *hundreds*:
  un centinaio di persone *about 100 people*
  centinaia di spettatori *hundreds of spectators*
- **migliaio** (m) *about a thousand* has the plural **migliaia** (f) *thousands*:
  un migliaio di turisti *about 1,000 tourists*
  migliaia di zanzare *thousands of mosquitoes*

ordinal numbers

1st	primo	1°	6th	sesto	6°
2nd	secondo	2°	7th	settimo	7°
3rd	terzo	3°	8th	ottavo	8°
4th	quarto	4°	9th	nono	9°
5th	quinto	5°	10th	decimo	10°

From 11th onwards, ordinal numbers are formed by adding -**esimo** to the cardinal number minus its final vowel:

11th	**undicesimo**	20th	**ventesimo**
12th	**dodicesimo**	50th	**cinquantesimo**
17th	**diciassettesimo**	100th	**centesimo**

The only irregularity to look out for is in 23, 33, 43, 53, etc., which keep the final e, but without its accent:

23 **ventitré**, 23rd **ventitreesimo**

Ordinal numbers are used much the same as in English except that:

- they're not used for dates (page 28) except for the first day of the month
- they agree with their noun because they're adjectives:
  primo amore *first love*; **primi piatti** *first courses*
  Consequently, the little ° changes to ª in the feminine:
  prima (1ª) classe *first class*
  per la terza (3ª) volta *for the third time*.

When relating to sovereigns or popes, ordinal numbers go after the name:

la regina Elisabetta Seconda *Queen Elizabeth II*
Papa Benedetto Sedicesimo *Pope Benedict XVI*

You'll sometimes hear an alternative for 11th to 19th using **decimo** *10th* + the relevant number: **Papa Benedetto Decimosesto**.

umpteenth *adj* ennesimo: *for the ~ time* per l'ennesima volta

There's nothing like seeing Italian words on a regular basis for them to become embedded in your memory. If you search on the internet for **calendario** and the relevant year you'll find downloadable calendars which will provide a daily reminder of the days and the months as well as lists of saint days and Italian public holidays.

time

The main points to remember about time are:
- the use of the 24-hour clock is widespread in Italy
- there's no translation of *o'clock*
- you need *the* before all times except *midday* and *midnight,* l' before **una**, **le** before other times
- you use **è** when the time includes *one o'clock*, **sono** for all other times.
  Che ora è? Che ore sono? *What time is it?*
  È l'una. *It's one o'clock.*
  Sono le due ... le undici ... *It's two o'clock ... 11 o'clock.*
  È mezzogiorno/mezzanotte. *It's midday/midnight.*

Sono ... *It's*
09.05 **le nove e cinque**
09.10 **le nove e dieci**
09.15 **le nove e quindici** or **le nove e un quarto**
09.20 **le nove e venti**
09.25 **le nove e venticinque**
09.30 **le nove e trenta** or **le nove e mezzo**
09.35 **le nove e trentacinque** or **le dieci meno venticinque**
09.40 **le nove e quaranta** or **le dieci meno venti**
09.45 **le nove e quarantacinque** or **le dieci meno un quarto**
09.50 **le nove e cinquanta** or **le dieci meno dieci**
09.55 **le nove e cinquantacinque** or **le dieci meno cinque**

A che ora ...? *(At) what time ...?*
l' and **le** after **a** *at* become **all'** and **alle** (see page 48):
all'una *at one o'clock*
alle due, alle tre ... alle undici *at two o'clock, three o'clock ... 11 o'clock*
alle otto e mezzo *at half past eight*

Da *from*, **di** *of*, **fino a** *until* and **prima di** *before* behave in the same way:
dalle nove alle sedici *from 09.00 to 16.00*
il treno delle 13 e 40 *the 13.40 train* lit. *the train of 13.40*
fino all'una *until one o'clock*
prima delle sette *before seven o'clock*

Mezzogiorno and **mezzanotte** aren't affected because they don't use *the*:
a mezzogiorno *at midday*; **prima di mezzanotte** *before midnight*.

date: days, months, years

- I giorni della settimana sono *the days of the week are:*

lunedì	*Monday*
martedì	*Tuesday*
mercoledì	*Wednesday*
giovedì	*Thursday*
venerdì	*Friday*
sabato	*Saturday*
domenica	*Sunday*

  > The days are masculine except for **domenica**. Like the months below, they're written without a capital letter.

  On isn't translated into Italian when talking about days:
  Lavoro lunedì. *I'm working on Monday.*
  Using **il/la** conveys that something is a regular event:
  Lavoro il/ogni lunedì. *I work on Mondays/every Monday.*

- I mesi dell'anno sono *the months of the year are:*

gennaio	*January*	**luglio**	*July*
febbraio	*February*	**agosto**	*August*
marzo	*March*	**settembre**	*September*
aprile	*April*	**ottobre**	*October*
maggio	*May*	**novembre**	*November*
giugno	*June*	**dicembre**	*December*

  Vado a Roma in/ogni agosto. *I go to Rome in/every August.*

- **Le quattro stagioni sono** *the four seasons are:*

la primavera	*spring*	**l'estate**	*summer*
l'autunno	*autumn*	**l'inverno**	*winter*

- **nel** (in + il combined, page 48) is used before a year:
  Sono nato/nata *I was born*
  ... **nel millenovecentosettantacinque** *in 1975*
  ... **nel settantacinque** *in '75*
  ... **nel duemiladue** *in 2002*

- With the date, ordinal numbers are used only for the first of the month; cardinal numbers are used after that. *On* isn't translated.
  il primo maggio *1 May, on the 1st of May*
  il ventidue agosto *22 August, on the 22nd of August*
  il quattordici dicembre *14 December, on the 14th of December*

word power

quando? when?
alle tre precise, alle tre in punto at three o'clock on the dot
verso le sei about six o'clock; **dopo le tre** after three o'clock
fra cinque minuti in five minutes' time

oggi today
alle dieci di mattina/di sera at ten in the morning/evening
alle tre di pomeriggio at three o'clock in the afternoon
stamattina this morning, **stasera** this evening

Keep an eye out for these words which look similar
but which have quite different meanings:

fa ago   **fra** within, in
oggi today   **ogni** every

ogni tanto every so often, once in a while
ogni giorno/due giorni/settimana every day/two days/week
una volta alla settimana/al mese once a week/month

domani tomorrrow
domani mattina/sera tomorrow morning/evening
dopodomani the day after tomorrow
fra due giorni within two days
la settimana prossima next week; **l'anno prossimo** next year

ieri yesterday
ieri mattina/sera yesterday morning/evening
ieri l'altro/l'altro ieri the day before yesterday
due giorni/una settimana fa two days/a week ago
la settimana scorsa last week; **l'anno scorso** last year

negli anni Sessanta in the '60s
nel ventesimo/ventunesimo secolo in the 20th/21st century
or you can say **nel Cinquecento/Settecento/Novecento etc.** in
the 16th/18th/20th century, i.e. the 1500s/1700s/1900s

checkpoint 2

1   What's the Italian for a *nil*, b three noughts?

2   Is **centosettantanove** greater or smaller than **centonovantasette**?

3   Write down the Italian for *8, 18, 28* and *88*.

4   Now write **due milioni quattrocentomila** in numbers, punctuating it the Italian way.

5   What do these mean?
   a sono le cinque   b alle sette di sera
   c dopo mezzanotte   d alle sette ieri sera
   e alle tre e mezzo   f prima delle undici di mattina
   g è l'una e un quarto   h l'una di pomeriggio
   i sabato alle sette in punto   j lunedì alle diciotto

6   And how do you say these times in Italian?
   a *It's 11 o'clock*   b *at nine am*
   c *at 12 noon*   d *after 18.00*
   e *at exactly 09.00*   f *at ten o'clock tomorrow*
   g *at ten yesterday*   h *on Sunday at 16.00*
   i *at seven o'clock every day*   j *before three o'clock in the afternoon*

7   What's the missing word? **Settembre ha** *has* .... **giorni**.

8   How do you say *about 40* in Italian?

9   In Italian, write the dates of New Year's Day, Christmas Day, New Year's Eve.

10 What does **per l'ennesima volta** mean?

11 What time is **il treno delle sedici e quarantatré** expected?

12 What comes between **sedicesimo** and **diciottesimo**?

13 In Italian, which century is **milleottocentocinquantasei** in?

14 Is **primavera, estate, autunno** or **inverno** the Italian for *spring*?

15 How do you say *75%* in Italian?

Nouns

Nouns are the words for
- living beings: man, sister, doctor, lion, Antonio
- things: table, water, night, lesson, sport
- places: country, town, Italy, Rome
- concepts: beauty, freedom, time, democracy

Every single Italian noun – not just the words for people – is either masculine (m) or feminine (f). This is its **gender**, and you need to know a noun's gender because words used with it, such as articles and adjectives, have corresponding masculine and feminine forms.

The majority of Italian nouns end in **o** or **a**, which is a guide to their gender because nearly all the ones ending in **o** are masculine while the majority of those ending in **a** are feminine. Some nouns end in **e**, and there are ways of recognising the gender of many of these too.

When you're talking about more than one of something, you don't add **s** as in English – you change the final vowel instead.

In an English-Italian dictionary, abbreviations to look out for include *n* noun, *m* masculine, *f* feminine, *sing* singular, *pl* plural.
If you look up *car* and *horse*, this is what you might find:

car *n* auto *f*, macchina *f*: *by* ~ in macchina; *~park n* parcheggio *m*, parking *m*

horse *n* cavallo *m*, *[gym]* cavallina *f*: ~ *racing* corsa *f* di cavalli; ~ *riding* equitazione *f*; *Trojan* ~ cavallo di Troia. *Don't look a gift* ~ *in the mouth* A caval(lo) donato non si guarda in bocca.

people: the family

Most of the nouns for people have corresponding masculine and feminine versions:

m		f	
neonato	*newborn boy*	neonata	*newborn girl*
bambino	*young boy*	bambina	*young girl*
ragazzo	*boy*	ragazza	*girl*
uomo	*man*	donna	*woman*
signore	*Mr*	signora	*Mrs*
figlio	*son*	figlia	*daughter*
fratello	*brother*	sorella	*sister*
madre	*mother*	padre	*father*
nonno	*grandfather*	nonna	*grandmother*
zio	*uncle*	zia	*aunt*
cugino	*cousin (male)*	cugina	*cousin (female)*
suocero	*father-in-law*	suocera	*mother-in-law*
cognato	*brother-in-law*	cognata	*sister-in-law*
genero	*son-in-law*	nuora	*daughter-in-law*
fratellastro	*stepbrother, half-brother*	sorellastra	*stepsister, half-sister*
padrino	*godfather*	madrina	*godmother*

Nipote is an exception. It can mean *nephew, niece, grandson* or *granddaughter*.

When talking about a mixed group of males and females, you use the plural of the masculine noun, changing the last **o** or **e** of e.g. **nonno, cugino, nipote** to **i**:
I nonni arrivano oggi. *My grandparents arrive today.*
I ragazzi sono a scuola. *The children are in school.*
Hai fratelli? *Do you have brothers and sisters?*

The plural of **figlio** is **figli**, which can mean *sons* or *children*. If you need to be specific, you use **maschio** and **femmina**:
Abbiamo tre figli. *We have three children.*
Abbiamo due femmine e un maschio. *We have two girls and a boy.*

... and at work

The words for some occupations end in **-o** or **-e**, changing to **-a** for the feminine; others add endings, much like *-ess* in English:

	cuoco	**cuoca**	*cook*
	cameriere	**cameriera**	*waiter/waitress*
	infermiere	**infermiera**	*nurse*
	parrucchiere	**parrucchiera**	*hairdresser*
-essa	**avvocato**	**avvocatessa**	*lawyer*
	campione	**campionessa**	*champion*
	professore	**professoressa**	*teacher*
	dottore	**dottoressa**	*doctor*
	studente	**studentessa**	*student*
-trice	**attore**	**attrice**	*actor/actress*
	direttore	**direttrice**	*manager/manageress*
	imperatore	**imperatrice**	*emperor/empress*

Traditional male roles are always masculine even when it's a woman:

architetto *architect* **chirurgo** *surgeon*
ingegnere *engineer* **medico** *doctor*
ministro *minister* **idraulico** *plumber*

Many opt for the generic noun, even when there's a feminine version:
Luisa è il direttore del personale. *Luisa's the personnel manager.*
La signora Ferrini è avvocato. *Mrs Ferrini's a lawyer.*

Like **nipote**, some words are the same for males and females:
- nouns ending in **-ista** (see page 36):
  giornalista *journalist* **pianista** *pianist*
  dentista *dentist* **economista** *economist*
- nouns ending in **-ga** and **-ta**:
  collega *colleague*, **atleta** *athlete*, **astronauta**, *astronaut*
- and many nouns ending in **-e**
  cantante *singer* **contabile** *accountant*
  insegnante *teacher* **agricoltore** *farmer*

Context, articles and/or adjectives ensure there's no confusion:
Mario è il nuovo dentista. *Mario is the new dentist.*
Anna è una brava dentista. *Anna is a good dentist.*
A few words are always feminine, even when they refer to a man:
persona *person*, **guida** *guide*, **spia** *spy*, **vittima** *victim*

animals

The words for many animals are the same for the male and the female of the species:

m		f	
orso	bear	scimmia	ape, monkey
elefante	elephant	giraffa	giraffe
leopardo	leopard	tigre	tiger
giaguaro	jaguar	pantera	panther
ghepardo	cheetah	zebra	zebra
gorilla	gorilla	tartaruga	turtle
cervo	deer	volpe	fox
delfino	dolphin	balena	whale
squalo	shark	rana	frog
coccodrillo	crocodile	foca	seal

- Exceptions include **leone/leonessa** *lion/lioness* and **lupo/lupa** *wolf/she-wolf*.

- If you need to be specific, you use **maschio** and **femmina**:
  una giraffa maschio *a male giraffe*
  un leopardo femmina *a female leopard*

Animali domestici *pets* and **bestiame** *livestock* tend to have distinct masculine and feminine versions:

m		f	
cane	dog	cagna	bitch
gatto	cat	gatta	she-cat
gallo	cockerel	gallina	hen
cavallo	horse	giumenta	mare
maiale	pig	scrofa	sow
toro	bull	mucca, vacca	cow
ariete, montone	ram	pecora	sheep
caprone	billy goat	capra	nanny goat

... and everything else

With objects and abstract ideas, the ending of the word is the only clue to its gender.

-o Nearly all nouns ending in **-o** are masculine:

passaporto *passport*	**supermercato** *supermarket*
vino *wine*	**albergo** *hotel*
vento *wind*	**entusiasmo** *enthusiasm*

Exceptions: **mano** *hand*, **dinamo** *dynamo* and a few established abbreviations of longer words – **auto**(mobile) *car*, **foto**(grafia) *photograph*, **radio**(fonia) *radio*, **moto**(cicletta) *motorbike,* (sedia di) **sdraio** *deckchair*

-a Nouns ending in **-a** are usually feminine:

energia *energy*	**montagna** *mountain*
birra *beer*	**casa** *house*
democrazia *democracy*	**tristezza** *sadness*

Exceptions: most things ending in **-ma** are masculine – **aroma, diagramma, diploma, dramma, enigma, panorama, problema, programma, sistema, clima** *climate*

-e Some things ending in **-e** are masculine while some are feminine. There's no apparent rationale, and it's a good idea to make a mental note of the gender of new **e** words as you come across them.

m		f	
cane	*dog*	carne	*meat*
nome	*name*	notte	*night*
valore	*value*	valle	*valley*
motore	*engine*	morte	*death*
mese	*month*	stagione	*season*

However, you can presume the gender of nouns with the following endings with only rare exceptions:

m		f	
-ore, -ere, -ale		**-ione, -ice, -udine**	
amore	*love*	occasione	*occasion*
cameriere	*waiter*	stazione	*station*
giornale	*newspaper*	vincitrice	*female winner*
canale	*canal*	solitudine	*loneliness*

making nouns plural

When there's more than one of something:

-o changes to **-i**

  bambino → **bambini** *young children*

  fratello → **fratelli** *brothers*

  vino → **vini** *wines*

  supermercato → **supermercati** *supermarkets*

  passaporto → **passaporti** *passports*

  Exceptions:

  - **auto, foto, moto, radio** – don't change.
  - **uomo** *man* **uomini** *men*; **dio** *god* **dei** *gods*

-a changes to **-e**

  ragazza → **ragazze** *girls*

  figlia → **figlie** *daughters*

  birra → **birre** *beers*

  montagna → **montagne** *mountains*

  studentessa → **studentesse** *female students*

  Exceptions:

  - **-ista** endings change to **-isti** for a male and **-iste** for a female: **turisti/turiste**; **giornalisti/giornaliste**
  - **-ta** endings change to **-ti** for a male and **-te** for a female **atleti/atlete**; **astronauti/astronaute**
  - **-ma** endings change to **-mi**: **problemi, programmi, sistemi**

-e changes to **-i**

  cane → **cani** *dogs*

  nome → **nomi** *names*

  valore → **valori** *values*

  motore → **motori** *engines*

  stagione → **stagioni** *seasons*

  canale → **canali** *canals, channels*

  cameriere → **camerieri** *waiters*

  carne → **carni** *meats*

  notte → **notti** *nights*

  valle → **valli** *valleys*

  mese → **mesi** *months*

  giornale → **giornali** *newspapers*

  stazione → **stazioni** *stations*

  abitudine → **abitudini** *habits*

Pasta dishes are all plural words: **spaghetti, ravioli, tortellini, rigatoni, lasagne, tagliatelle, penne, orecchiette, farfalle** to name but a few.

... and related spelling detail

- Nouns ending in **-io** only end in **-ii** when the **i** is stressed:

zio *uncle*	**zii** *uncles*
esempio *example*	**esempi** *examples*
bacio *kiss*	**baci** *kisses*
figlio *son*	**figli** *sons, children*
occhio *eye*	**occhi** *eyes*

- The few nouns ending in **-ea** have the plural ending **-ee**:

assemblea *assembly*	**assemblee** *assemblies*
dea *goddess*	**dee** *goddesses*
idea *idea*	**idee** *ideas*
marea *tide*	**maree** *tides*

- Nouns ending in consonant + **-cia/-gia** drop the **i** in the plural:

arancia *orange* **arance** *oranges*

provincia *province*	**province** *provinces*
spiaggia *beach*	**spiagge** *beaches*
striscia *stripe*	**strisce** *stripes*

whereas nouns ending in vowel + **-cia/-gia** tend to retain the **i**:

ciliegia *cherry*	**ciliegie** *cherries*
farmacia *chemist's*	**farmacie** *chemists'*
valigia *suitcase*	**valigie** *suitcases*
camicia *shirt*	**camicie** *shirts*

- Most nouns ending in consonant + **-co/-ca** or **-go/-ga** add **h** before the plural vowel **i/e**, keeping the hard sound of the **c** and **g**:

fico *fig*	**fichi** *figs*
parco *park*	**parchi** *parks*
amica *f friend*	**amiche** *f friends*
barca *boat*	**barche** *boats*
albergo *hotel*	**alberghi** *hotel*
lago *lake*	**laghi** *lakes*
droga *drug*	**droghe** *drugs*
casalinga *housewife*	**casalinghe** *housewives*

but some masculine nouns with a vowel before **-co/-go** don't add the **h**:

amico *friend*	**amici** *friends*
medico *doctor*	**medici** *doctors*
asparago *asparagus*	**asparagi** *asparagus*
geologo *geologist*	**geologi** *geologists*

and other professions ending in **-ologo** (see page 40).

irregular plurals

The endings of these three groups don't change in the plural:

- Nouns with an accent on the final vowel and nouns of one syllable:

città *town, city*	difficoltà *difficulty*
caffè *coffee, bar*	tassì *taxi*
virtù *virtue*	bambù *bamboo*
sci *ski*	re *king*

- The few nouns ending in -i or -ie:

analisi *analysis*	brindisi *toast (drink)*
crisi *crisis*	diagnosi *diagnosis*
enfasi *emphasis*	ipotesi *hypothesis*
paralisi *paralysis*	sintesi *synthesis*
serie *series*	specie *species*

  except **moglie** *wife*, which becomes **mogli** *wives*

- Words borrowed from other languages:

bar	chef	computer
dessert	film	garage
puzzle	sport	weekend

Some masculine nouns become feminine in the plural:

m sing		f pl	
braccio	*arm*	braccia	*arms*
dito	*finger*	dita	*fingers*
ginocchio	*knee*	ginocchia	*knees*
labbro	*lip*	labbra	*lips*
centinaio	*about 100*	centinaia	*hundreds*
miglio	*mile*	miglia	*miles*
mille	*1,000*	duemila	*2,000*
migliaio	*about 1,000*	migliaia	*thousands*
lenzuolo	*sheet*	lenzuola	*sheets*
paio	*pair*	paia	*pairs*
uovo	*egg*	uova	*eggs*

A few nouns change in the middle because they're actually two words joined together. The most noticeable are the ones with **capo** head:

capofamiglia *head of the family* → **capifamiglia** *heads of family*
capostazione *stationmaster* → **capistazione** *stationmasters*

adding endings to nouns

Endings such as **-etto** or **-one**, added to a noun without its final vowel, are called suffixes. They alter the noun's meaning and are often used instead of an adjective. Some refer to size, but others reflect the speaker's emotions, whether it's affection or antipathy.

- **-ino, -etto, -ello, -ellino, -icello** *little, small, cute, nice*

pane *bread*	**panino** *bread roll*
letto *bed*	**lettino** *cot*
vino *wine*	**vinello** *nice wine*
telefono *phone*	**telefonino** *mobile phone*
isola *island*	**isoletta** *small island*
vento *wind*	**venticello** *breeze*

- **-one** *big, large*

ragazzo *boy*	**ragazzone** *big boy*
ombrello *umbrella*	**ombrellone** *beach umbrella*

Many feminine nouns become masculine when you add **-one**:

minestra *soup*	**minestrone** *thick soup*
palla *ball*	**pallone** *football*

- **-accio** *bad, poor, horrible*

ragazzo *boy*	**ragazzaccio** *lout*
roba *goods, stuff*	**robaccia** *rubbish*
strada *road*	**stradaccia** *track, road in poor condition*
parola *word*	**parolaccia** *swearword, bad language*

Other suffixes with negative connotations (but slightly less disparaging than **-accio**) include **-uzzo, -onzolo, -astro** and **-uncolo**.

ladro *thief*	**ladruncolo** *small-time crook*
medico *doctor*	**medicastro** *quack*

Adding a suffix is regularly used in Italian to great effect – but it's something to approach with a little caution. Don't assume, for example, that all nouns ending in **-ino** or **-one** are examples of using a suffix: **un tacco** is *a heel of a shoe* but **un tacchino** is *a turkey*; **un lampo** is *a flash* whereas **un lampone** is a *raspberry*. The difficulty when you're learning is that there are no absolute and consistent rules, not all nouns can be modified, and meaning often depends on the attitude of the speaker.

word power

There are hundreds of English nouns which you can easily convert to Italian if you know the endings to look out for. Don't forget to factor in any consonant changes (page 37). If in doubt, say the word out loud and the meaning will often become obvious.

🇬🇧	🇮🇹	
-al	-ale	animale, canale, carnevale, cattedrale, ideale, minerale, ospedale
-nt	-nte	consonante, corrente, elefante, paziente, presidente
-ism	-ismo	comunismo, realismo, futurismo, turismo
-ist	-ista	dentista, terrorista, ottimista, pessimista, pianista
-nce/ncy	-nza	danza, distanza, emergenza, indipendenza, innocenza, esistenza
-ologist	-ologo	archeologo, astrologo, cardiologo, ecologo, ginecologo, patologo, psicologo, radiologo
-or/our	-ore	creatore, dottore, motore, odore, professore, settore, trattore
-sion	-sione	confusione, conversione, fusione, impressione, occasione, passione
-tion	-zione	ambizione, attenzione, conversazione, integrazione, petizione, soluzione, stazione, promozione
-ction	-zione	azione, introduzione, funzione, produzione, condizione
-ty	-tà	abilità, città, enormità, difficoltà, possibilità, velocità, autorità, obesità, università, qualità, quantità, umanità
y	ia	economia, energia, geografia, industria, storia, coreografia

false friends

Not all nouns mean what they appear to mean:

argomento means *topic*	*argument* is **litigio, discussione**
camera means *room*	*camera* is **macchina fotografica**
cantina means *cellar*	*canteen* is **mensa**
carta means *paper*	*cart* is **carretto**
confidenza *secret, familiarity*	*confidence* is **fiducia**
criceto means *hamster*	*cricket* is **cricket** *(game)*
grillo means *cricket (insect)*	*grill* is **griglia**
delusione means *disappointment*	*delusion* is **illusione**
fabbrica means *factory*	*fabric* is **tessuto**
libreria means *bookshop*	*library* is **biblioteca**
mobile means *furniture*	*mobile (phone)* is **telefonino**
pavimento means *floor*	*pavement* is **marciapiede**
preservativo means *condom*	*preservative* is **conservante**
incidente is *accident*	*incident* is **avvenimento**
parenti means *relatives*	*parents* is **genitori**
ostriche means *oysters*	*ostrich* is **struzzo**
stormo means *flock*	*storm* is **temporale**
tasto means *key (on keyboard)*	*taste* is **gusto**
vacanza means *holiday*	*vacancy* is **posto vacante**

Look out too for these nouns, which have entirely different meanings
depending on whether they end in **-o** or **-a**:

m		f	
baleno	*flash*	**balena**	*whale*
cappello	*hat*	**cappella**	*chapel*
caso	*case*	**casa**	*house*
modo	*way, manner*	**moda**	*fashion*
pizzo	*lace*	**pizza**	*pizza*
porto	*port*	**porta**	*door*
posto	*place*	**posta**	*post, mail*
torto	*wrong, fault*	**torta**	*cake*

and these, which are identical apart from their gender:

capitale	*money*	**capitale**	*capital city*
fine	*aim*	**fine**	*end*
fronte	*front*	**fronte**	*forehead*
morale	*morale, mood*	**morale**	*moral*

checkpoint 3

1 Write m, f, or m/f in the boxes depending on whether the noun is masculine, feminine or could be either?

vino ☐   dentista ☐   problema ☐

amore ☐   mercato ☐   posizione ☐

spiaggia ☐   mano ☐   nipote ☐

città ☐   vittima ☐   settore ☐

2 What are these in the plural?

ragazza	conversazione
caffè	cappuccino
sistema	sport
ciclista	amica
difficoltà	analisi
figlio	figlia
serie	sci
uomo	luogo
foto	braccio

3 Is **mano** *hand* masculine or feminine?

4 What two meanings does **fratelli** have?

5 **leone, leopardo, ghepardo**: which is the odd one out and why?

6 Does **colleghe** mean one male colleague, one female colleague, several male colleagues or several female colleagues?

7 Think of a word that's feminine even when it refers to a man.

8 Can you work out the Italian for a) *biology*, b) *science*, c) *probability*, d) *difference*, e) *nation*, f) *situation*, g) *feminism*?

9 What kind of creatures are **ostriche** and **grilli**?

10 Does **librone** or **libretto** mean *big book*?

11 What do you think is the plural of **capogruppo** *group leader* and **caporeparto** *head of department*?

12 Given that **imperatore** is *emperor* and **imperatrice** *empress*, what's the female equivalent of **redattore** *editor*?

Articles: the, a, some

An article is used with a noun to show whether you're talking about something which is specific or defined: ***the** house*, ***the** houses*, or something which is not: ***a** house*, ***some** houses*.

Grammatically, articles fall into three categories:
- the definite article: *the*
- the indefinite article: *a/an*
- the partitive article: *some/any*

Articles are very different in English and Italian. For example, there are seven versions of *the* in Italian, the one you use depending on whether the following noun is masculine or feminine, singular or plural; whether it begins with a vowel or a consonant. And there are four words for *a/an* as well as various ways of saying *some* and *any*.

There's a difference too in the way articles are used. Italian uses the definite article more than English – most noticeably when generalising – but doesn't use the indefinite article in a sentence like *He's a doctor*.

As a beginner, it can be easy to get bogged down with the sheer number of articles in Italian, especially since they combine with **a**, **da**, **di**, **in** and **su** to form single words such as **alla** *to the* or **nel** *in the*. The trick is to be aware of the rules and to get used to these gradually, bearing in mind that you'll be understood even if you get a few wrong at first.

a: un, uno, una, un'

English has two forms of the indefinite article: *a* and *an*. Italian has four: **un**, **uno**, **una** and **un'**. Which one you use depends on:

- the gender of the noun that's with the article

- the first letter(s) of the word immediately following the article, which is usually the noun but can also be an adjective describing that noun.

masculine

The words for *a/an* with masculine nouns are **un** and **uno**:

- **un** before vowels and most consonants:
  un padre *a father*
  un bicchiere di vino *a glass of wine*
  un altro bicchiere di vino *another glass of wine*
  un segreto *a secret*

- **uno** before words beginning with:
z	**uno zio** *an uncle*
s + consonant	**uno sbaglio** *a mistake*, **uno sconto** *a discount*
	uno smeraldo *emerald*, **uno stivale** *a boot*

Uno is also used before words beginning with **gn**, **ps** and **x** as well as with foreign words that start with one of the **uno** sounds: **uno gnomo**, **uno psicologo**, **uno xilofono**, **uno chef**, **uno scanner**. There are so few of these that all you need do in practice is keep an eye out for words beginning with **z** or with **s** followed by a consonant.

feminine

The words for *a/an* with feminine nouns are **una** and **un'**:

- **una** before a consonant:
  una casa *a house*
  una birra *a beer*
  una zia *an aunt*
  una stella *a star*
  una buona idea *a good idea*

- **un'** before a vowel:
  un'idea *an idea*
  un'altra birra *another beer*

... and how to use them

Un, **uno**, **una** and **un'** are used in pretty much the same circumstances as *a/an* in English, i.e. before a noun that isn't referring to a specific person or thing.

However, unlike English, they're <u>not</u> used:

- with nouns denoting occupation, nationality, religion, marital status:
  Sono studente. *I'm a student.*
  Luciano è avvocato. *Luciano's a lawyer.*
  Mio zio è cuoco. *My uncle's a cook.*
  È australiano. *He's (an) Australian.*
  Anna è cattolica. *Anna's a Catholic.*
  Sono vedova. *I'm a widow.*

  unless those nouns have additional information added to them:
  Sono uno studente di venti anni. *I'm a 20-year old student.*
  Mio zio è un cuoco molto bravo. *My uncle's a very good cook.*

- before 100, 1000 and ½:
  Ci sono cento persone. *There are a hundred people.*
  L'ho detto mille volte. *I've said it a thousand times.*
  un chilo e mezzo di mele *a kilo and a half of apples*
  mezza bottiglia di acqua *half a bottle of water*

- after **che** in exclamations:
  Che buona idea! *What a good idea!*
  Che bella giornata! *What a lovely day!*
  Che bravo cuoco! *What a good cook!*
  Che seccatura! *What a nuisance!*
  Che peccato! *What a pity!*

the: il, l', lo, i, gli, la, le

English has one word for *the*; Italian has seven: **il, l', lo, i, gli, la, le**.
Which one you use depends on three things:
- the gender of the noun that's with the article

- whether that noun is singular or plural

- the first letter(s) of the word immediately following the article, which is usually the noun but can also be an adjective describing that noun.

masculine
The words for *the* with masculine nouns are **il, l', lo, i** and **gli**:
- il before most singular words:
  il giardino *the garden*, **il direttore** *the manager*

- l' before singular words starting with a vowel:
  l'ufficio *the office*, **l'altro direttore** *the other manager*

- lo before singular words that have **uno** as *a/an* (see page 44):
  lo zaino *the rucksack*, **lo squalo** *shark*
  lo champagne, **lo yoga**

- i before most plural words:
  i giardini *the gardens*, **i direttori** *the managers*

- gli before plural words beginning with a vowel or letter associated with **lo**:
  gli uffici *the offices*, **gli zaini** *the rucksacks*, **gli squali** *the sharks*, **gli stessi giardini** *the same gardens*

feminine
The words for *the* with feminine nouns are **la, l'** and **le**:
- la before singular words beginning with a consonant:
  la spiaggia *the beach*, **la marea** *the tide*

- l' before singular words beginning with a vowel:
  l'escursione *the trip*, **l'alta marea** *the high tide*

- le before all plural words:
  le spiagge *the beaches*, **le escursioni** *the trips*
  le alte maree *the high tides*

... and how to use them

Like *the* in English, **il, l', lo, i, gli, la, le** are used before a noun referring to a specific person or thing. In Italian they're also needed:

- when making generalisations:
  I leoni mangiano la carne. *Lions eat meat.*
  L'esercizio non basta. *Exercise isn't enough.*
  Ti piace la pizza? *Do you like pizza?*

- with abstract nouns and illnesses:
  La vita è bella. *Life is beautiful.*
  Che cosa sono i diritti umani? *What are human rights?*
  Ha il morbillo/la varicella. *He's got measles/chicken pox.*

- when talking **about** someone and referring to them by their title but not when talking **to** someone:
  La signora Bellini non c'è. *Mrs Bellini isn't here.*
  Buongiorno, signora Bellini.

- with the names of continents, countries, large islands and regions:
  l'Asia, l'Australia, gli Stati Uniti, la Sardegna, la Toscana

- with languages, although it is often omitted immediately after **parlare**:
  Studio l'italiano. *I'm learning Italian.*
  Parla molto bene il cinese. *You speak Chinese very well.*
  Parla tedesco? *Do you speak German?*

- with dates and times (pages 27-28):
  il duemiladodici *2012*; **l'otto maggio** *8th May*
  l'una e dieci *ten past one*; **le nove e mezzo** *half past nine*

- When talking about possession, except when referring to a singular member of the family (page 32):
  la mia macchina *my car*; **i nostri figli** *our children*
  but **mia sorella e suo marito** *my sister and her husband*

- Instead of *my*, *your*, etc. with parts of the body or when it's clear who something belongs to:
  Apri la bocca. *Open your mouth.*
  Ho perso l'ombrello. *I've lost my umbrella.*

the + a, da, di, in, su

When *the* follows **a** *at, to, in*; **da** *from, by*; **di** *of*; **in** *in*; **su** *on* they combine to form a single word.

	il	lo	la	l'	i	gli	le
a	al	allo	alla	all'	ai	agli	alle
da	dal	dallo	dalla	dall'	dai	dagli	dalle
di	del	dello	della	dell'	dei	degli	delle
in	nel	nello	nella	nell'	nei	negli	nelle
su	sul	sullo	sulla	sull'	sui	sugli	sulle

- **alla stazione** *at the station*; **all'aria aperta** *in the open air*; **abituato al sole** *used to the sun*; **vicino allo zoo** *near the zoo*

- **dal cuore** *from the heart*; **libero dalla paura** *free from fear*; **lontano dagli uffici/dai negozi** *far from the offices/from the shops*

- **il piatto del giorno** *dish of the day*; **i margini della terra** *the ends of the earth*; **stanco delle scuse** *tired of the excuses*

- **nel 1995** *in 1995*; **nella macchina di Carlo** *in Carlo's car*; **nei dintorni** *in the vicinity*; **negli Stati Uniti** *in the US*

- **sul mercato** *on the market*; **sulla pianta** *on the map*; **sui letti** *on the beds*; **sugli scaffali** *on the shelves*

The key to remembering these combinations is to focus on learning the first column. Once your brain has accepted that, for example, **in** and **il** become **nel**, you won't have a problem with remembering that **in** and **la** become **nella**, **in** and **le** become **nelle** and so on.

Con *with* sometimes combines with **il** and **i** to form **col** and **coi**: **col coltello** *with the knife*; **coi figli** *with the children* but it's **con la famiglia** *with the family* and **con gli altri** *with the others*.

some/any

Del, dello, dell', della, dei, degli, delle are used in a similar, but not identical, way to *some* and *any* in English.

Mi dà del pane. *I'll have some bread.*
Vorrei delle albicocche mature. *I'd like some ripe apricots.*
Avete degli asparagi? *Do you have any asparagus?*

They're used in this sort of way even when English might leave them out, and they're repeated before each noun in a list:

Ho comprato degli zucchini. *I've bought (some) courgettes.*
Mi dà del vino, delle olive e dell'olio. *I'll have some wine, (some) olives and (some) oil.*
but it's also correct to say:
Abbiamo comprato vino e olio. *We bought wine and oil.*

They're not used for *any* in negative statements:
Non ho comprato zucchero. *I haven't bought any sugar.*
Non abbiamo fragole. *We don't have any strawberries.*
Non c'è ghiaccio. *There isn't any ice.*

There are other ways of translating *some* and *any*:

- **Qualche** is always followed by a singular noun even when the English translation is plural:
  Ho qualche problema. *I've got some problems.*
  qualche tempo fa *some time ago*
  qualche anno fa *some years ago*
  qualche volta *sometimes, occasionally*
  Qualche can't be used in the negative.

- **Alcuni** (m) and **alcune** (f), on the other hand, are always used with a plural noun.
  Ho alcuni problemi. *I've got some/a few problems.*
  alcuni anni fa *some/a few years ago*
  alcune settimane fa *some/a few weeks ago*

  In the negative, the singular **alcuno** is used. It behaves like **uno** (page 44), changing to **alcun**, **alcuna** or **alcun'**.
  Non ha alcun problema. *He hasn't any problems.*
  Non esiste alcuna alternativa. *There are no alternatives.*
  Non ho alcun'idea. *I've no idea.*

checkpoint 4

1   Choose **un, uno, una** or **un'** for these nouns. If in doubt about what gender they are, check with pages 31 - 35.

sorella	fratello	tigre
zio	attrice	albergo
elefante	giornale	cameriera
occasione	specchio	professoressa
bicchiere	madre	sistema

2   Now put **il, lo, l'** or **la** in front of the same nouns.

3   Put **i, gli** or **le** in front of these plural nouns.

bambini	zie	studenti
arance	sport	stazioni
giaguari	persone	baci
squali	giornali	pecore
idee	valli	capifamiglia

4   Combine *the* with a, da, di, in and su.

a + la	casa	di + lo	zio
da + l'	albergo	in + la	scatola *box*
su + le	scale *stairs*	su + lo	scalino *step*
di + gli	zucchini	a + i	fratelli
in + il	cuore	da + le	spiagge

One of the classic differences between Italian and English is the use of *the* with abstract nouns and nouns used in a general sense. To get a feel for this, have a look at the examples on page 47 then see if you can come up with at least a dozen sentences in English where you would need to include the definite article in Italian.

Adjectives

Adjectives are words that describe nouns or pronouns:
We have a **small** garden.
The film was **superb**.
She is **Italian**.
Take the **second** turning.
I prefer **red** wine.

There are two major differences in the way Italian and English adjectives are used:

- **Position**

  Italian adjectives generally – though not always – go after the noun:
  Unione Europea *European Union*; **Croce Rossa** *Red Cross*; **parco nazionale** *national park*; **Giochi Olimpici** *Olympic Games*.

- **Agreement**

  The ending of an Italian adjective varies depending on the noun it's describing; it has to be masculine or feminine, singular or plural to agree with, i.e. match, that noun: **Regno Unito** *United Kingdom*; **Stati Uniti** *United States*; **Nazioni Unite** *United Nations*.

The dictionary abbreviations for *adjective* are *adj* in English and **agg** in Italian (from **aggettivo**).

If you look up **clear**, this is what you might find:

clear *adj* **1.** chiaro, trasparente, luminoso **2.** manifesto, evidente: *as ~ as daylight* chiaro come il sole **3.** netto: *~ profit* guadagno netto **4.** libero: *all ~* cessato allarme

word power

There are hundreds of English adjectives which you can easily convert to Italian when you know the endings to look out for. While they look similar, some have the stress in a different place. On this page the stress is highlighted, and once you've repeated a few out loud, you'll get a feel for the difference.

🇬🇧	🇮🇹	
-al	-ale	artificiale, centrale, digitale, federale, finale, generale, (in)formale, locale, musicale, naturale, normale, originale, personale, reale, sociale, speciale
-ary	-ario	letterario, mercenario, necessario, ordinario, secondario, volontario
-ic(al)	-ico	classico, diplomatico, domestico, economico, erotico, fantastico, geografico, islamico, microscopico, periodico, politico, romantico, rustico, tipico, tragico and many more adjectives ending in -ological: archeologico, astrologico, cardiologico, ecologico, geologico, ginecologico, psicologico, radiologico
-ive	-ivo	aggressivo, comunicativo, eccessivo, impulsivo, inclusivo, informativo, intensivo, offensivo, negativo
-nt	-nte	arrogante, differente, eccellente, elegante, evidente, frequente, importante, intelligente, paziente, permanente, persistente
-ble	-bile	accessibile, impossibile, immobile, incompatibile, inevitabile, navigabile, nobile, possibile, probabile, tollerabile
-ous	-oso	ambizioso, delizioso, famoso, geloso, generoso, grazioso, nervoso, numeroso, prezioso, spazioso

The consonants in many corresponding Italian and English adjectives are different in a predictable way (page 21):
assente *absent*, **assoluto** *absolute*, **assurdo** *absurd*, **osceno** *obscene*, **oscuro** *obscure*, **cattolico** *catholic*, **matematico** *mathematical*, **ibrido** *hybrid*, **igienico** *hygienic*, **patetico** *pathetic*, **patologico** *pathological*, **omeopatico** *homeopathic*, **orrendo** *horrendous*, **orribile** *horrible'* **intellettuale** *intellectual*, **ottagonale** *octagonal*, **ottimistico** *optimistic*

But there are many more that you'll recognise instantly because the Italian simply has **o** at the end of its English equivalent:
rapido, splendido, stupido, timido, moderno
materialistico, realistico, modesto
italiano, americano, arabo and many other nationalities.

false friends

Look out for these adjectives:

abusivo means *illegal*	*abusive* is **offensivo**
attuale means *current*	*actual* is **reale**
bravo means *good, clever*	*brave* is **coraggioso**
caldo means *hot*	*cold* is **freddo**
casuale means *random*	*casual* is **informale**
educato means *polite*	*educated* is **colto, istruito**
effettivo means *actual*	*effective* is **efficace**
largo means *wide*	*large* is **grande**
morbido means *soft*	*morbid* is **morboso**
noioso means *boring*	*noisy* is **rumoroso**
portabile means *wearable*	*portable* is **portatile**
sensibile means *sensitive*	*sensible* is **sensato**
successivo means *next*	*successful* is **riuscito**
triviale means *vulgar*	*trivial* is **banale**

If you use an adjective after **qualcosa** *something* or **niente** *nothing*, you need to put **di** between them:
qualcosa di strano *something odd*
qualcosa di terribile *something awful*
niente di interessante *nothing interesting*
niente di grave *nothing serious*.

adjective endings and agreement

In a dictionary, adjectives are listed in the masculine singular, ending in either -o or -e. These endings change, depending on whether the noun being described is masculine or feminine, singular or plural.

- Adjectives that end in -o have four possible endings:

-o	m sing	un albergo moderno *a modern hotel* il film famoso *the famous film*
-a	f sing	una città moderna *a modern town* l'attrice famosa *the famous actress*
-i	m pl	i tempi moderni *modern times* i quadri famosi *famous paintings*
-e	f pl	le stazioni moderne *modern stations* le parole famose *famous words*

- Adjectives that end in -e have only two possible endings:

-e	m sing	un rimedio naturale *a natural remedy* un momento importante *an important moment*
	f sing	la selezione naturale *natural selection* una vittoria importante *an important victory*
-i	m pl	i parchi naturali *natural parks* i dettagli importanti *important details*
	f pl	le terapie naturali *natural therapies* le partite importanti *important matches*

As you can see from the examples, it's not about the noun and the adjective necessarily ending in the same letter – the issue is that they agree in terms of gender and number.

- An adjective describing more than one noun has the masculine plural ending except when both the nouns are feminine:
Lorenzo e Paolo sono italiani.
Maria e Paolo sono italiani.
Maria e Giulietta sono italiane.

plural spellings

- Adjectives ending in **-io** drop the **-i** in the masculine only:

	m pl	f pl
vecchio, vecchia *old*	vecchi	vecchie
grigio, grigia *grey*	grigi	grigie
ampio, ampia *ample*	ampi	ampie
serio, seria *serious*, *reliable*	seri	serie

- Most adjectives ending in **-co** and **-go** add **h** before the final vowel, retaining the hard **c/g** sound:

	m pl	f pl
bianco, bianca *white*	bianchi	bianche
ricco, ricca *rich*	ricchi	ricche
tedesco, tedesca *German*	tedeschi	tedesche
largo, larga *wide*	larghi	larghe
lungo, lunga *long*	lunghi	lunghe

- Most adjectives with a vowel before **-co** add **h** in the feminine only:

	m pl	f pl
comico, comica *comical*	comici	comiche
simpatico, simpatica *friendly*	simpatici	simpatiche
magnifico, magnifica *magnificent*	magnifici	magnifiche
politico, politica *political*	politici	politiche
greco, greca *Greek*	greci	greche

A common exception is:

	m pl	f pl
antico, antica *ancient*	antichi	antiche

In English we use the word *one(s)* with adjectives to avoid repeating a noun:
Which car? The big one/The red one.
Which cars? The big ones/The red ones.

In Italian you simply use *the* and the adjective or **quello/a**:
Quale macchina? La grande/La rossa/Quella rossa.
Quali macchine? Le grandi/Le rosse/Quelle rosse.

position of adjectives

When adjectives and nouns are next to each other, the adjective usually goes after the noun:

un documento importante *an important document*
la musica classica *classical music*
i prezzi alti *high prices*
le attrazioni fatali *fatal attractions*

Some adjectives ***always*** go after the noun:

- colour: **un gatto nero** *a black cat*
            i vini rossi *red wines*

- shape: **un tavolo rotondo** *a round table*
            una torta quadrata *a square cake*

- nationality: **la cucina italiana** *Italian cooking*
            la bandiera americana *the American flag*

- an adjective with an adverb, e.g. *very, too, fairly*
            un posto molto tranquillo *a very quiet spot*
            una casa piuttosto piccola *a rather small house*

A few adjectives go before the noun most of the time:

- ordinal numbers
    primo soccorso *first aid*
    seconda classe *second class*
    terzo mondo *third world*

- the following common adjectives:
    bello *beautiful*, **bravo** *good, clever*, **brutto** *ugly, nasty*
    breve *short*, **lungo** *long*
    buono *good*, **cattivo** *bad*
    giovane *young*, **nuovo** *new*, **vecchio** *old*
    grande *big*, **piccolo** *small*
    stesso *same*, **vero** *real*, **caro** *dear*

    una bella giornata *a beautiful day*
    un brutto periodo *an unpleasant time*
    un breve/lungo soggiorno *a short/long stay*
    vecchi edifici e grandi chiese *old buildings and large churches*
    una cara amica *a dear friend*
    un bravo artista *a good artist*

Most adjectives which normally go after the noun can be put beforehand for emphasis, and vice versa:

un importante documento *a (particularly) important document*
un soggiorno breve *a very brief stay*
una casa piccola ma bella *a small but beautiful house*
un artista bravo *a good artist (not bad or mediocre)*
Che periodo brutto! *What an unpleasant time!*

A few adjectives actually change their meaning depending on whether they go before or after the noun:

un grand'uomo *a great man*; **un uomo grande** *a big man*
la stessa cosa *the same thing*; **la cosa stessa** *the thing itself*
diversi problemi *various problems*; **problemi diversi** *different problems*
un paese povero *a poor country*; **Povera Maria!** *Poor Maria!*
una semplice idea *just an idea*; **un'idea semplice** *a simple idea*
un vecchio amico *an old friend*; **un amico vecchio** *an elderly friend*
una vera storia *a real story*; **una storia vera** *a true story*
Santo means *holy* after a noun: **il pozzo santo** *the holy well*, but in front of a noun it means *saint* and is irregular: **san Cristoforo**; **santo Stefano**; **santa Maria**; **sant'Angela**

When two adjectives are used to describe the same noun:

- they can both follow the noun:
  un vino rosso corposo *a full-bodied red wine*
- they can be separated by **e** and:
  un vino giovane e leggero *a light young wine*
- one can go before the noun and one after:
  un robusto vino rosso *a robust red wine*

Learning words in sets is more effective than learning them individually. This doesn't only mean learning words relating to a particular topic or situation but, for example, learning an adjective together with its opposite or a word with a similar meaning: **bello/brutto**, **grande/piccolo**, **breve/lungo**, **vecchio/antico**. If you have to search for the partner word, so much the better because the more active your learning is, the more you will remember. Create your own associations. If you were asked to think of a partner for **bianco** *white*, would you choose **nero** *black* or **rosso** (wine connection)? Both? Or another word altogether?

irregular adjectives

Adjectives ending in **-ista** e.g. **egoista** *selfish*:

- are the same in both the masculine and feminine singular:
  un uomo egoista *a selfish man*; **una donna egoista** *a selfish woman*

- end in **-i** in the masculine plural and **-e** in the feminine plural:
  gli uomini egoisti *selfish men*; **le donne egoiste** *selfish women*

Colours are not always straightforward:

- Some behave normally:
  il vino rosso *red wine*; **una giacca nera** *a black jacket*

- Others are invariable, i.e. have only one possible ending. These include
  colours borrowed from other languages such as **blu** *dark blue* and **beige**
  beige and colours which are the names of objects, e.g.
  rosa *(rose) pink*, **lilla** *lilac*, **nocciola** *hazel*:
  un vestito rosa *a pink dress*; **le scarpe blu** *the dark blue shoes*

- Colours using a combination of two words are invariable too:
  una camicia azzurro chiaro *a pale blue shirt*
  le tende verde scuro *the dark green curtains*
  i pantaloni grigio carbone *the charcoal grey trousers*

A handful of adjectives ending in **-i** are also invariable:
un numero pari/dispari *an even/odd number*
case altrui *other people's houses*

Bello, **buono** and **grande** can be used before or after the noun. After the
noun, they follow the regular patterns for adjectives ending in **-o** and **-e**: **una
casa grande e bella** *a big and beautiful house*. Before the noun they have
some irregular endings. Like articles (pages 44 and 46), these depend not
only on the gender of the noun but also on its initial letter.

bello *beautiful* behaves in a similar way to the definite article:

il	**un bel sorriso** *a lovely smile*
lo	**un bello spettacolo** *a fine sight*
l'	**un bell'uomo** *a handsome man*
	una bell'avventura *a fine adventure*
la	**una bella giornata** *a lovely day*
i	**bei ricordi** *beautiful memories*
gli	**begli occhi** *beautiful eyes*
le	**belle montagne** *beautiful mountains*

buono *good* in the singular behaves like **un/uno/una/un'**:
buongiorno *hello, good day*
un buon libro *a good book*
buon appetito *enjoy your meal*
un buono studente *a good student*
buonanotte *good night*
una buona notizia *a piece of good news*
di buon'ora *early*; **una buon' idea** *a good idea*

In practice, **buon** tends to be used before all masculine singular nouns and **buona** before all feminine singular nouns:
un buon studente, una buona idea

grande *big* is irregular in the singular only:
un gran piacere *a great pleasure*
un grand'errore *a big mistake*
un grande spettacolo *a great show*
una gran parte *a large part*
una grand'avventura *a great adventure*

In practice, **grande** tends to be used instead of **gran** and **grand'**:
un grande piacere, un grande errore
una grande parte, una grande avventura

---

bello: **le belle arti** *the fine arts*; **il bel mondo** *high society*; **nel bel mezzo** *right in the middle*; **un bel niente** *absolutely nothing*; **belle notizie** *good news*; **un bel pasticcio** *a fine mess*

buono: **buono a niente** *good for nothing*; **buono da mangiare** *edible*; **a buon mercato** *cheap*; **una buona volta** *once and for all*; **alla buona** *easy-going, informal*; **di buona voglia** *willingly*

grande: **in grande** *on a large scale*; **il grande pubblico** *the general public*; **fa un gran caldo** *it's really hot*; **non è un gran che** *it's nothing special*;
la Grande Guerra *the Great War*
*grande isn't used for *great* in genealogy. *Great-grandparents* are **bisnonno/bisnonna**; *a great-grandchild* is **un/una pronipote**.

checkpoint 5

1   Add the ending to these adjectives and work out or guess what
    the phrases mean:

    a il prim___ ministro   b la Casa Bianc___
    c gli itinerari alpin___   d la musica popolar___
    e il turismo verd___   f le grandi città italian___
    g la Costa Azzurr___   h una pantera maschi___
    i in second___ classe   j delle strisce ross___ scur___
    k la danza modern___   l un uomo materialist___

2   Find adjectives in this unit with the opposite meaning from
    these:

    a maleducato   b antipatico
    c raro   d difficile
    e noioso   f insignificante
    g informale   h intelligente

3   Guess the Italian for the following. There are no false friends,
    but you do need to consider the internal consonants of two of
    them.

    a professional   b evident
    c terrible   d romantic
    e generous   f absolute
    g neutral   h indifferent
    i electric   j possible

4   If **straricco** means *ultra rich* and **strapieno** means *full to
    overflowing*, what do you think **stragrande**, **stravecchio** and
    straordinario mean?

5   How would you say in Italian:
    a *the white one (wine); the big ones (houses); the old one
    (a man); the dark green one (jacket);*
    b *something impossible; something different; nothing new;
    nothing special?*

Adverbs and comparisons

Adverbs are words that add an extra dimension to:

- adjectives:

  Our garden is **very** small.

  I'm **really** tired, **too** tired to go out.

- verbs:

  They cooked it **perfectly**.

  He's walking **quickly**.

- other adverbs:

  They cooked it **absolutely** perfectly.

  He's walking **extremely** quickly, **rather** quickly for me.

- whole sentences:

  Unfortunately we have to leave.

  They would be here **otherwise**.

Just as many English adverbs end in **-ly**, many Italian ones end in **-mente**. But words like **sempre** *always* and **già** *already*, which say when something happens, are also adverbs. As are words which say where things happen, such as **lontano** *far away*, **vicino** *nearby* and **altrove** *elsewhere*.

Adverbs are easy to use because their endings never change and most of the time they fit within a sentence in the same way as their English equivalent. However, in Italian they don't go between the subject and its verb as they often do in English, for example in sentences like *I sincerely apologise* or *Anna often works*. In Italian the order is *I apologise sincerely* or *Anna works often*.

The dictionary abbreviations for *adverb* **avverbio** are *adv* in English and **avv** in Italian. If you look up **clearly** and **nicely**, this is what you might find:

clearly *avv* **1.** chiaramente, distintamente, con chiarezza **2.** *[obviously, without doubt]* evidentemente, ovviamente, decisamente

nicely *avv* **1.** bene: *she paints* ~ dipinge bene **2.** *[politely, kindly]* cortesemente, gentilmente **3.** *[in a pleasant way]* piacevolmente

word **power**

- Many adverbs are formed by adding **-mente** to the feminine singular of an adjective (a or e):

es**a**tto *exact*	esatt**a**mente *exactly*
evid**e**nte *evident*	evidentemente *evidently*
fant**a**stico *fantastic*	fantasticamente *fantastically*
forte *strong*	fortemente *strongly*
fortunato *fortunate*	fortunatamente *fortunately*
frequente *frequent*	frequentemente *frequently*
giusto *just, right*	giustamente *justly, rightly*
immediato *immediate*	immediatamente *immediately*
necessario *necessary*	necessariamente *necessarily*
psicol**o**gico *psychological*	psicologicamente *psychologically*
s**e**mplice *simple*	semplicemente *simply*
sincero *sincere*	sinceramente *sincerely*
vero *true, real*	veramente *truly, really*

Exceptions: ben**e**volo *benevolent* → benevolmente, mal**e**volo *malevolent* → malevolmente, violento *violent* → violentemente, leggero *light* → leggermente

- Adjectives that end in **-le** or **-re** drop the e before adding **–mente**.

f**a**cile *easy*	facilmente *easily*
gentile *kind*	gentilmente *kindly, nicely*
incred**i**bile *incredible*	incredibilmente *incredibly*
normale *normal*	normalmente *normally*
not**e**vole *notable*	notevolmente *notably*
particolare *particular*	particolarmente *particularly*
regolare *regular*	regolarmente *regularly*
speciale *special*	specialmente *especially*
uguale *equal*	ugualmente *equally*

Take care with the pronunciation of adverbs. In English they're pronounced with the stress in the same place as the adjective they come from: n**a**tural, n**a**turally. This isn't the case in Italian, where the stress is always on the first syllable of -mente, naturale, naturalmente; diff**i**cile, difficilmente.

There are also many adverbs that don't end in -mente:

- **bene** *well*   **male** *badly*

   così *so*   **piuttosto** *rather*   **troppo** *too*

   molto *very*   **poco** *not very*   **un po'** *a bit*, *a little*

   anche *also*   **forse** *perhaps*   **soprattutto** *especially*

> More on ***molto, poco, un po'*** and ***troppo*** on page 70.

Parli bene l'italiano, molto bene. *You speak Italian well, very well.*
La casa è così piccola. *The house is so small.*
Viene anche Giovanna. *Giovanna's coming too.*
Mi piace soprattutto il rosso. *I especially like the red one.*

- **già** *already*   **sempre** *always*   **spesso** *often*

   insieme *together*   **lontano** *far*   **vicino** *nearby*

Sono sempre in ritardo. *They're always late.*
Fabio ha già mangiato. *Fabio has already eaten.*
Abitano lontano/vicino. *They live a long way away/nearby.*

Phrases are often used as alternatives to adverbs:
in modo spettacolare *spectacularly*
in modo elegante *stylishly, in a stylish way*
in modo poco elegante *without much style*
all'improvviso *unexpectedly, all of a sudden*
con cautela *carefully, with caution*
con difficoltà *with difficulty*; **con successo** *successfully*
in fretta *hastily/in haste*
senza entusiasmo *unenthusiastically, without enthusiasm*
senza sforzo *effortlessly*

false friends

attualmente means *currently*   *actually* is **in realtà**
eventualmente means *if needs be*   *eventually* is **alla fine**
definitivamente means *conclusively*   *definitely* is **certamente**
fatalmente means *inevitably*   *fatally* is **mortalmente**
finalmente means *at last*   *finally* is **alla fine**
possibilmente means *if possible*   *possibly* is **forse**
scarsamente means *sparsely*   *scarcely* is **appena**
ultimamente means *recently*   *ultimately* is **in fin dei conti**

più and meno

Più and **meno** are used in several ways:

- *plus* and *minus*, with numbers:

  due più due uguale quattro $2 + 2 = 4$

  otto meno uno uguale sette $8 - 1 = 7$

  La temperatura è più tre. *The temperature's plus three.*

  Fa meno cinque fuori. *It's minus five outside.*

- *more*, *less/fewer*, followed by a noun:

  Hai più pazienza di me. *You have more patience than me.*

  Hanno più soldi di Mario. *They have more money than Mario.*

  Ho meno appetito oggi. *I'm less hungry today.* lit. *I have less appetite.*

  Ci sono meno ristoranti qui. *There are fewer restaurants here.*

- *more than/less than*, followed by **di** + noun:

  più di due giorni fa *more than two days ago*

  fra meno di una settimana *in less than a week's time*

They also feature in many everyday phrases:

mai più *never again*

non più *not any more, no longer*

più o meno *more or less*

x volte più grande *x times bigger*

niente di più *nothing more*

Meno male! *Just as well!/Thank goodness!*

parlare del più e del meno *to chat, make small talk*

al più presto *at the earliest*

al più tardi *at the latest*

sempre più caro *more and more expensive, dearer and dearer*

sempre meno contento *less and less happy*

Per di più ... *And what's more ...*

comparisons

When making comparisons – both with adverbs and adjectives – **più** and **meno** are the key words. There's no equivalent of the English -*er* ending for adjectives, as in *faster*, *cheaper*, *nicer* or *bigger*.

Questo metodo è più facile. *This method is easier (more easy).*
Vuoi dimagrire più facilmente? *Do you want to lose weight more easily?*
Il corso è meno intensivo. *The course is less intensive.*
Ho studiato meno intensivamente. *I studied less intensively.*

Than is either **di** or **che**:

● **di** (or **del, della, dei,** etc.) before nouns, pronouns and numbers:
  Marta è più giovane di Marco. *Marta is younger than Marco.*
  È più giovane della sorella. *She's younger than her sister.*
  È più giovane di me. *She's younger than me.*
  Lavora più regolarmente di Marco. *She works more regularly than Marco.*
  Guadagna meno di 10 000 euro. *She earns less than 10,000 euro.*

● **che** in all other cases, i.e. when comparing two nouns, two adjectives, two adverbs, two verbs or two phrases:
  Hanno più soldi che gusto. *They have more money than taste.*
  Mi piace più Londra che Parigi. *I like London more than Paris.*
  È più furbo che intelligente. *He's more cunning than clever.*
  Meglio tardi che mai. *Better late than never.*
  Preferirei uscire che stare qui. *I'd rather go out than stay here.*
  Fa più caldo in Sicilia che in Sardegna. *It's hotter in Sicily than in Sardinia.*

as ... as

Tanto ... quanto or **così ... come** can be used to say *as ... as*:
Il tè non è tanto buono quanto il caffè. *The tea isn't as good as the coffee.*
Non faccio esercizio così regolarmente come vorrei. *I don't exercise as often as I'd like to.*
Tanto and **così** can be omitted, with no change in meaning:

Il tè non è buono quanto il caffè.
Non faccio esercizio regolarmente come vorrei.

superlatives: il più, il meno, -issimo

- To say the *most/least …* you use *the* + **più/meno**, + adjective or adverb. There's no equivalent of the English *-est* ending for adjectives, as in *fastest, cheapest* or *biggest*.

  Questo piatto è il più gustoso. *This dish is the tastiest/most tasty.*
  È la camera meno cara. *It's the least expensive room.*
  Sono i più interessanti. *They're the most interesting.*
  il più/meno rapidamente *the most/least quickly*

  In after a superlative is **di** or **del, della**, etc. (page 48):
  Sono i più grandi del mondo. *They're the biggest in the world.*
  È la camera meno cara dell'albergo. *It's the least expensive room in the hotel.*

- Adding **-issimo** to an adjective without its final vowel is a particularly Italian way of expressing an ultimate degree of something.

  È caro quel ristorante? *Is that restaurant expensive?*
  È carissimo. *It's extortionate/very expensive indeed.*
  La città è bella, vero? *Isn't the town beautiful?*
  È bellissima. *It's extremely beautiful.*
  Siete stanchi? *Are you tired?*
  Siamo stanchissimi. *We're absolutely shattered.*

  -issimo can also be added to a few adverbs, such as **bene** *well* and **spesso** *often*:
  Tu parli benissimo l'italiano. *You speak Italian very well indeed.*
  Vado spessissimo a Roma. *I go to Rome really often.*
  A few others add **-mente** to the **-issima** form of the adjective:
  Cammina lentissimamente. *He walks incredibly slowly.*
  but it's more common to use **molto** *very* or **assai** *extremely*:
  Ci vado molto spesso. *I go there very often.*
  Cammina assai lentamente. *He walks extremely slowly.*

Possibile *possible* can be added to a superlative to mean *as … as possible*: **il più lentamente possibile** *as slowly as possible*. If you add **il più possibile** to a verb, it means *as much as possible*: **dare il più possibile** *to give as much as possible*.

irregular comparatives and superlatives

- As in English, **buono** *good* and **cattivo** *bad* have irregular comparatives and superlatives. Unlike English, you can also use the regular **più buono**, **il più cattivo**, etc.

buono *good*	**migliore** *better*	**il migliore** *best*
cattivo *bad*	**peggiore** *worse*	**il peggiore** *worst*

  Il tempo è migliore di ieri. *The weather's better than yesterday.*
  È la peggiore squadra. *It's the worst team.*
  È più buono questo vino. *This wine's better.*

- English uses the words *better/best* and *worse/worst* as adjectives and adverbs. In Italian this isn't the case – there are separate words which are not interchangeable:

bene *well*	**meglio** *better*	**il meglio** *best*
male *badly*	**peggio** *worse*	**il peggio** *worst*

  Sta meglio di ieri. *He's feeling better than yesterday.*
  È possibile giocare peggio? *Is it possible to play worse?*

- **Piccolo** *small* and **grande** *big* also have irregular comparatives and superlatives:

piccolo *small*	**minore** *smaller*	**il minore** *smallest*
grande *big*	**maggiore** *bigger*	**il maggiore** *biggest*

  They're used mostly to talk about people's age, alongside **(il) più giovane** *younger, (youngest)*:
  la mia figlia minore *my youngest daughter*
  il mio fratello maggiore *my older brother*

  To talk about size, you tend to use **più piccolo** and **più grande**.
  Questa macchina è più piccola. *This car is smaller.*
  È la più grande che abbiamo. *It's the biggest we have.*

You'll notice **maggiore** and **minore** in the names of places and natural features: **Lago Maggiore, Gorla Minore, Orsa Maggiore e Orsa Minore** *Great Bear and Little Bear*.
They also translate the English *major* and *minor*:
Maggiore *Major (Army)*, **chiave maggiore/minore** *major/minor key (music)*; **elemento maggiore** *major element*, **danni minori** *minor damages*, **reato minore** *minor offence*.

checkpoint 6

1   What's the dictionary form of the adjective these adverbs come from?

   a assolutamente   b velocemente   c tipicamente

   d raramente   e normalmente   f simbolicamente

   g abitualmente   h misteriosamente   i dolcemente

2   And what's the adverb from these adjectives?

   a paziente   b incidentale   c logico

   d scientifico   e diverso   f regolare

   g relativo   h estremo   i indifferente

3   Find the opposites of these adverbs. They're all in this unit.

   a sfortunatamente *unfortunately*   b peggio *worse*

   c difficilmente *with difficulty*   d vicino *nearby*

   e ogni tanto *occasionally*   f ingiustamente *unjustly*

4   Fill the gaps by translating the words in brackets.

   a L'aereo è .... (*faster*)

   b Però, il treno è .... (*less expensive*)
   Costa .... venti euro. (*less than*)

   c Secondo me, quei film sono .... (*the most interesting*)

   d Gianfranco è più alto .... Enrico. (*than*)

   e Questo menù è .... (*better*)

   f Loro hanno giocato .... di noi. (*better*)

   g Preferirei giocare a tennis .... nuotare. (*than*)

   h Questa chiesa è .... della città. (*the biggest*)

   i Mia figlia è .... oggi. (*really exhausted*)

   j Questa è .... biblioteca ....
   (*the most important library in the world*)

5   Make four pairs from these adverbs. There's one left over – what does it mean?

   onestamente ovviamente drammaticamente crudelmente
   subito evidentemente sinceramente immediatamente
   brutalmente

Multi-function words

It isn't always possible to slot Italian and English words neatly into corresponding grammatical boxes. Language isn't like that. Just as there are English words that have several translations in Italian, there are Italian words that correspond to two or more different words in English.

Among the most widely-used are:

- **molto**, **poco**, **tanto** and **troppo**, which can mean *a lot of*, *few*, *so much/many*, *too much/many*, or they can mean *very*, *not very*, *so*, *too*

- **questo** and **quello**, which mean *this* and *that* and also *this one/that one*

- the Italian words for *my*, *our*, *your*, *his/her*, *their*, which are the same as *mine*, *ours*, *yours*, *his/hers*, *theirs*

The grammatical explanation is that these words can belong in more than one category: whether adjectives (describing a noun), adverbs (adding information to an adjective, a verb or another adverb) or pronouns (standing in for a noun).

It's important to understand which they happen to be in a sentence because, not only is the English translation slightly different, but adjectives and pronouns change their ending to agree with the noun they relate to, whereas adverbs don't.

The words in this unit aren't the only words to fit in more than one grammatical category. The following are regularly used as both adjectives and adverbs:

chiaro *clear; clearly, openly*	**diritto** *straight; straight on*
forte *loud, strong; loudly*	**piano** *slow, soft; slowly, quietly*
lontano *faraway; far*	**vicino** *near; nearby*
solo *alone, lonely; only*	**giusto** *right, correct; correctly*

molto, poco, tanto, troppo

Molto, **poco**, **tanto** and **troppo** can be adjectives, pronouns or adverbs.

- When they're adjectives, they mean:
  molto *much, many, a lot of*   **poco** *not much, little, few*
  tanto *so much/many*   **troppo** *too much/many*
  and, like other adjectives ending in **-o**, the **-o** can change to **-a**, **-i** or **-e** to agree with the noun/pronoun they describe (page 54).

  Non ho molto tempo oggi. *I don't have a lot of time today.*
  Accetto con molto piacere. *I accept with much pleasure.*
  C'è molta rabbia. *There's a lot of/a great deal of anger.*
  Non ho molti soldi. *I don't have much/a lot of money.*
  Ci sono stato molte volte. *I've been there many times.*

  C'è poco spazio. *There's little room/not much room.*
  Ha poca pazienza. *He doesn't have much patience.*
  Arriverà fra pochi minuti. *He'll be here in a few minutes.*
  Ho ricevuto poche risposte. *I've received few replies.*

  C'è tanto rumore *There's so much/such a lot of noise*
  ... e tanta emozione. *... and so much emotion.*
  Tanti auguri! *All the best.* lit. *So many good wishes.*
  Tante grazie. *Thank you so much.* lit. *So many thanks.*

  Ho troppo lavoro. *I've got too much work.*
  Esiste troppa burocrazia. *There's too much bureaucracy.*
  C'erano troppi turisti. *There were too many tourists.*
  ... e troppe macchine. *... and too many cars.*

- They can also be pronouns:
  Non ne ho molto. *I don't have a lot (of it).*
  Me ne hai dato troppo. *You've given me too much (of it).*

  The masculine plural **molti**, **pochi**, **tanti** and **troppi** are often used to mean people in a general sense:
  È un problema per molti. *It's a problem for many people.*
  Pochi sanno la verità. *Few people know the truth.*
  La pizza piace a tanti. *So many people like pizza.*
  Troppi sono obesi. *Too many people are obese.*

- When they're adverbs, they mean:

  molto *very (much), a lot*   **poco** *not very, not much*
  tanto *so (much)*   **troppo** *too (much)*

  and, like all adverbs, their ending never changes.

  Anna è molto simpatica. *Anna's very nice.*
  Mi piace molto l'idea. *I like the idea very much.*
  Mangio molto a mezzogiorno. *I eat a lot at midday.*

  Lui/lei è poco affidabile. *He/She's not very reliable.*
  Abbiamo dormito poco. *We haven't slept much.*

  Sono tanto bravi. *They're so good/clever.*
  Questa mi piace tanto. *I like this one so much.*

  Sono arrivati troppo presto. *They arrived too early.*
  Ho speso troppo. *I've spent too much.*

- They can be followed by **da** and a verb:

  C'è molto da vedere? *Is there a lot to see?*
  C'è poco da mangiare. *There's not much to eat.*
  Rimane tanto da scoprire. *There's still so much to find out.*
  Ho troppo da fare. *I've got too much to do.*

Don't confuse **poco** *not very* with **un poco** *a little, a bit*, which is usually shortened to **un po'** and can be used:
- on its own:
  Solo un po' per me. *Just a little for me.*
  Aspetto da un po'. *I've been waiting for a little while.*
- with an adjective:
  Sono un po' stanco. *I'm a bit tired.*
  È un po' troppo piccolo. *It's a bit too small.*
  Comincia un poco più tardi. *It starts a little later.*
- with **di** and a noun:
  Vorrei un po' di zucchero. *I'd like a little sugar.*
  Ecco un poco del vino locale. *Here's a little of the local wine*

questo and quello

Grammatically speaking, **questo** *this* and **quello** *that* are called **demonstratives** and they're used in two ways: with a noun as adjectives or on their own as pronouns.

When **questo** and **quello** are adjectives, they:
- go in front of the noun they describe
- change their ending to agree with that noun.

Questo, like other adjectives ending in **o**, changes to **questa**, **questi** or **queste**:

in questo modo *this way*; **in questo momento** *at this moment*
questa casa *this house*; **questa settimana** *this week*
questi vini *these wines*; **questi mesi** *these months*
queste parole *these words*; **queste macchine** *these cars*

Questo and **questa** (but never **questi** and **queste**) can be shortened to **quest'** before a vowel:

quest'anno *this year*; **quest'estate** *this summer*

Quello behaves in a similar way to the definite article (page 46) and **bello** *beautiful* (page 58):

il treno *the train*	**quel treno** *that train*
lo sciopero *the strike*	**quello sciopero** *that strike*
l'uomo *the man*	**quell'uomo** *that man*
l'intervista *the interview*	**quell'intervista** *that interview*
la sera *the evening*	**quella sera** *that evening*
i giorni *the days*	**quei giorni** *those days*
gli ospiti *the guests*	**quegli ospiti** *those guests*
le persone *the people*	**quelle persone** *those people*

You can use the adjectives **questo** and **quello** with other adjectives or with numbers:

questo inutile sito web *this useless website*
questa grande passione *this great passion*
quel posto tranquillo *that quiet place*
quell'altra avventura *that other adventure*
quegli ultimi giorni *those last days*
queste due settimane *these two weeks*

When **questo** and **quello** are used without a noun (i.e. are pronouns):

- they agree with the noun they stand for
- **quello** has only four forms: **quello, quella, quelli, quelle**
- **questo/a** is translated into English as *this* or *this one* and **quello/a** as *that* or *that one*.

Questo is often used in introductions:
Questo è mio marito. *This is my husband.*
Questa è mia moglie. *This is my wife.*
Questi sono i miei amici. *These are my friends.*
Queste sono le nostre figlie. *These are our daughters.*

Questo and **quello** are used for comparing and contrasting:
Ecco le camere – questa è più grande di quella.
Here are the bedrooms – this one's bigger than that one.
Prendo quelli in vetrina, non mi piacciono questi.
I'll take those in the window, I don't like these.

For emphasis, you can add **qui** or **qua** *here* to **questo**, and **lì** or **là** *there* to **quello**. There's no real difference in meaning between **qui** and **qua** or **lì** and **là**:
Abbiamo due tavoli, questo qui e quello lì in fondo.
We have two tables, this one and that one at the end.
Questa qua è per te, quella lì per me.
This one's for you, that one for me.

You can use **questo** and **quello** with other pronouns:
Preferisco quest'altra. *I prefer this other one.*
Mi piacciono quelli neri. *I like those black ones.*

Ciò can be used for *this* or *that* when you're referring to a whole idea or situation rather than to a specific noun. **Ciò** is singular and it never changes.
Ciò mi sorprende. *That surprises me.*
Ciò non ti riguarda. *This has nothing to do with you.*
Ciò nonostante, vincerò. *In spite of this/that, I'll win.*
Puoi fare ciò che vuoi. *You can do what you want.*
E con ciò? *So what?* lit. *And with that?*

possession

When you're talking about ownership and possession in Italian, there are four things to remember:

- There's no equivalent of the English apostrophe -s ('s) as in *Paul's* house or the *company's address*. Neither is there the equivalent of two nouns together as in *company address* or *telephone number*.

  Instead, you always say *the house of Paul; the address of the company. Of* is **di**, changing to **del**, **della**, etc. (page 48) when followed by *the*.
  la casa di Paolo *Paul's house*
  l'indirizzo della società *the company's address*
  il numero di telefono *the phone number*

- There's only one set of possessive words, with no difference between *my, our, your, his/her, their* and *mine, ours, yours, his/hers, theirs*.

- The possessive words all have *the* in front of them.

	singular		plural	
m	f	m	f	
il mio	la mia	i miei	le mie	*my, mine*
il tuo	la tua	i tuoi	le tue	*your, yours* **tu**
il suo	la sua	i suoi	le sue	*his/her, hers, its, your, yours* **lei**
il nostro	la nostra	i nostri	le nostre	*our, ours*
il vostro	la vostra	i vostri	le vostre	*your, yours* **voi**
il loro	la loro	i loro	le loro	*their, theirs*

- The possessive words agree with what's owned, not with the owner. *My house* is **la mia casa**, regardless of whether it's a man or a woman talking.

  It's particularly important to bear this in mind with **suo/sua/suoi/sue**, which can mean *his, her, its* or *your* (when *you* is someone you call **lei**).

  Roberto guida la sua macchina. *Robert drives his car.*
  Paola guida la sua macchina. *Paola drives her car.*
  Lei guida la sua macchina. *You drive your car.*

Possessive adjectives *my, our, your, his/her, its, their:*
- agree with the noun that follows them:
  il mio nome *my name*   **la nostra casa** *our house*
  il loro indirizzo *their address*   **i loro indirizzi** *their addresses*

- are used less in Italian than in English – they're omitted when it's clear who the possessor is.
  Gabriele è con la madre. *Gabriele's with his mother.*
  Mi fa male la spalla. *My shoulder hurts.*
  Ho qualcosa nell'occhio. *I have something in my eye.*
  Hai trovato gli occhiali? *Have you found your glasses?*

- can be used with **un/una**:
  un mio fratello *one of my brothers*
  una mia amica *a friend of mine, one of my friends*

- are used without *the* when talking about one individual family member:
  mia figlia *my daughter*   **sua moglie** *his wife*
  nostro cugino *our cousin*   **vostro padre** *your father*
  except with **loro** and when the person is described in some way:
  la loro sorella *their sister*   **il loro nonno** *their grandfather*
  la tua sorellina *your little sister*
  la sua seconda moglie *his second wife*
  il nostro zio americano *our American uncle*

- can also be used without *the*:
  a) when possession is being stressed: **Questa valigia è mia.** *This case is mine* (and nobody else's).
  b) in a few colloquial expressions: **amore mio** *my love*; **cara mia** *my dear*; **è colpa mia** *it's my fault*; **a casa nostra** *to our house.*

Possessive pronouns *mine, ours, yours, his/hers, theirs*
- are used without a noun but agree with the noun they stand for:
  La mia è qui. *Mine's here.* (referring to something feminine)
  I passaporti? Ecco il mio. Dov'è il tuo? *Passports? Here's mine. Where's yours?*
  E le valigie? Le nostre sono con le loro. *And the cases? Ours are with theirs.*

- are often used in the masculine plural to mean *family*:
  Vi presento i miei. *Let me introduce my family to you.*
  Di dove sono i tuoi? *Where's your family from?*

1   Choose the right word for the gap.

   a **Ci sono** _____ monumenti. (molto, molti)

   b **Lucia è** _____ simpatica. (tanto, tanta)

   c **Ho** _____ da fare oggi. (molto, molti)

   d **È** _____ utile. (poca, poco)

   e **Le scarpe sono un po'** _____ grandi. (troppo, troppe)

2   Which of these four sentences means something completely different from the others?

   a **Raffaele è poco intelligente.**

   b **Raffaele è un po' stupido.**

   c **Raffaele è intelligente.**

   d **Raffaele non è molto intelligente.**

3   What would you need to add to **un po'** in a sentence like _I'd like a little milk please._

4   Which form of **questo** would you use to introduce

   a your sister   **b** two colleagues   **c** your boyfriend

   d your father   **e** your daughter   **f** two aunts

5   Put the correct form of **quello** before these nouns:

   a _____ **chef**   b _____ **casa**

   c _____ **donne**   d _____ **alberghi**

   e _____ **uomo**   f _____ **parco**

   g _____ **turisti**   h _____ **ragazzo**

6   What words can you add to **questo** and **quello** when you're contrasting two items?

7   When would you use **ciò**?

8   What are the Italian words for _my_ with the people in Question 4 above?

9   If you hear someone talking about **i miei**, who or what are they referring to?

10 What are the three ways of saying _your car_? How would you say _yours_ (referring to the car)?

11 And to say _their car_, do you need **loro**, **la loro** or **le loro** before **macchina**? How would you say _It's theirs_?

12 Still on the subject of cars, what's the Italian for _my new car_?

Personal pronouns

A pronoun is a word which replaces a noun to avoid repeating it:
The plumber called – **he**'s going to be late.
Have you seen **the children**? I can't find **them**.
Where's **my key**? I've lost **it**?

The main pronoun groups are:
- demonstrative, e.g. *this one, those* (page 73)
- possessive, e.g. *mine, yours, theirs* (page 75)
- relative, e.g. *who, which, that* (pages 90-91)
- interrogative, e.g. *what, which* (page 128)
- personal, e.g. *I, she, we, us, them*.

Personal pronouns can be:
- the subject of a verb: *I, we, you, he, she, they*;
- the direct object of a verb: *me, us, you, him, her, them*;
- the indirect object of a verb: *(to/for) me, (to/for) us, (to/for) you, (to/for) him, (to/for) her, (to/for) them*. Italian has single words for these.

There are differences in the way personal pronouns are used in English and Italian. Subject pronouns are used far less often – you don't need them to tell you who's doing what because that information is carried in the ending of the verb. Object pronouns usually go before the verb, not after it – except in certain circumstances, such as when you're emphasising them: *I love **you** not **her***. A few pronouns combine when there are two next to each other.

subject pronouns

io *I*	noi *we*
tu *you*	voi *you*
lui *he*	loro *they*
lei *she, you*	

Io is only written with a capital letter when it starts a sentence.

There are three words for *you*:
- **tu**: someone you call by their first name;
- **lei**: someone you don't know well, someone older than you. It can be written with a capital letter in formal correspondence, and the verb with it has the same ending as for **lei** *she*;
- **voi**: more than one person. In a really formal situation, you might hear **loro** used instead of **voi**.

Subject pronouns, which can go before or after the verb in Italian, are used much less than in English because the verb ending shows who's doing what. So they tend to be used only when you want to emphasise them:

Lui lavora qui ... *He works here* ...
... mentre io lavoro a Roma. ... *while I work in Rome.*
Noi non possiamo andare ma tu sì. *We can't go but you can.*
Io non so dov'è. *I don't know where it is.*
Pagano loro? *Are they paying?*
Come si chiama lei? *What's your name? What's her name?*
Lui, come si chiama? *What's his name?*

For even greater emphasis, you can add **stesso/a/i/e**:
Io stesso credo che ... *I myself believe that* ...
L'ha scritto lei stessa? *Did she write it herself?*
Voi stessi l'avete visto. *You saw him yourselves.*

Subject pronouns are also used in phrases like these:
Sono io. *It's me.*
Chi, io? *Who, me?*
È lui! È lei! *It's him! It's her!*
Anche noi. *Us too. So are we. So have we.*
Neanch'io. *Nor me./Neither am I./Nor did I.*

si: undefined subject

When the subject of a verb is nobody in particular, **si** is often used.
The English equivalent is *one, you, we, they, people*, or sentences like *English is spoken here; Fine wines are produced in Italy*.

- The verb with **si** has the same ending as *he/she*.
  Si può parcheggiare qui? *Can you park here?*
  Si compra online o in negozio. *You can buy it/It can be bought online or in the shops.*
  Si deve riciclare. *People should recycle.*
  Non si sa mai. *You never know.*

- An adjective used with **si** is masculine plural, even though it comes after **è** *is* or **era** *was*:
  quando si è stanchi/soli *when one is tired/alone*
  si era disorientati *people were disorientated*
  una volta che si è nominati *once you're nominated*

- When there's a direct object after **si** + verb, that verb is singular with a singular object and plural with a plural object:
  A Natale si mangia il tacchino. *At Christmas, people eat turkey.*
  A Pasqua si mangiano le uova di cioccolato. *At Easter, people eat chocolate eggs.*

- When **si** is used with a reflexive verb (page 116), **ci si** is used instead of **si si**.
  Come ci si innamora? *How does one fall in love?*
  Ci si è incontrati la sera. *We met up in the evening.*
  Non ci si può fare niente. *It can't be helped.*

You can find out how to do almost anything by using **come si** + the third person of a verb:
Come si dice ... in italiano? *How do you say ... in Italian?*
Come si pronuncia questa parola? *How do you say this word?*
Come si scrive? *How do you write it? How is it written?*
Come si usa questo coso? *How do you use this thingummy?*
Come si apre/chiude? *How do you open/close it?*
Come si paga? *How do you pay?*
Come si fa il panettone? *How do you make panettone?*
Come si fa a iscriversi? *How do you go about joining?*

object pronouns

Object pronouns (*me, us, you, him, her, them*) can either be:

- the direct object of a verb: *Anna knows <u>me</u>, the children saw <u>him</u>, I've invited <u>them</u>*
- or the indirect object of a verb: *Anna writes <u>to me</u>, the children listened <u>to him</u>; I've made a cake <u>for them</u>*.

In Italian, there's no distinction made between these four direct and indirect object pronouns:

mi *me, to/for me*	**ti** *you, to/for you* **(tu)**
ci *us, to/for us*	**vi** *you, to/for you* **(voi)**

Anna mi/ci conosce. *Anna knows me/us.*
Anna mi/ci scrive. *Anna writes to me/to us.*

However, the pronouns *him, her, them, you* **(lei)** are entirely different words from *to/for him, to/for her, to/for them, to/for you*.

direct	**indirect**
lo *him, it* (m)	**gli** *to/for him*
la *her, it* (f), *you* **(lei)**	**le** *to/for her, to/for you* **(lei)**
li *them* (m)	**gli** or **loro** *to/for them* (m & f)
le *them* (f)	

Anna lo/la conosce. *Anna knows him/her/you.*
Anna gli/le scrive. *Anna writes to him/to her/to you.*
Li ho invitati. *I've invited them.*
Gli ho fatto una torta. *I've made a cake for them.*

- **Li** is used when *them* refers to a mixed masculine and feminine group:
  Anna e Giorgio? Li conosco bene. *I know them well.*

- **Le** can mean *them* (f plural), *to her* and *to you* **(lei)**.
  Le conosco bene. *I know them* (f) *well.*
  Le hanno scritto? *Have they written to her/to you?*

- **Gli** can mean *to him* or *to them*:
  Gli ho dato le chiavi. *I gave the keys to him/to them.*
  If there's any ambiguity, **loro** can be used instead of **gli** for *to them*. **Loro** goes after the verb:
  Ho dato loro le chiavi. *I gave the keys to them.*

- **Lo** *it* is often not translated into English:
  Non lo so. Lo sai tu? *I don't know (it). Do you know (it)?*

direct or indirect object?

In general, the same verbs take a direct or indirect object in English and Italian. However, there are some to look out for.

- With some verbs it's not immediately obvious that the object is indirect because there are two ways of using them in English – with or without a preposition before the pronoun:
  Gli ho spedito una mail. *I sent an email to him./I sent him an email.*
  Le ho comprato un gelato. *I bought an ice cream for you./I bought you an ice cream.*
  Gli può dare questo? *Can you give this to them?/Can you give them this?*

  Similar verbs include **chiedere, domandare** *to ask,* **dare** *to give,* **dire** *to tell,* **insegnare** *to teach,* **mandare** *to send,* **mostrare** *to show,* **offrire** *to offer, give,* **regalare** *to give, present,* **portare** *to bring,* **restituire** *to give back,* **scrivere** *to write.*

- Unlike English, the following have an indirect object in Italian:
  telefonare *to phone*   **piacere** *to please* (page 177)
  fare male *to hurt*   **volere bene** *to love*

  Le ho telefonato. *I phoned you.* lit. *I phoned to you.*
  Le piacciono i fichi? *Do you like figs?* lit. *Are figs pleasing to you?*
  Gli fanno male i piedi. *His feet are hurting him.* lit. *His feet are doing harm to him.*
  La odio o le voglio bene? *Do I hate her or love her?* lit. *Do I hate her or want good for her?*

- In English, these verbs are followed by a preposition before a noun whereas in Italian they have a direct object:
  ascoltare *to listen to*   **chiedere** *to ask for*
  aspettare *to wait for*   **cercare** *to look for*
  guardare *to look at*   **pagare** *to pay for*

  Lo ascolto spesso. *I listen to him/to it often.*
  Sto aspettando un'amica. La sto aspettando. *I'm waiting for a friend. I'm waiting for her.*
  Il caffè ... chi lo paga? *The coffee ... who's paying ?*

position of object pronouns

- Object pronouns, direct and indirect, generally go before a verb:
  Mi capisce? *Do you understand me?*
  Mi dia la valigia. *Give me your case. Give your case to me.*
  Ti credo. *I believe you.*
  Ti mostro la casa. *I'll show the house to you.*
  Lo conosci? *Do you know him?*
  Gli hai scritto? *Have you written to him?*
  Li conosco bene. *I know them well.*
  Gli ho chiesto di aspettare. *I asked them to wait.*

- When the verb is an infinitive (i.e. ending in **-are**, **-ere** or **-ire**) pronouns follow it, attaching themselves to it without its final **e**:
  È difficile crederti. *It's difficult to believe you.*
  Posso mostrarvi la casa? *Can I show the house to you?*
  Bisogna scrivergli. *You have to write to him.*

- When the infinitive is after **dovere** *to have to*, **potere** *to be able to* or **volere** *to want to*, pronouns can either be attached to the infinitive or they can go before **dovere**, **potere**, **volere**:
  Voglio mostrarti la casa/Ti voglio mostrare la casa. *I want to show the house to you.*
  Puoi spiegarmi le regole?/Mi puoi spiegare le regole?
  Can you explain the rules to me?

- Object pronouns follow **ecco**, some imperatives (page 165) and usually the gerund (page 162), attaching themselves to them:
  Eccola! *Here she is! There she is!*
  Scusatemi. *Please excuse me.*
  Chiediamogli. *Let's ask him. Let's ask them.*
  Guardandola, ho visto che … *Looking at her, I saw that ….*

You'll find that **ci** *there* (page 93) and **ne** *of it/of them* (pages 94-95) follow the same rules as object pronouns where position is concerned.

object pronouns and the past tense

When you're talking about the past and using third person object pronouns, i.e. *him*, *her*, *it*, *them*:

- **lo** and **la** usually shorten to **l'** before **h** or a vowel
- the past participle (page 148) has to agree with the noun represented by direct pronouns **l'**, **lo**, **la**, **li** or **le**. However, there's no agreement with indirect pronouns.

L'ho visto ieri. *I saw him yesterday.*
Francesca? L'ho vista oggi. *Francesca? I saw her today.*
Dov'è il cane? L'hai lasciato da Marco? *Where's the dog? Have you left it at Marco's?*
I biglietti! Li ha dimenticati. *The tickets! He's forgotten them.*
Le lettere? Le ho spedite. *The letters? I've posted them.*
Le abbiamo invitate tutte. *We invited them* (f) *all.*

emphatic pronouns

To emphasise an object pronoun you use the following – which are the same as the subject pronouns (page 78) except for **me** and **te**.

me *me*	**noi** *us*
te *you*	**voi** *you*
lui *him*	**loro** *them*
lei *her, you*	

Ho visto lei, non lui. *I saw her, not him.*
Hanno dato i soldi a me. *They gave the money to me.*

These are the pronouns you use after a preposition (page 107):
Secondo me, è troppo presto. *In my opinion it's too early.*
Posso viaggiare con te? *Can I travel with you?*
Cesare è più giovane di lei. *Cesare is younger than her/you.*
Elena è andata da loro. *Elena's gone to their house.*
Era seduta fra lui e me. *She was sitting between him and me.*
Questi sono per te/lei/voi. *These are for you.*

combined object pronouns

When indirect object pronouns are used in the same sentence as direct object pronouns or **ne** (page 95):

- they change:

mi, ti, ci, vi	change to	me, te, ce, ve
gli and le	change to	glie-

- they go before the direct pronoun or **ne**:

  Me lo spedirà? *Will you send it to me?*
  Ve li mostro subito. *I'll show them to you straightaway.*
  Te ne ho comprato uno. *I've bought you one.*

- glie combines with **lo, la, li, le, ne**:

	lo	la	li	le	ne
mi	me lo	me la	me li	me le	me ne
ti	te lo	te la	te li	te le	te ne
gli/le	glielo	gliela	glieli	gliele	gliene
ci	ce lo	ce la	ce li	ce le	ce ne
vi	ve lo	ve la	ve li	ve le	ve ne
gli	glielo	gliela	glieli	gliele	gliene

La fotografia – gliela regalo. *The photo – I'm giving it to him/her/them.*
Il vino – gliene regalo una bottiglia. *The wine – I'm giving him/her/them a bottle of it.*
Gliene regalo cinque. *I'm giving him/her/them five of them.*

Glie combined with another pronoun has several possible meanings:
Gliel'ho mandato can mean *I sent it to him/I sent it to her/I sent it to you/ I sent it to them.*

However, this rarely causes confusion because the meaning is usually obvious from the context. If there is any potential ambiguity or if you want to emphasise who the recipient is, then you can use **a lui, a lei** or **a loro** instead of **glie-**:

L'ho mandato a lui. *I sent it to him.*
L'ho mandato a lei. *I sent it to her./I sent it to you.*
L'ho mandato a loro. *I sent it to them.*

reflexive pronouns

mi	myself
ti	yourself **tu**
si	himself, herself, itself, yourself **lei**
ci	ourselves
vi	yourselves **voi**
si	themselves

These pronouns are an integral part of reflexive verbs (pages 116-117), and as such are often not translated into English:

Mi diverto tanto. *I enjoy myself so much.*
Mi alzo alle otto. *I get (myself) up at eight o'clock.*
Si è ucciso. *He killed himself.*
Quando vi siete sposati? *When did you get married?*

Ci, **vi** and **si** (plural) can mean *each other* or *one another*:
Ci vediamo ogni giorno. *We see each other every day.*
Vi conoscete da molto tempo? *Have you known each other long?*
Si aiutano molto. *They help one another a lot.*

Direct object pronouns and **ne** go after **mi**, **ti**, **si**, **ci**, **vi**, **si**, which change to **me**, **te**, **se**, **ce**, **ve**, **se**. Except for **si**, they result in the same combinations as direct and indirect object pronouns.

	lo	la	li	le	ne
mi	me lo	me la	me li	me le	me ne
ti	te lo	te la	te li	te le	te ne
si	se lo	se la	se li	se le	se ne
ci	ce lo	ce la	ce li	ce le	ce ne
vi	ve lo	ve la	ve li	ve le	ve ne
si	se lo	se la	se li	se le	se ne

Me lo compro. *I'm buying (myself) it.*
Io me ne compro due. *I'm buying myself two (of them).*
Quella canzone? Te la ricordi? *That song? Do you remember it?*
Se ne occupa mio padre. *My father's dealing with it.*
Quei cocomeri – ce ne compriamo uno? *Those watermelons – shall we buy one?*

checkpoint 8

1   How would you say *Hi, it's me* in Italian?

2   Would you use **tu**, **lei** or **voi** for these people?
    a a six-year-old child   b an elderly neighbour
    c two friends   d a new client to your office
    e a student friend   f the person on the hotel reception desk

3   What do these mean?
    a **L'hai visto tu stesso?**   b **Anche loro.**
    c **Non lo conosco bene.**   d **Gli ho parlato.**
    e **Li abbiamo mangiati.**   f **Non l'hai vista?**
    g **Glielo spiego.**   h **Scusateci.**

4   Fill the gap with the correct object pronoun.
    a **Tu** _____ **credi?** *him*   b **Tu** _____ **credi?** *me*
    c **Ho parlato** _____ . *to them*   d **Che cosa** _____ **serve?** *you pl.*
    e _____ **ho mangiato.** *it*   f _____ **telefona ogni giorno.** *to us*
    g _____ **ho mangiate.** *them (f)*   h _____ **dica di aspettare.** *to her*

5   Replace **il caffè** and **i biglietti** with *it* and *them*. There are two
    possible ways of arranging the words.
    Volete assaggiare il caffè?   Devo comprare i biglietti.

6   What's the Italian for these?
    a *with them*   b *for me*
    c *in her opinion*   d *at his place*
    e *Do you (tu) know her?*   f *I phoned you (pl)*
    g *I saw him.*   h *I saw her*
    i *I sent it to him.*   j *Anna sent it (m) to me*

7   What do you think **Qui si parla inglese** means?

8   To emphasise that you've made something yourself, what could you
    add to **L'ho fatto io**?

9   What do the English translations of **pagare**, **cercare** and **aspettare**
    have in common?

10 In *I phoned them yesterday*, what's the Italian for *them*?

Sentence structure

The more Italian you learn, the more you'll progress from simple short phrases to longer sentences which express your needs and opinions in more detail. The two main things to consider when constructing more complex sentences are word order and how to join together the various parts of the sentence.

- Word order is broadly similar in English and Italian although there are some fundamental differences, such as the position in Italian of adjectives after nouns, and pronouns (e.g. *us, him, them*) before verbs.

- To join together the various elements of what you want to say, you can use conjunctions – words like *and, but, since, so, however*. You also need words that save you having to repeat nouns or phrases when you're giving additional information about them: words like **che** and **quale** *who, which*, and the very useful little words **ci** *there* and **ne** *of it/them, about it/ them*.

Progressing isn't simply about more and more grammatical rules. If you listen to native speakers of any language, you'll find that they use words like *well then*, *let's see*, *anyway*, *furthermore*, which bring a sense of continuity to what they say and take it beyond the strictly functional. When you learn a new language, it's an effort at first to remember to use these words as well as everything else – but when you get used to them you'll find not only that they make you sound more fluent but also that they give you useful thinking time when you're stuck for a word.

word order

English and Italian word order is broadly similar – but there are four striking differences between the two languages.

1   When a noun and an adjective are used together, the noun often comes first in Italian whereas in English the adjective always comes first: **una decisione importante** *an important decision*. Even more striking is that Italian has the flexibility to change the position of the adjective for emphasis: **un'importante decisione** *a (truly) important decision*. (pages 56-57)

2   To ask a yes/no question, English brings in words like *do/does* or reverses the order of the subject and noun. *Do you work here? Is she ill?* Italian simply makes the statements *You work here* and *She is ill* sound like questions: **Lavori qui? È ammalata?**

In open questions using words like **quando** *when*, **perché** *why*, the question word can go at the beginning of the question with the verb straight after it: **Quando comincia la partita?** *When does the match start?* or it can go where the answer will be: **La partita comincia quando?** *The match starts when?* (page 126)

3   Where in English you might emphasise a word or phrase with your tone of voice, in Italian you move it to the end: **Camilla è andata?** *Did Camilla go?* **È andata Camilla?** *Did Camilla go?*

This is particularly common with subject pronouns (**io** *I*, **noi** *we*, **loro** *they*, etc) which aren't used routinely in Italian because the information they carry is already stored in the ending of the verb: **Sono andata** *I went*; **Sono andata io** *I went*. (page 78)

4   When the object of a verb is a pronoun (*me, us, you, him, her, it, them*: page 80) it generally goes in front of the verb in Italian and after it in English (page 82):
Guido mi telefona ogni giorno. *Guido phones me every day.*
L'ho lasciato sul treno. *I left it on the train.*

joining parts of a sentence

The words on this page will help you join together the various elements of what you say, and bring logic and continuity to your sentences.

- Draw things together with **e** *and*, **anche** *also*, **né** *neither/nor*.

- Express reservation with **però** *however* or **ma** *but*. For emphasis you can add **invece** *instead* to **ma**.

- Introduce alternatives with **o**, **oppure** *or*, **altrimenti** *otherwise*, **invece** *instead, rather*.

- Contrast two elements with **da una parte** *on the one hand* and **dall'altra** *on the other (hand)*.

- Show you're about to infer a conclusion with **dunque**, **perciò**, **quindi** which all mean *so, therefore*.

- Reinforce or clarify what you've said with **cioè** *that is, i.e.*, **anzi** *in fact, indeed*, **per esempio** *for example*.

- Provide detail with **dove** *where*, **quando** *when*, **mentre** *while, whereas*.

- Introduce an explanation with **perché** *because*, **siccome** or **poiché**, *since*, **dato che** *given that*.

- Show there's a consequence with **allora** or **poi**, both meaning *then*, **di conseguenza** *as a result*.

- Introduce a condition with **se** *if*.

- Introduce further information about something you've just mentioned with **che** or **il/la quale**, **i/le quali** *who, which, that*.

Dal momento che means *since/given that*, not to be confused with **al momento di** *at the moment of* and **nel momento in cui** *at the moment in which*.

Infatti is closer to *indeed* or *as a matter of fact* than to *in fact*, which is **in effetti**, **anzi** or **in realtà**.

which, who, whom, whose, that

These words save you having to repeat a noun or a phrase when you're giving additional information about it. Grammatically they're known as *relative pronouns*, and the one used most in Italian is **che**.

- **Che** can mean *who*, whom*, which, that*. It never changes and it isn't omitted as its equivalent often is in English.
  mio fratello, che vive con me *my brother, who lives with me*
  l'uomo che tu non conosci *the man (whom) you don't know*
  le foto che ti ho promesso *the photos (which) I promised you*
  gli stivali che ho comprato *the boots (which) I bought*
  È il rosso che preferisci? *Is it the red one (that) you prefer?*

- **Cui** is used instead of **che** after a preposition. In Italian, prepositions never go at the end of a sentence as in the second translations below:
  l'uomo con cui vivo *the man with whom I live, the man I live with*
  la casa in cui vivo *the house in which I live, the house I live in*
  i film per cui è famoso *the films for which he's famous, the films he's famous for*
  le musiciste di cui parlavo *the musicians about whom I was talking, the musicians I was talking about*

- **Il, la, i, le + cui** mean *whose** or *of which*. The agrees with the noun which follows **cui**.
  L'uomo la cui moglie è m̲edico. *The man whose wife is a doctor.*
  Una bella villa, il cui giardino dà sul mare. *A beautiful house, whose garden looks over the sea.*

- **Il che** is used when you're referring to a whole idea rather than to a particular noun: conveying the English *which* or *and this*.
  Lui dice che è impossi̲bile, il che non è vero. *He says it's impossible, which isn't true.*
  Non è andato, il che mi sorprende. *He didn't go, which surprises me.*
  L'alloggio è lussuoso, il che si riflette nel prezzo. *The accommodation is luxurious, and this is reflected in the price.*

*In a statement only. In a question, *who/whom* is **chi**, *whose* is **di chi** (page 127).

- **Quale** also means *which* or *who* but, unlike **che**, **quale** is always preceded by *the*, and it has a plural:

  il terzo concerto, il quale era il migliore *the third concert, which was the best*

  mia sorella, la quale vive con me *my sister, who lives with me*

  gli altri biglietti, i quali sono più cari *the other tickets, which are more expensive*

  le foto ingrandite, le quali ti ho promesso *the enlarged photos, which I promised you*

- **Il quale, la quale, i quali, le quali** can be used instead of **cui** after prepositions. Some prepositions combine with **il/la/i/le** (page 48).

  l'uomo con il quale vivo *the man I live with*

  la casa nella quale vivo *the house I live in*

  i colleghi con i quali lavoro *the colleagues I work with*

  le scarpe delle quali parlavo *the shoes I was talking about*

Quale is more formal and less widely used than **che**. It's useful, though, in sentences such as **la madre di Marco che lavora con me** *the mother of Marco who works with me*, where **che** doesn't make it clear whether it's Marco or his mother who works with me: **La madre di Marco il quale lavora con me.** i.e. *Marco works with me* or **La madre di Marco la quale lavora con me.** i.e. *his mother works with me*.

checkpoint 9

Fill the gaps with **che**, **cui**, **il che**, **quale** or **quali**.

1 Questo è Guido .... lavora con me.
2 Sono i tre amici con .... gioco a tennis.
3 La bistecca .... ho mangiato al ristorante era deliziosa.
4 Marta non è arrivata .... è strano.
5 Ecco l'ospedale nel .... la vittima è morta.
6 Hai visto lo zaino .... ho comprato ieri?
7 Conosci il signor Ponza la .... figlia abita qui?
8 La macchina nella .... siamo andati a Roma.

making conversation flow

Words that help the flow of conversation, such as *well*, are difficult to translate exactly – making it more effective to focus on the context they're used in.

- **Allora** can convey *Well then…*, *So …*, *Right then…* at the start of a sentence. Other words used in the same way include **ecco**, **dunque**, **mah**.

- **Beh**, also meaning *well*, suggests a bit of uncertainty or hesitation.

- **Boh** shrugs something off, conveying *I don't really know and frankly I don't care. Whatever!*

- **Però** and **comunque** mean *however*, indicating that you're about to offer an alternative viewpoint. You could also use **tuttavia** *still*, *nevertheless*, *anyway*.

- **Insomma** is used where English might use *basically*, *all in all*, *on the whole*.

- **Addirittura** *even* can be used to reinforce what you're saying.

- **Anzi** *in fact* can either add further weight to what you've just said or introduce contrary information.

opinions

When giving your opinion, you can start with **secondo me** or **a mio parere** *in my view*. To strengthen your argument you can use **chiaramente** *clearly* or **ovviamente** *obviously*.

As you get into your stride you can punctuate what you're saying with **in primo luogo** *first of all*, **in secondo luogo** *secondly*, and summarise with **in breve** *in short*.

And you can show that you're coming to a conclusion with **quindi** or **perciò** *so*, *therefore*, **in conclusione**, **per finire** or **alla fine** *finally*.

Cosa ne pensi?, **Cosa ne pensa?** *What do you think about it?* bring others into the discussion. Or you can use **secondo te/lei**, **a tuo/suo parere** *in your opinion* instead.

To agree with someone you can say **sono d'accordo** *I agree* or **ha/hai ragione** *you're right*, and when you disagree you use **non sono d'accordo**.

ci

Ci is a very frequently used word in Italian, with several different meanings. Its use as *us, ourselves* and *each other* is explained on pages 80, 84-85, whereas here the focus is on its other meanings and its role in drawing sentences together. Although usually before the verb, **ci** attaches itself to the end of infinitives, imperatives (page 165) and gerunds (page 162).

- **Ci** can mean *there*. It shortens to **c'** before **e** and changes to **ce** when it's followed by **ne** (page 94):

  C'è una banca in centro. *There's a bank in the centre.*
  C'era troppo rumore. *There was too much noise.*
  Ci sono molti negozi. *There are a lot of shops.*
  Ce n'è una in centro. *There's one in the centre.*
  Ce ne sono molti. *There are lots of them.*
  È inutile andarci. *It's no use going there.*
  Andiamoci. *Let's go there.*

- It saves you having to repeat a phrase when talking about places:

  A Roma? Non ci siamo mai stati. *To Rome? We've never been there.*
  Vai in Australia quest'anno? No, non ci vado. *Are you going to Australia this year. No, I'm not going there.*
  Vado all'albergo. Ci vado subito. *I'm going to the hotel. I'm going there straightaway.*

- Some Italian verbs are followed by **a**. **Ci** can replace the phrase introduced by **a**:

  Non credo alle voci. Ci credi tu? *I don't believe in the rumours. Do you believe them?*
  Sei riuscito a chiudere la valigia? No, non ci sono riuscito. *Did you manage to shut the case? No, I didn't manage (to do it).*
  Stai pensando alla crisi? Sì, pensandoci … *Are you thinking about the crisis? Yes, thinking about it …*

Ci features in many idiomatic phrases:
Ce l'hai la chiave? *Have you got the key?*
Sì, ce l'ho in tasca. *Yes, I've got it in my pocket*
Cosa c'entra? *What's that got to do with it?*
Ci vuole pazienza. *It takes patience.*
Non ce la faccio. *I just can't do it.*
Non ci capisco niente. *I don't understand a thing.*

---

ne

Ne, which usually goes before the verb, is a pronoun, saving the need to repeat a noun that's previously been mentioned. It's often not translated in English – but you don't leave it out in Italian.

It corresponds to *some*, *any*, *of it*, *of them* in phrases involving quantity and numbers.

Ne ho/non ne ho. *I have some./I don't have any.*
Quanto ne vuole? *How much (of it) would you like?*
Quanti ne vuole? *How many (of them) would you like?*
Ne prendo due bottiglie. *I'll take two bottles (of it).*
Figli? Ne abbiamo tre. *Children? We have three (of them).*
Banche? Ce ne sono alcune. *Banks? There are a few (of them).*

When used in this way in the past tenses that use **avere** (page 00), the past participle has to agree with what **ne** stands for:

Abbiamo acqua minerale, ne ho comprata una bottiglia. *We've got mineral water, I've bought a bottle.*
Zucchini? Ne ho comprati un chilo. *Courgettes? I bought a kilo (of them).*

- **Ne** can translate *of it/them*, *about it/them*:
  Ne sono molto contento. *I'm very happy about it.*
  Ne sei fiero? *Are you proud of it/them?*
  Ne siete sicuri? *Are you sure?*
  Ne siamo stufi. *We're fed up with it.*
  It's used in this way with some adjectives that are followed by **di** e.g.

conscio di *aware of*	contento di *happy about*
soddisfatto di *satisfied with*	fiero di *proud of*
pieno di *full of*	certo di *certain of*
sicuro di *sure of*	stufo di *fed up of*

- Similarly, it can replace a phrase introduced by **di** after verbs, e.g.:

accorgersi di *to realise*	parlare di *to talk about*
ricordarsi di *to remember*	vantarsi di *to boast about*
avere bisogno di *to need*	avere paura di *to be afraid of*
avere voglia di *to feel like*	avere vergogna di *to be ashamed of*

  Ne parlo spesso. *I often talk about it.*
  Non se n'è ricordato per niente. *He didn't remember about it at all.*
  Non ne abbiamo bisogno. *We don't need one/any.*
  Sono italiano e me ne vanto! *I'm Italian and proud of it!*

- Although usually before the verb, **ne** attaches itself to the end of infinitives without their final **e**, imperatives (page 165) and gerunds (page 162):
  Vorrei assaggiarne un po'. *I'd like to taste a bit (of it/of them).*
  Ricordatene! *Remember it!*
  Parlandone, ha capito. *Talking about it, he understood.*

- **Ne** comes after indirect object pronouns (page 82) and reflexive pronouns (page 85):
  Gliene posso ordinare tre. *I can order three (of them) for him/her/them/you* (sing.).
  Me ne ha parlato. *He's spoken to me about it.*
  Gliene ha parlato. *He's spoken to him/her/them/you* (sing.) *about it.*
  Se ne occuperà Emilio. *Emilio will deal with it.*

- **Ne** is an integral part of verbs like **andarsene** *to go away,* **starsene** *to stay/remain,* **fregarsene** *to give a damn*:
  Me ne vado domani. *I'm going away tomorrow.*
  Se ne sono andati. *They've gone away.*
  Devo andarmene. *I have to go away.*
  Vattene! *Go away!*
  Devi startene quieto. *You must keep very quiet.*
  Chi se ne frega? *Who cares?/Who gives a damn?*

Little words like **ci** and **ne** can be very confusing at first: not only do they have so many meanings and uses but they often have no English equivalent to relate to. To help you get used to them, choose about six random examples from this page and the previous two. Then see if you can come up with a similar phrase for each one.

For example, based on **ne siamo stufi** *we're fed up with it,* you might come up with:
Ne siamo contenti. *We're happy with it.*
Ne sono stufo/a. *I'm fed up with it.*
Ne siete fieri? *Are you proud of it?*

checkpoint 10

1 Which of these would you use:

Sono d'accordo.

Secondo me...

Cosa ne pensi?

Boh!

Allora...

Da una parte

a when you're about to contrast or compare?
b when asking someone for their opinion?
c if you don't know and don't much care?
d when offering your opinion?
e to say you agree with someone?
Which one is left over and what does it mean?

2 What's the English for che, cui and quale in the following?
a la frutta che ho comprato   b l'uomo che vive qui
c l'amico che abbiamo invitato d l'anno in cui sono nato
e lo zio, il quale tu non conosci f Che bello!
g una persona a cui puoi dire h Arrivano oggi, il che mi
                                    fa tutto molto piacere.

3 Do you need il cui, la cui, i cui or le cui in the gap?
Ho parlato con Laura, ... figli conoscono Giancarlo.

4 Fill these gaps with ci, c' or ne.
a .... sono tante chiese in Italia.
b Macchine: .... abbiamo due.
c Ce .... sono tanti in Italia.
d .... era una grande processione.
e Non .... sono mai stata.
f .... sei sicura?

5 Perciò, poiché, dal momento che, siccome: which is the odd one out?

6 How do you say *I'm going away* in Italian?

7 Which two of these mean the same as però: oppure, ma, comunque, allora?

Prepositions

Prepositions are words like *at, in, on, of, with, to, between*:
I'm **at** home.
He's going **to** Italy, **with** her.
It's **in** the office, **by** the phone.

They have a noun or a pronoun after them; they never go at the end of a sentence or question as in English:
Con chi vai? *Who are you going with?* lit. *With whom are you going?*

A few Italian and English prepositions correspond directly: **attraverso** *through*, **con** *with*, **durante** *during*, **senza** *without*, **sopra** *above*, **sotto** *under*. But this isn't the case for the widely used **a**, **da**, **di** and **in**. For example:

- Italian **in** is used where English uses *in*, *to* and *into*.

- **Da** can mean *from* as in **Leonardo da Vinci** but it also has other meanings, such as **da Fabrizio** *at Fabrizio's place*, **da venerdì** *since Friday*, **da solo** *by oneself*.

- Certain verbs are always followed by **a** or **di**. They're not translated into English; they're simply part of that verb: **giocare a tennis** *to play tennis*; **aver bisogno di aiuto** *to need help*.

It's therefore more effective to associate a preposition with the way it's used than to look for a straight translation.

> Don't forget that when **a**, **da**, **di**, **in** and **su** are followed by *the*, they combine to make **alla**, **dal**, **dei**, **nelle**, etc. (page 48).

a

A, which sometimes becomes ad before a vowel, is used for:

- *to* + a person:
  Ho scritto ... *I've written* ...
  ... a Luciano ... *to Luciano*
  ... a mio padre ... *to my father*
  ... al direttore ... *to the manager*
  ... agli studenti ... *to the students*

- *at, to, in* + places (except see page 104):
  a casa, a letto, a scuola *at home, in bed, at/in school*
  È all'aeroporto. *He's at the airport.*
  È andato all'aeroporto. *He's gone to the airport.*
  Vado a Roma. *I'm going to Rome.*
  Sono a Torino. *I'm in Turin.*
  A̲bito ad Arezzo. *I live in Arezzo.*
  Lidia lavora a Capri. *Lidia works in Capri.*

- *at, in* + time and occasions:
  A che ora arriva/parte? *What time does it arrive/leave?*
  a mezzogiorno/mezzanotte *at 12 noon/midnight*
  all'una *at one o'clock*
  alle dieci *at ten o'clock*
  a Natale/a Pasqua *at Christmas/at Easter*
  a febbraio *in February*

- *to, until*:
  da martedì a giovedì *from Tuesday until Thursday*
  dalle otto alle u̲ndici *from eight to 11 o'clock*
  A domani. *See you tomorrow.* lit. *Until tomorrow.*
  All'anno pro̲ssimo. *See you next year.*

- *a/per*:
  100 chilo̲metri all'ora *100 kph*
  tre volte al giorno *three times per day*
  quattro euro al chilo *four euro per kilo*
  due euro all'etto *two euro per 100 grams*

A is also used:

- when talking about direction, distance and location:
  la prima a destra/sinistra *the first on the right/left*
  È a due chilometri/tre ore. *It's two kilometres/three hours away.*
  È a cinque minuti dal centro. *It's five minutes from the centre.*
  Perugia è a nord di Roma. *Perugia is north of Rome.*

- to describe food and drink:
  agnello alle erbe *lamb cooked with herbs*
  bistecca alla brace *barbecued steak*
  lasagne al forno *baked lasagne*
  fegato alla veneziana *liver, Venetian style*
  gelato al cocco/all'arancia *coconut/orange ice cream*

- after certain adjectives and other prepositions
  abituato al sole *used to the sun*
  bravo a golf *good at golf*
  pronto ad uscire *ready to go out*
  Attenti al cane! *Beware of the dog!*
  accanto alla/di fronte alla banca *next to/opposite the bank*

- after certain verbs (pages 184-185)
  Andiamo a vedere. *Let's go and see.*
  Comincia a piovere. *It's starting to rain.*
  Continua a fare caldo. *It's still hot.*
  Sono riuscito a trovarlo. *I managed to find it.*

Many everyday expressions use **a**:
al dente *not over-cooked (pasta)*; **al sangue** *rare (meat)*
al chiuso *indoors*; **al buio** *in the dark*
alla pari *au pair*; **al verde** *broke*; **a metà** *in half*
addio al celibato/nubilato *stag/hen party*
alla buona *informal*; **alla ribalta** *in the limelight*
alla follia *to distraction*; **agli antipodi** *poles apart*
al contrario *on the contrary*; **al di là** *beyond*
al giorno d'oggi *nowadays*; **a due a due** *two by two*
a bordo *on board*; **a braccio** *off the cuff*; **a piedi** *on foot*

da

Da is used for:

- *from* + time and place:
  dalla A alla Z *from A to Z*
  dalle nove alle undici *from nine to 11 o'clock*
  da lunedì a venerdì *from Monday to Friday*
  dal diciassette al ventisette maggio *from the 17th to 27th May*
  Comincio da domani. *I start from tomorrow.*
  Vengo da Londra. *I come from London.*
  È lontano dal mare. *It's a long way from the sea.*
  Quanto dista da Verona? *How far is it from Verona?*

- *by*:
  il film commissionato da RAI 3 … *the film commissioned by RAI 3 …*
  … e diretto da Luca … *and directed by Luca*
  una poesia scritta da me *a poem written by me*
  una torta fatta dalla nonna *a cake made by my grandmother*
  leggibile dal computer *machine readable*

- *since, for* (page 134):
  Imparo l'italiano *I've been learning Italian*
  … da settembre. *… since September.*
  … da oltre un anno. *… for over a year.*
  Abito qui dal 2008. *I've been living here since 2008.*
  Da quanto tempo aspetti? *How long have you been waiting?*

- *…'s house/place/business*:
  Mangiamo da mia cugina. *We're eating at my cousin's.*
  Andiamo da Giovanna. *Let's go to Giovanna's.*
  Da noi è diverso. *In our house/country it's different.*
  Vado dal dentista. *I'm going to the dentist's.*

- *as a*:
  Da studente era sportivo. *As a student he was sporty.*
  Da bambina, avevo un gatto. *When I was little I had a cat.*
  Che farai da grande? *What will you do when you grow up?*
  È vestita da uomo. *She's dressed as a man.*
  vivere da re/da eremita *to live like a king/ like a hermit*

Da is also used:

- when attaching a price or value to a noun:
  un francobollo da novanta cent̲e̲simi *a €0.90 stamp*
  il menù da quaranta euro *the 40-euro menu*
  una villa da cinque milioni *a five million (euro) house*
  diamanti da un milione *diamonds worth a million*

- to indicate purpose, followed by a noun or a verb:
  occhiali da sole *sunglasses*
  un bicchiere da vino *a wine glass (not a glass of wine)*
  scarpe da tennis *tennis shoes*
  un film da ridere *a comedy film*
  un orologio da uomo *a man's watch*
  una villa da affittare *a villa to let*
  qualcosa da bere *something to drink*
  Cosa c'è da vedere qui? *What is there to see here?*

- when describing a person:
  il ragazzo dai capelli lunghi *the boy with the long hair*
  Lisa dagli occhi blu *Lisa with the blue eyes*
  l'uomo dalla barba grigia *the man with the grey beard*

There are many expressions with **da**:
da solo/a *alone, by oneself*; **l'ho fatto da solo** *I did it by myself*
bello/a da morire *drop-dead gorgeous*
dal sangue freddo/blu *cold/blue blooded*
fuori dal comune *out of the ordinary*
fuori dal mondo *out of this world*
preso dal p̲a̲nico *panic stricken*
fuori dai guai *out of the woods*
a un pelo da ... *within an inch of ...*
cominciare dal niente *to start from scratch*
morire dalla voglia di ... *to be dying to ...*
pi̲a̲ngere dal dolore *to cry from the pain*

di

Di is used for:

- *of*:

  un bicchiere di vino *a glass of wine*
  un chilo di pomodori *a kilo of tomatoes*
  un bambino di cinque anni *a child of five*
  ciascuno di noi *each of us*

- *(made) of*:

  una camicia di seta *a silk shirt*
  stivali di pelle *leather boots*
  botti di legno *wooden barrels*
  È di lana? Di cotone? *Is it wool? Cotton?*

- *some/any* (page 49):

  Mi dà del pane e delle uova. *I'll have some bread and some eggs.*
  Avete delle camere? *Do you have any rooms?*
  Ho comprato delle belle cose. *I've bought some lovely things.*

- *than* with numbers, pronouns and nouns (page 64):

  Ho meno di cinquanta euro. *I've got less than 50 euro.*
  Lui guadagna più di lei. *He earns more than her.*
  È meno dotato del padre. *He's less talented than his father.*
  Giada è più giovane di Martina. *Giada is younger than Martina.*

- *in* after superlatives:

  È l'uomo più alto del mondo. *He's the tallest man in the world.*
  È la più grande città d'Italia. *It's the largest town in Italy.*

- *in, at, on* with some expressions relating to time:

  alle sette di mattina/del mattino *at seven in the morning*
  alle tre di/del pomeriggio *at three in the afternoon*
  alle sette di/della sera *at seven in the evening*
  di domenica *on Sundays*
  d'inverno/d'estate *in winter/in summer*
  (although you say **in primavera** *in spring*, **in autunno** *in autumn*)

Di is also used:

- to indicate possession, belonging (page 74) and provenance:
  la casa di Giorgio *Giorgio's house*
  i figli della padrona *the landlady's children*
  Di chi è questo? *Whose is this?*
  Di dove sei? *Where are you from?*
  Sono di Napoli. *I'm from Naples.*

- where English uses *'s*
  il giornale di oggi *today's paper*
  la fine del viaggio *journey's end*
  l'arrivo del treno *the train's arrival*

- where English uses two nouns together
  una casa di campagna *a country house*
  un film di guerra *a war film*
  una rivista di attualità *a news magazine*
  i drammi di Shakespeare *Shakespeare plays*
  la buccia di limone *lemon peel*
  i numeri di telefono *phone numbers*
  il treno delle undici e cinque *the 11.05 train*

- after **qualcosa** *something* and **niente** *nothing*
  qualcosa di diverso *something different*
  qualcosa di molto piacevole *something very pleasant*
  niente di nuovo *nothing new*
  niente di personale *nothing personal*

- after some adjectives
  coperto di neve *covered in snow*
  contento di essere qui *pleased to be here*
  stanco di viaggiare *tired of travelling*
  sicuro di pagare *sure to pay*

- after some verbs (pages 186-187)
  Spero di andare a Venezia. *I hope to go to Venice.*
  Abbiamo deciso di rimanere. *We've decided to stay.*
  Ho intenzione di ritornare. *I intend to come back.*

in

- *in/into* + place (*the* is often omitted):
  una casa in campagna *a house in the country*
  Devo andare in banca. *I must go to the bank.*
  Vado in città. *I'm going into town.*
  Andiamo in giardino. *Let's go into the garden.*
  Sono in montagna. *They're in the mountains.*
  Si trova nel sud della Spagna. *It's in the south of Spain.*

- *in* + years, months, seasons:
  Ci sono andato nel 2009. *I went there in 2009.*
  Vado in agosto. *I'm going in August.*
  in primavera/in autunno *in spring/in autumn*
  in estate/in inverno *in summer/in winter*

- *by* + means of transport:
  in aereo *by plane*
  in barca *by boat*
  in bicicletta *by bike*
  in corriera *by coach*
  in macchina *by car*
  in treno *by train*

- *in/to* + regions, states, continents, countries and most large islands:
  in Europa *in Europe, to Europe*
  in California *in California, to California*
  Abitano in Australia. *They live in Australia.*
  Siamo andati in Australia. *We went to Australia.*
  È in Germania/in Portogallo. *He's in Germany/in Portugal.*
  Abito in Galles. *I live in Wales.*
  Sei mai stato in Sicilia? *Have you ever been to Sicily?*

  You add *the* after *in* for the UK, countries with a plural name and place names that are described in some way:
  nel Regno Unito *in the UK/to the UK*
  negli Stati Uniti *in the USA/to the USA*
  nell'Italia meridionale *in southern Italy/to southern Italy*
  nel profondo Sud *in/to the deep South*
  nell'Europa dell'Est *in/to Eastern Europe*

per

- *for*:

  Vorrei rimanere per dieci giorni. *I'd like to stay for ten days.*
  Sarà pronto per le otto? *Will it be ready for eight o'clock?*
  Lavora per la banca. *He works for the bank.*
  Cosa c'è per pranzo? *What's for lunch?*
  I fiori sono per te. *The flowers are for you.*
  Siamo in viaggio per la Francia. *We're en route for France.*
  However, you don't need **per** when using **aspettare** *to wait for*, **cercare** *to look for* or **pagare** *to pay for (an item)*.

- *in order to* + infinitive – often translated in English simply as *to*:

  Lavoro per sopravvivere. *I work (in order) to survive.*
  Vado per guardare le balene. *I'm going to watch the whales.*
  Sono venuto per parlarti. *I've come in order to talk to you.*
  E per concludere … *And to finish …*

- *through, along, by*:

  Il treno passa per Bologna. *The train passes through Bologna.*
  per strada *along the street*
  per email *by email*; **per posta** *by post*; **per via aerea** *by air mail*
  per telefono *by phone*; **per iscritto** *in writing*

- *through, because of, from*:

  tremare per la paura/il freddo *to shiver through fear/from the cold*
  parlare per esperienza *to talk from experience*

- **Stare per** means *to be about to* do something:

  Sto per uscire. *I'm just about to go out.*
  Stanno per vincere. *They're about to win.*

---

per is also used in dozens of expressions:
per favore/per piacere/per cortesia *please*
cento per cento *100%*; **il dieci per cento** *10%*
due per cinque *2 x 5*; **per lo meno** *at least*
per esempio *for example*; **per caso** *by chance*
andare pazzo per … *to go mad for …*
per sempre *for ever*; **occhio per occhio** *an eye for an eye*
per così dire *as it were*; **per di più** *and what's more*

su

- *on*:
  seduto su una sdraio *sitting on a deckchair*
  sul tavolo *on the table*
  un libro sulla guerra *a book on/about the war*
  basato su una storia vera *based on a true story*
  concentrare su *to concentrate on*
  salire sul treno *to get on/into the train*

- *over*:
  il ponte sul Po *the bridge over the river Po*
  portare sulle spalle *to carry over/on the shoulders*
  C'è nebbia sulla città. *There's fog over the town.*

  su features in many expressions:
  sul giornale *in the paper*
  su misura *made to measure*; su richiesta *on request*
  sul momento *there and then*
  sul mare *by the sea*; dare sul mare *to have a sea view*
  errore su errore *mistake after mistake*
  nove volte su dieci *nine times out of ten*

  > Su can also be an adverb, meaning *up*:
  > su e giù *up and down*
  > guardare in su *to look up*
  > Su le braccie. *Raise your arms up.*
  > Su! *Come on!*

fra and tra

- fra and tra, which are interchangeable, can mean *between, among* and *in* (a period of time).
  Puoi scegliere fra questo e quello. *You can choose between this one and that one.*
  Arriva tra le due e le tre. *She's arriving between two and three o'clock.*
  Silvia è fra i feriti. *Silvia's among the injured.*
  Parlate fra di voi. *Talk amongst yourselves.*
  Parto tra due ore. *I'm leaving in a couple of hours.*
  Sarà pronto fra un settimana. *It will be ready in a week.*

preposition phrases using a and di

Some prepositions are made up of two words, the second of which is **a** or **di**:

accanto a *next to*
davanti a *in front of, before*
di fronte a *opposite, in front of*
fino a *until, as far as*
insieme a *together with*
intorno a *around*
oltre a *besides, as well as*
quanto a *as regards*
vicino a *near*
fuori di *outside*
invece di *instead of*
prima di *before*

È di fronte alla stazione. *It's opposite the station.*
Vada fino al semaforo. *Go as far as the traffic lights.*
Cosa fai oltre a studiare? *What do you do besides studying?*
Vive fuori del paese. *He lives outside the village.*
Vuoi un tè invece di un caffè? *Would you like tea instead of coffee?*

The following prepositions can be followed directly by a noun, but they require **di** before personal pronouns, i.e. **me** *me*, **noi** *us*, **te**, **lei**, **voi** *you*, **lui** *him*, **lei** *her*, **loro** *them*:

contro *against*
dentro *inside*
dietro *behind*
dopo *after*
presso *near, c/o*
senza *without*
sopra *above*
sotto *beneath*

dietro la banca *behind the bank*; **dietro di te** *behind you*
dopo mezzanotte *after midnight*; **dopo di noi** *after us*
È partito senza Alfredo e senza di me. *He left without Alfredo and without me.*

checkpoint 11

1 Choose a preposition from the box to fill the gap. Each can only be used once.

a Ho cominciato due anni fa, _____ 2008.
b Grazia è la ragazza _____ capelli biondi.
c Conosci il vecchio ponte _____ fiume?
d I fiori sono _____ tua moglie.
e Voglio qualcosa _____ mangiare.
f Il treno parte _____ sette.
g Mio fratello abita _____ Australia.
h Abitiamo _____ Firenze, _____ Palazzo Pitti e Ponte Vecchio.

> alle, da, dai, fra, a, in, sul, nel, per

2 How are each of these houses described?

a una casa al mare
b la casa di mio zio
c una casa per le vacanze
d una casa di legno
e una casa in montagna
f una casa alle Azzorre
g una casa ai piedi dell'Etna
h una casa su misura
i la casa dei miei nonni
j una casa su tre piani
k una casa da trentacinque milioni di euro
l una casa tra due strade

3 Translate these into Italian.

a *Stefano's car*
b *a phone number*
c *orange peel*
d *each of us*
e *the end of the film*
f *my mother's cousin*
g *the doctor's address*
h *the 09.55 train*

4 Is a *champagne glass* un bicchiere da champagne or un bicchiere di champagne?

5 In la riserva marina più grande del mondo, what does del mean?

6 What are scarpe da ginnastica, scarpe di pelle, and scarpe da uomo?

7 How do you say *He's behind you* in Italian?

8 Which prepositions are missing from _____ macchina *by car*, _____ via aerea *by airmail* and dipinto _____ me *painted by me*?

Verbs: overview

Verbs are the words we use to say:

- what people and things are and have: *be, exist, have*
- what happens to them: *live, die, become, change, break*
- what they do physically: *breathe, eat, run, wait, arrive*
  and mentally: *like, believe, decide, respect, dream, analyse*.

In a dictionary you find the **infinitive** of a verb. In English this is the basic verb, which can have *to* in front of it: *(to) arrive, (to) decide, (to) finish*.
In Italian, infinitives are identified by their ending, which can be **-are**, **-ere** or **-ire**: **arrivare**, **dec_idere**, **finire**. When you remove **-are**, **-ere**, **-ire**, you're left with the stem of the verb: **arriv-**, **decid-**, **fin-**. A range of other endings can now be added to this stem, each of them conveying precise information about:

- how the verb is being used = **mood**
- when it's happening: present, past or future = **tense**
- who/what is doing it = **person**.

Each of the **-are**, **-ere** and **-ire** verb groups has sets of regular endings, and most verbs use these endings. However, some verbs are irregular and need to be learnt individually.

A group of verbs called **reflexive verbs** always have **-si** at the end of the infinitive: **sposarsi** *to get married*, **chi_edersi** *to wonder/to ask oneself*, **divertirsi** *to enjoy oneself*.

When they're not in the infinitive, reflexive verbs have the same endings as other verbs, but they also have to be accompanied by a reflexive pronoun, e.g. **mi**, **ti**, **si** (page 85).

moods and tenses

Modo *mood* refers to how the verb is being used. Moods include:

Infinitive	the name of the verb, i.e. the basic dictionary form: (*to*) *work*.
Indicative	indicating that facts are being talked about: *I work, they were working, he doesn't work, do you work?*
Conditional	referring to a hypothetical situation, often involving conditions: *we would work if … /but …*
Subjunctive	conveying that the verb is not fact but is subject to opinion, speculation, attitude or emotion: *if you were to work, should I ever work, if only I'd worked.*
Imperative	giving an instruction: *Work! Let's work!*

Tempo *tense* refers to when the verb is happening: in the past, present or future. Tenses have names, e.g. present, perfect, imperfect.
English has

- two simple one-word tenses: *I work, I worked;*

- many compound tenses which use extra words with the basic verb, e.g. *I am working, do I work? I will work, I was working, I have worked, I had worked.*

Italian too has simple and compound tenses but, as you see from the table opposite, the balance is different. In Italian there are far more simple tenses, where the ending of the verb supplies all the necessary information without the need for any extra words.

You'll find it much easier to use Italian tenses correctly if you make a point of remembering that the only extra words you'll use relate to *have* and *had*.
You can then concentrate on endings. Even if you think these look complicated at first, you'll find that you soon start to make subconscious associations. For example, you'll associate endings with a distinctive **v** sound with *was/were doing something* and those with a distinctive **r** sound with *will do something*.

Infinitive	aspettare	to wait
stem	aspett	

Indicative

Present	aspetto	*I wait, I'm waiting*
Future	aspetterò	*I will/shall wait*
Imperfect	aspettavo	*I was waiting, I used to wait*
Simple past	aspettai	*I waited*
Perfect	ho aspettato	*I have waited, I waited*
Future perfect	avrò aspettato	*I will have waited*
Pluperfect	avevo aspettato	*I had waited*

Conditional

Present	aspetterei	*I would wait*
Past	avrei aspettato	*I would have waited*

Subjunctive

Present	aspetti	*I wait*
Imperfect	aspettassi	*I waited*
Perfect	abbia aspettato	*I waited*
Pluperfect	avessi aspettato	*I had waited*

Imperative

	Aspetta! Aspetti! Aspettate!	*Wait!*
	Aspettiamo!	*Let's wait!*

Verbs also have:

Past participle	aspettato	*waited*
Gerund	aspettando	*waiting*

person

The person of a verb refers to who/what is making the verb happen.

A verb has three persons in the singular and three in the plural:

1st person singular	io	*I*
2nd person singular	tu	*you*
3rd person singular	lui, lei	*he, she/you*

1st person plural	noi	*we*
2nd person plural	voi	*you*
3rd person plural	loro	*they*

This is the order verbs are set out in, with each group of verbs (**-are**, **-ere** and **-ire**) having a specific ending for each of these six persons in each of the various moods and tenses.

The precise information transmitted by verb endings is the reason why **io**, **tu**, **lui**, **lei**, **noi**, **voi**, **loro** aren't really needed and why they're omitted more often than not. They're only really used for emphasis (page 78) or to make it clear who the third person singular is (i.e. *he*, *she* or *you*).

In English there's only one word for *you*, while Italian has three:
tu: someone you call by their first name;
lei: someone you don't know well, someone older than you;
voi: more than one person.

Each of these is linked to a different verb ending, and when you're talking to someone you call **lei**, you use the third person singular of the verb, the same ending as for **lui** *he* and **lei** *she*:

One ending for each of six persons in each of the moods and tenses sounds like a huge number of endings to learn – but in reality you'll find that the various endings for each person have a similarity across the tenses that makes most of them instantly recognisable. For example, the first person plural ending in the present tense is **-iamo**, and the imperfect, future, conditional, simple past and subjunctive all also end in **-mo**.

verb groups and irregular verbs

Many English verbs follow predictable patterns. These verbs are called regular verbs and once you know the patterns you can apply them to all regular verbs:

to wait	*I wait*	*I waited*	*I have waited*
to believe	*I believe*	*I believed*	*I have believed*

Irregular verbs are verbs that deviate from the regular patterns.

to be	*I am*	*I was*	*I have been*
to go	*I go*	*I went*	*I have gone*
to hide	*I hide*	*I hid*	*I have hidden*

Italian verbs divide into three groups, according to whether the infinitive ends in **-are**, **-ere** or **-ire**. Each group has sets of endings for each of the tenses and moods; and once you know a set of endings you can apply them to all the regular verbs in that group.

Each group also includes some irregular verbs which have to be remembered separately. A small number of these have a stem that's different from the infinitive.

- **-are** verbs form the largest group. Nearly all of them are regular, with only these four irregular ones:
  andare *to go*　　　　**dare** *to give*
  fare *to do, to make*　　**stare** *to stay*

- Many **-ere** verbs are irregular, some in the past tenses only, others across the board.

- **-ire** verbs form the smallest group, and most of them are regular. In some persons of some tenses they subdivide into two groups.

A few irregular verbs have infinitives ending in **-arre**, **-orre** or **-urre**, e.g.

attrarre *to attract*　　　**distrarre** *to distract*
imporre *to impose*　　　**supporre** *to suppose*
dedurre *to deduce*　　　**introdurre** *to introduce*

They behave in the same way as **trarre** *to pull* (page 234), **porre** *to put* (page 220) and **produrre** *to produce* (page 223).

the infinitive

The infinitive is the basic form of a verb that you find in a dictionary, ending in **-are**, **-ere** or **-ire**: **visitare** *visit*, **spendere** *spend*, **dormire** *sleep*. The final -e is sometimes dropped with no impact at all on meaning.

The infinitive isn't the main verb of a sentence. Corresponding to both *to …* and *… ing* in English; it's used:

- after another verb, sometimes separated by **a(d)** or **di** (pages 184-187):
  Devo andare da solo. *I have to go alone.*
  Preferisco andare da solo. *I prefer going alone.*
  Esito ad andare da solo. *I hesitate to go alone.*
  Ho intenzione di andare da solo. *I intend going alone.*

- after adjectives, either directly or linked by **a**, **di** or **da**:
  È inutile andare. *It's no use going.*
  Non è possibile prenotare? *Isn't it possible to book?*
  Stai attento a non cadere. *Mind you don't fall.*
  Lei è pronto a partire? *Are you ready to leave?*
  Sono stufo di aspettare. *I'm fed up of waiting.*
  È così difficile da credere. *It's so difficult to believe.*

- after some prepositions:
  invece di emigrare *instead of emigrating*
  oltre ad avere paura *besides being afraid*
  prima di partire *before leaving*
  È partito senza telefonarmi. *He left without phoning me.*

- as a noun, sometimes with *the*, where in English we use *-ing*:
  Vivere qui è un privilegio. *Living here is a privilege.*
  (Il) camminare fa bene al cuore. *Walking is good for the heart.*
  Sbadigliare è contagioso. *Yawning is contagious.*
  Tra il dire e il fare c'è di mezzo il mare. *Easier said than done.*
  lit. *Between saying and doing there's a sea in the middle.*
  Viaggiare allarga la mente. *Travelling broadens the mind.*

Italian has a verb form called the gerund which also translates as *–ing*, but don't be tempted to use it in any of the circumstances listed opposite. Its use is mainly limited to sentences like *While **walking** along, we chatted*, when two things are happening at the same time (page 162).

The infinitive is also used for orders and instructions:
Spingere. *Push.* **Tirare** *Pull.*
Allacciare le cinture di sicurezza. *Fasten your safety belts.*
Compilare il questionario. *Complete the questionnaire.*
Non premere questo pulsante. *Don't press this button.*
Mescolare tutti gli ingredienti ... *Mix all the ingredients ...*
... e mettere sul fuoco. *... and heat.*

verbs in a dictionary

In a dictionary, *v* stands for **verbo** *verb*. Next to the *v*, you'll find further information:
irr: irregular;
pp: past participle, if this is irregular;
rfl: reflexive;
i: intransitive, needing only a subject; does not have a direct object: *go, fly, laugh*;
t or *tr*: transitive, needing a subject and a direct object: *give, use*.

Many verbs can be both transitive and intransitive: *he's reading, he's reading a book; I continued, I continued the story.*

If you look up *change*, this is what you might find:

change 1. *vt* cambiare, trasformare: *to ~ the topic* cambiare argomento
2. *vi* cambiare: *his voice ~d* la sua voce è cambiata **3.** *v rfl* cambiarsi:
to get ~d cambiarsi i vestiti

Next to it, you'll find the translations for *change* when it's not a verb:

1. *n* cambiamento *m*, variazione *f* **2.** *[money]* resto *m*, spiccioli *m* pl.
3. *the ~ [of life]* la menopausa *f*

reflexive verbs: the infinitive

Reflexive verbs have -si at the end of the infinitive. There's no consistent English equivalent although many reflexive verbs include *get* or *oneself* in the translation:

abituarsi *to get used to*
accorgersi *to realise*
addormentarsi *to fall asleep*
alzarsi *to get up*
annoiarsi *to get bored*
chiamarsi *to be called* lit. *to call oneself*
divertirsi *to enjoy oneself*
domandarsi *to wonder* lit. *to ask oneself*
lamentarsi *to complain*
lavarsi *to wash (oneself), to get washed*
presentarsi *to introduce oneself*
ricordarsi *to remember* lit. *to remind oneself*
riposarsi *to rest (oneself)*
scusarsi *to apologise (excuse oneself)*
sedersi *to sit (oneself) down*
sentirsi *to feel*
sposarsi *to get married*
stancarsi *to get tired*
stufarsi *to get fed up*
svegliarsi *to wake (oneself) up*
ubriacarsi *to get drunk*
vestirsi *to get dressed*

Si means *oneself*, so when you want to say *myself, yourself, ourselves*, etc., you need to replace **si** with one of the other reflexive pronouns – **mi**, **ti**, **si**, **ci**, **vi** or **si** (page 85):

Vorrei scusarmi. *I'd like to apologise.*
Vuoi riposarti? *Would you like to rest (yourself)?*
Cominciavamo a stufarci. *We were beginning to get fed up.*

When they have a subject, reflexive verbs:
- have exactly the same endings as non-reflexive verbs;
- are always accompanied by a separate reflexive pronoun – **mi**, **ti**, **si**, **ci**, **vi** or **si** depending on who the subject is (page 85).

... and various tenses

alzarsi *to get up* lit. *to raise oneself*

present	mi alzo	*I get up*
	ti alzi	*you get up*
	si alza	*he, she gets up, you get up*
	ci alziamo	*we get up*
	vi alzate	*you get up*
	si alzano	*they get up*
future	mi alzerò	*I will get up*
conditional	mi alzerei	*I would get up*
imperfect	mi alzavo	*I used to get up*
simple past	mi alzai	*I got up*

In compound tenses (page 153), reflexive verbs use **essere**, and the past participle agrees with the subject:

perfect	mi sono alzato/alzata	*I* (m/f) *got up*
	ti sei alzato/alzata	*you* (m/f) *got up*
	si è alzato	*he got up, you* (m) *got up*
	si è alzata	*she got up, you* (f) *got up*
	ci siamo alzati/alzate	*we* (m/f) *got up*
	vi siete alzati/alzate	*you* (m/f) *got up*
	si sono alzati/alzate	*they* (m/f) *got up*
pluperfect	mi ero alzato/a	*I had got up*
future perfect	mi sarò alzato/a	*I will have got up*
past conditional	mi sarò alzato/a	*I would have got up*

When a reflexive verb has the direct object **lo**, **la**, **li** or **le**, the past participle agrees with it, not with the subject:
La password? Te la sei ricordata? *The password? Did you remember it?*

word **power**

While hundreds of verbs are very similar in English and Italian, there's a vital difference in the position of the stress. In English verbs it varies: <u>i</u>mitate, im<u>ag</u>ine, cont<u>ro</u>l – but it never moves from that syllable. In Italian verbs ending in **-are**, the stress on the infinitive is always on the ending: imit<u>a</u>re, immagin<u>a</u>re, controll<u>a</u>re, but this changes when the verb has other endings: contr<u>o</u>llo / *control*, controller<u>ò</u> / *will control*.

🇬🇧	🇮🇹	
_	-are	abbandonare, calmare, confessare, consultare, controllare, costare, depositare, detestare, informare, insultare, inventare, meritare, passare, presentare, protestare, telefonare, visitare
-e	-are	accusare, adorare, approvare, arrivare, basare, causare, combinare, conservare, consumare, continuare, immaginare, invitare, preservare, usare, votare
-ate	-are	celebrare, collaborare, comunicare, creare, dedicare, disintegrare, educare, elevare, eliminare, emigrare, implicare, indicare, interrogare, illuminare, nominare, penetrare
-ise	-izzare	anglicizzare, antagonizzare, criminalizzare, fraternizzare, marginalizzare, materializzare, modernizzare, naturalizzare, neutralizzare, organizzare, paralizzare, polverizzare, socializzare, terrorizzare, vaporizzare but not *fantasise* fantasticare, *recognise* ricon<u>o</u>scere or *apologise* scusarsi.
-ify	-ficare	amplificare, certificare, classificare, falsificare, gratificare, modificare, notificare, pacificare, qualificare, quantificare, semplificare, significare, solidificare, unificare, verificare but not *terrify* atterrire or *horrify* inorridire.

The meaning of many Italian verbs is obvious from the context, e.g. technology: **cliccare**, **copiare**, **programmare**, **digitalizzare**

You can work out what others mean from related English words: **bere** *to drink (beer, beverage)*, **dimenticare** *to forget (dementia)*, **odiare** *to hate (odious)*, **pensare** *to think (pensive)*, **respirare** *to breathe (respiration)*, **sposare** *to marry (spouse)*.

Don't forget to take predictable letter changes into account in verbs such as **accettare, accompagnare, rispettare, amministrare, ammirare, caratterizzare, osservare, calcolare, trasformare, trasportare, esportare, fissare, studiare, fotocopiare, fotografare**. If you're not sure what any of these mean, say the word out loud. If still in doubt, check with page 21.

false friends

attendere means *to expect*   *to attend* is **assistere a**

cancellare means *to delete*   *to cancel* is **disdire, annullare**

confrontare means *to compare*   *to confront* is **affrontare**

domandare means *to ask*   *to demand* is **esigere**

importare means *to be important* as well as *to import*

pretendere means *to claim/demand*   *to pretend* is **fingere, fare finta**

realizzare means *to realise/*   *to realise (become aware)* is
carry out   **accorgersi**

restare means to stay   *to rest* is **riposare**

salutare means *to greet*   *to salute* is **fare il saluto**

tranquillizzare means to *calm down* as well as *to tranquillise, reassure*

checkpoint 12

1 Two of these words are not verbs. Can you identify them?*
know, negotiate, applaud, arrival, disintegrate, play, depend, deep, realise, depart.

2 Which of these words can be a verb and a noun in English?
disturb, describe, deny, distribute, deliver, dream.

3 What are the infinitive endings for the three groups of Italian verbs? Which is the largest group? And the smallest?

4 Does *Mood* or *Tense* refer to the time something takes place?

5 Who's doing something when a verb is in the first person singular? And the third person plural?

6 Which verb ending do you need for **lei** *you*?

7 How many irregular verbs end in **-are**? Can you list them?

8 If you saw **Tirare** on a door, would you push or pull?

9 What does *v irr* signify next to a word in a dictionary? And *v rfl*?

10 What's the English for *salutare*?

11 Work out the Italian for *to accelerate*, *to illustrate*, *to separate*, *to navigate*, and the English for **commercializzare**, **utilizzare** and **monopolizzare**.

12 Given that **s-** can signify an opposite meaning, and **ri-** is often the equivalent of *re-/again* in English, guess what these verbs mean: **sbloccare, sbottonare, squalificare, ricominciare, ripensare, riciclare, ricreare**.

*If ever you're not sure, remember that you can put *to* in front of a verb and *the* in front of a noun.

Negatives and questions

There are two structural differences in the way English and Italian negatives are formed:

- In the simple (one-word) tenses, as well as using *not*, English introduces the words *do*, *does*, or *did*. These have no equivalent in Italian, which just inserts **non** before the verb:
  A̲bito qui. *I live here.*
  Non a̲bito qui. *I do not live here.*

- In Italian, unlike English, both **non** and a negative word like **niente** *nothing* or **mai** *never* can be used in the same sentence:
  Non voglio niente. *I want nothing.* lit. *I don't want nothing.*

English also uses *do*, *does* and *did* to ask questions, or it reverses the order of the subject and noun: *Do you live here? Is she ill?* Italian simply makes the statements *You live here* and *She is ill* sound like questions: **A̲biti qui? Lei è ammalata?**

In questions using words like **quando** *when*, **perché** *why*, the question word can go in one of two places:

- usually at the beginning of the question, in which case the verb comes straight after it: **Quando comincia la partita?** *The match starts when? When does the match start?*
- sometimes where the answer will be: **La partita comincia quando?**

Most question words don't change. But **quale** *which* and **quanto** *how much* agree with the noun they relate to.

negatives: non

To say something negative in Italian the key word is **non**, which you put before the verb. You don't translate the English words *do*, *does* or *did*.

Sono italiano. *I'm Italian.*
Non sono italiano. *I'm not Italian.*
Parlo italiano. *I speak Italian.*
Non parlo italiano. *I do not/don't speak Italian.*
Laura non parla italiano. *Laura does not/doesn't speak Italian.*
Laura non parla italiano? *Doesn't Laura speak Italian?*
Hanno due figli. *They have two children.*
Non hanno figli. *They don't have children; They haven't got children.*

In compound (two-word) tenses, **non** goes before **avere** or **essere**:
Ho finito. *I finished, I have finished.*
Non ho finito. *I haven't finished.*
È arrivata. *She arrived./She has arrived.*
Non è arrivata. *She didn't arrive./She hasn't arrived.*
Avevamo pagato. *We had paid.*
Non avevamo pagato. *We hadn't paid.*

Non normally goes before personal pronouns (page 77):
Non mi piace questo. *I don't like this one.*
Non si può negare che … *One can't deny that …*
Non ti credo. *I don't believe you.*
Non gli hai scritto? *Haven't you written to them?*
Non ti alzi alle sette? *Don't you get up at seven o'clock?*
Non me lo ricordo. *I don't remember (it).*

In Italian, unlike English, you also use **non** in the same sentence as a negative word like **niente** *nothing* or **mai** *never*. The way this works is explained on the next two pages.

nessuno, niente, nulla, né

With simple (one-word) tenses, these four negative words are used in this order:

non + verb + **nessuno** *nobody/not … anybody*, **niente/nulla** *nothing/not … anything*, **né … né** *neither…nor:*

Non vedo nessuno qui. *I don't see anyone here.*
Luisa non mangia niente. *Luisa isn't eating anything.*
Non capiscono nulla. *They understand nothing.*
Non mangio né carne né pesce. *I don't eat meat or fish.*

With compound (two-word) tenses, they go after the past participle:
Non ho visto nessuno. *I haven't seen anybody.*
Luisa non ha mangiato niente. *Luisa hasn't eaten anything.*
Non hanno capito nulla. *They haven't understood anything.*
Non ho mangiato né carne né pesce. *I haven't eaten meat or fish./I ate neither meat nor fish.*

Non + verb + **nessuno** + noun translates *not … any (at all)*.
When used in this way, **nessuno**:
- is only used with a singular noun – even though the English translation might be plural;
- is an adjective and so agrees with the noun;
- has similar forms to the indefinite article (page 44):
  Non ho nessun problema. *I have no problems (at all).*
  Non c'è nessuno sbaglio. *There's no mistake.*
  Non rispetta nessuna regola. *He doesn't respect any rules.*
  Non c'è nessun'altra soluzione. *There's no other solution.*

With an adjective, **niente** needs **di**: **niente di interessante** *nothing interesting*; **niente di nuovo** *nothing new*.
With a noun **niente** means *no* or *any*. It can be used with a singular or plural noun and its ending doesn't change.
Niente zucchero, grazie. *No sugar, thanks.*
Niente domande. *No questions.*
Niente domande? *Any questions?*

mai, neanche, ancora, più, affatto, mica

With simple tenses these six negative words follow the same rules as **nessuno**, **niente** and **nulla**, i.e. **non** + verb + negative word:

- **non ... mai** *never, not ever*
  Non mangio mai la carne. *I never eat meat.*

- **non ... neanche, non ... neppure, non ... nemmeno** *not even*
  Non mangi neanche le uova? *Don't you even eat eggs?*
  No, non mangio neppure/nemmeno le uova. *No, I don't even eat eggs.*

- **non ... ancora** *not yet*
  Non è ancora qui. *He's not here yet.*

- **non ... più** *no longer, not any more*
  Non abito più in Italia. *I no longer live in Italy.*

- **non ... per niente, non ... affatto** *not at all*
  Non mi piace per niente. *I don't like it at all.*
  Non è affatto vero. *It's not true at all.*

- **non ... mica** *not in the least, not as if*
  Non ho mica fame. *I'm not in the least hungry.*
  Non ho mica ucciso qualcuno. *It's not as if I killed someone.*

With compound tenses, these go ***before*** the past participle:
Non sono mai stato in India. *I've never been to India.*
Non ha nemmeno telefonato. *He hasn't even rung.*
Non ho neppure cominciato. *I haven't even started.*
Non hanno ancora finito. *They haven't finished yet.*
Non mi è piaciuto per niente. *I didn't like it at all.*
Non ha affatto contribuito. *She hasn't contributed at all.*
Non ho mica chiesto la luna. *It's not as if I asked for the moon.*

negative words without non

You don't use **non**:

- when a negative word/phrase is used on its own:

  Who did you see?   **Nessuno.** *Nobody.*
  What did you do?   **Niente.** *Nothing.*
  Did you enjoy yourself?   **Niente affatto.** *Not at all.*
  Will you go again?   **Mai.** *Never.*

- when a negative word starts the sentence:

  Nessun dorma. *Let nobody sleep/No-one shall sleep.*
  Nessuno vuole andare? *Doesn't anybody want to go?*
  Niente è impossibile. *Nothing is impossible.*
  Mai dire mai. *Never say never.*
  Neppure Anna sa dov'è. *Not even Anna knows where he is.*

- after **senza** *without*:

  Va via senza salutare nessuno? *Is he going away without saying goodbye to anyone?*
  È morto senza mai sapere. *He died without ever knowing.*
  È tornata senza aver vinto niente. *She came back without having won/ without winning anything.*

Negative words feature in many phrases.
Di niente. Non è niente. *It's nothing. Don't mention it.*
Non fa niente. *It doesn't matter.*
poco o niente *little or nothing, next to nothing*
niente di più *nothing more*
Niente affatto! *No way!*
Mica male. *Not bad.*
Come mai? *How come?*
ora o mai più *now or never*
buono a nulla *good for nothing*
svanire nel nulla *vanish into thin air*
Non ci pensare neanche! *Don't even think of it!*
Nemmeno per sogno! *In your dreams!*

asking questions

To ask a closed question, expecting the answer *yes* or *no*, English brings in words like *do/does* or reverses the order of the subject and noun:
Does he live in Rome?
Is Anna with them?

Italian does neither of these, simply making the statements *He lives in Rome* and *Anna is with them* sound like questions by raising the voice at the end:
Abita a Roma?
Anna è con loro?

You can add **vero** to your question. It corresponds to all English question tags like *isn't it, is he, don't we, aren't you, did she, have you, won't they…*, making it very easy to use.

Lavori qui, vero? *You work here, don't you?*
Non lavori qui, vero? *You don't work here, do you?*
È ammalata, vero? *She's ill, isn't she?*

Open-ended questions use question words such as **dove** *where*, **perché** *why*. These usually go at the beginning of the question. Unlike English, Italian puts the verb straight after the question word and doesn't use extra words like *do/does*:
Quando finisce il concerto? *When does the concert finish?*

They can also go where the answer will be:
Il concerto finisce quando? *The concert finishes when?*

Italian question words fall into two groups:
- **chi** *who*, **di chi** *whose*, **come** *how*, **dove** *where*, **perché** *why*, **quando** *when*
- **che (cosa)** *what*, **quale** *which*, **quanto** *how much*

These are explained on the next three pages.

chi? come? dove? quando? perché?

These question words never change:

- chi *who, whom*
  Chi vuol essere milionario? *Who wants to be a millionaire?*
  Sai chi è? *Do you know who he is?*
  Chi conosci a Roma? *Who do you know in Rome?*
  Di chi stanno parlando? *Who are they talking about?*
  Con chi lavori? *Who do you work with?*
  Secondo chi? *According to whom?*

- di chi *whose*
  Di chi è questo? *Whose is this?*
  Di chi sono queste scarpe? *Whose are these shoes?*
  Di chi è la macchina rossa? *Whose is the red car?*

- come *how*
  Come stai? *How are you?*
  Come si dice ... in italiano? *How do you say ... in Italian?*
  Sai come funziona? *Do you know how it works?*
  Come ti chiami? *What's your name?* lit. *How do you call yourself?*

- dove *where*, which becomes dov' before è:
  Di dove sei? *Where are you from?*
  Dov'è la fermata? *Where's the bus stop?*
  Dove sono le chiavi? *Where are the keys?*
  Dove posso parcheggiare? *Where can I park?*

- quando *when*
  Quando arrivano? *When are they arriving?*
  Quando apre la banca? *When does the bank open?*
  Fino a quando siete qui? *Until when are you here?*
  Da quando siete qui? *Since when have you been here?*

- perché *why*
  Perché è in ritardo? *Why is she late?*
  Perché non andiamo? *Why don't we go?* Perché no? *Why not?*
  Perché tanto interesse? *Why so much interest?*
  Perché risparmiare energia? *Why save energy?*

che? quale?

Che and **quale** are used in a very similar way, just as *what* and *which* are in English.

Che? *what?*, which doesn't change, is used in two ways:

- followed by a noun:
  Che lavoro fai? *What (work) do you do?*
  Che differenza c'è? *What difference is there?*
  A che ora? *(At) what time?*
  Che biglietti volete? *What tickets do you want?*
  Che prove avete? *What proof do you have?*

- without a noun:
  Che posso fare? *What can I do?*
  Che succede dopo? *What happens afterwards?*
  Che hai comprato? *What did you buy?*

Cosa is often used with **che**. And, informally, **che** is dropped, with **cosa** then used on its own. They all mean the same.
Che cosa hai comprato? *What did you buy?*
Di che cosa sta parlando? *What's he talking about?*
Cosa? Cos'hai detto? *What? What did you say?*
Cosa facciamo? *What shall we do?*
Cos'è questo? *What's this?*

Quale? *which? what?* is also used in two ways:

- as an adjective with a noun, becoming **quali** in the plural:
  Quale telefonino ti piace di più? *Which mobile do you like best?*
  Quale pizza vuole? *Which pizza would you like?*
  Quali sintomi ha? *What symptoms does she have?*
  Quali garanzie offre? *What guarantees is he offering?*

- as a pronoun meaning *which one(s)? what?*, becoming **qual** in the singular before è and **quali** in the plural:
  Qual è il migliore? Quale? *Which is the best? Which one?*
  Quale preferisci? Quale? *Which do you prefer? Which one?*
  Qual è l'indirizzo? *What (lit. which one) is the address?*
  Quali sono i rischi? *What (lit. which ones) are the risks?*

quanto?

Quanto *how much, how many, how …* can be used in three ways:

- with a verb, i.e. as an adverb. It doesn't change to agree with anything, but it can shorten to **quant'** before a vowel:
  Quanto costa? *How much does it cost?*
  Quanto costano questi? *How much do these cost?*
  Quanto sei alto? *How tall are you?*
  Quanto dura? *How long does it last?*
  Quant'è? *How much is it?*
  Quanto puoi mangiare? *How much can you eat?*

- with a noun, i.e. as an adjective, so it has to agree with the noun like any other adjective ending in **-o** (page 54):
  Quanto tempo rimane? *How much time is left?*
  Quanta acqua c'è? *How much water is there?*
  Quanti anni hai? *How old are you?* lit. *How many years do you have?*
  Quante persone ci sono? *How many people are there?*

- instead of a noun, i.e. as a pronoun, so it has to agree with the noun it refers to:
  Vino: quanto ne vuoi? *Wine: how much would you like?*
  Birra: quanta ne vuoi? *Beer: how much would you like?*
  Gelati: quanti ne vuoi? *Ice creams: how many would you like?*
  Mele: quante ne vuoi? *Apples: how many would you like?*

Both **quanto** and **come** translate the English *how*. However, there is a basic difference, and the way to remember it is to associate **quanto** with *quantity* as in the examples on this page. **Come**, on the other hand, usually refers to the way something is done, and on page 127 there's a list of questions using it in this way.

checkpoint 13

1 Write the negatives of these sentences.
  a Lavorano con noi.   b Giovanni è andato via.
  c Mi piace il tè.   d Sono stato in Perù.
  e Abbiamo figli.   f So dove abitano.

2 What do these mean? niente, nessuno, mai, nulla, non ...
  affatto, non ... per niente, non ... mica, non ... più

3 Non c'è _____ sbaglio. Is the missing word nessun,
  nessuno, nessun' or nessuna?

4 What's missing from this sentence? niente _____ importante.

5 Rearrange these words to form two sentences.
  a i piacciono né né le non cipolle mi pomodori
  b le mangiato Salvatore mai ha non ostriche

6 Which two question words change to agree with a noun?

7 What are the three versions of *What?* in Italian?

8 Rearrange these words to form two questions.
  a parte per treno quando il Roma
  b parlare sorella vuoi mia perché con

9 What's the Italian for *isn't it?* And for *haven't we?*

10 Complete these questions with a word from the box.
  a _____ studente è inglese?
  b _____ facciamo questa sera?
  c Di _____ siete voi?
  d Di _____ sono questi giornali?
  e _____ vuoi partire subito?
  f _____ camere desiderate?

  > chi perché
  > dove quante
  > quale cosa

Verbs: simple tenses

The following pages guide you through the moods and tenses of Italian verbs, showing you how to choose the one you need and which endings are involved.

You need to be familiar with the information on pages 109-115, briefly:

- Verb endings tell you a) how the verb is being used, b) when it's happening, and c) who/what is doing it. The endings fit onto the stem of the verb, which you find by removing **-are**, **-ere**, **-ire** from the end of the infinitive:

  aspettare *to wait* → **aspett**   **vendere** *to sell* → **vend**
  partire *to leave* → **part**   **capire** *to understand* → **cap**

  The replacement endings are similar – but not identical – for the three groups of verbs. Irregular verbs deviate from the standard patterns in some way, but even most of these have endings that are similar to regular verb patterns.

- The balance of simple and compound tenses is different in English and Italian, with Italian verb endings doing away with the need for support words like *am*, *is*, *are*, *will*, *was*, *would*.

On the whole it's easy to relate Italian and English tenses, but there are two things to watch out for.

The Italian simple past tense, which appears to provide a handy translation for e.g. *I worked*, *I ate*, is in fact not widely used. What's used instead is the perfect tense: *I have worked, I have eaten*.

English uses the word *would* in two senses: *We would buy it if we had the money*, which is the conditional, and *We would see the same things every time we went there*, which is the imperfect. They have no connection in Italian.

present tense

	aspettare	vendere	partire*	capire*
	to wait	*to sell*	*to leave*	*to understand*
io	aspetto	vendo	parto	capisco
tu	aspetti	vendi	parti	capisci
lui/lei	aspetta	vende	parte	capisce
noi	aspettiamo	vendiamo	partiamo	capiamo
voi	aspettate	vendete	partite	capite
loro	aspettano	vendono	partono	capiscono

*In the present tense, verbs in the **-ire** group divide into two sub-groups, one of them inserting **-isc** before all endings except **noi** and **voi** (page 145). The **-isc** group is the one you'll come across most often.

- The stress on the **noi** and **voi** forms is on the ending, while on all the other forms - including **loro** - it's on the stem.

- There are changes in the spelling of the **tu** and **noi** persons of some verbs, keeping the sounds of **c** and **g** the same as in the infinitive.
  Verbs ending in **-ciare** and **-giare** drop the **i**:
  cominciare *to start*   **tu cominci**   **noi cominciamo**
  mangiare *to eat*   **tu mangi**   **noi mangiamo**
  whereas verbs ending in **-care** and **-gare** insert **h**:
  giocare *to play*   **tu giochi**   **noi giochiamo**
  spiegare *to explain*   **tu spieghi**   **noi spieghiamo**

- There are no spelling changes for verbs ending in **-cere**, **-gere**, **-gire**, therefore the **io** and **loro** forms sound different from the others:
  vincere *to win*   io vinco   tu vinci   loro vincono
  leggere *to read*   io leggo   tu leggi   loro leggono
  fuggire *to run away*   io fuggo   tu fuggi   loro fuggono

common irregular verbs

There are verbs which deviate from the regular present tense patterns in some way. These are called irregular verbs. Many have only minor differences, with the verb still instantly recognisable. However, the most commonly used verbs have substantial irregularities in the present tense.

essere *to be*	avere *to have*	andare *to go*	fare *to do/make*
sono	ho	vado	faccio
sei	hai	vai	fai
è	ha	va	fa
siamo	abbiamo	andiamo	facciamo
siete	avete	andate	fate
sono	hanno	vanno	fanno

dovere *to have to*	potere *to be able to*	volere *to want to*	dire *to say*
devo	posso	voglio	dico
devi	puoi	vuoi	dici
deve	può	vuole	dice
dobbiamo	possiamo	vogliamo	diciamo
dovete	potete	volete	dite
devono	possono	vogliono	dicono

sapere *to know*	venire *to come*	tenere *to hold*	porre *to put*
so	vengo	tengo	pongo
sai	vieni	tieni	poni
sa	viene	tiene	pone
sappiamo	veniamo	teniamo	poniamo
sapete	venite	tenete	ponete
sanno	vengono	tengono	pongono

Other irregular verbs are written out in full in the verb tables (pages 191-241).

when to use the present tense

- Present tense endings replace the **-are**, **-ere**, **-ire** of the infinitive when in English you say *I do something* or *I'm doing something*:
  Lavoro a Londra. *I work in London.*
  Lavoriamo oggi. *We're working today.*
  Lavorano domani. *They're working tomorrow.*
  Anna capisce il francese. *Anna understands French.*
  Vende gelati. *He sells/he's selling ice cream.*
  Partono domani. *They leave/they're leaving tomorrow.*
  Vado in vacanza in agosto. *I'm going on holiday in August.*

- You also use the present tense in questions like these, where English uses *shall*:
  Ti aspetto? *Shall I wait for you?*
  Pago adesso? *Shall I pay now?*
  Mangiamo? *Shall we eat?*

- In questions and negatives, Italian doesn't use extra words like *do*, *does*, *am*, *is*, *are*:
  Lavori? *Do you work?*
  Lavori domani? *Are you working tomorrow?*
  Non lavoro. *I'm not working./I don't work.*
  Anna capisce il francese? *Does Anna understand French?*
  Vende gelati? *Is he selling ice cream?*
  Non partono domani. *They're not leaving/they don't leave tomorrow.*

- You use the present tense with **da** *since/for* to talk about something which started in the past and is still going on, where English uses *have/has been … ing*.
  Lavoro qui da aprile. *I've been working here since April.*
  Lavoro qui da tre anni. *I've been working here for three years.*

present continuous

If you need to emphasise that something's happening right now, differentiating between, e.g. *I'm learning Italian* and *I'm learning about tenses (right now),* you can use an alternative to the simple present tense (page 132) called the present continuous. This is made up of:

the present tense of **stare: sto stai sta stiamo state stanno**

+ the gerund (page 162) of the main verb, formed by changing the infinitive endings as follows:

-are → -ando	aspettare *to wait*	aspettando *waiting*
-ere → -endo	v<u>e</u>ndere *to sell*	vendendo *selling*
-ire → -endo	partire *to leave*	partendo *leaving*

Cosa stai scrivendo? *What are you writing?*
Ti sto pensando. *I'm thinking about you.*
Stiamo mangiando. *We're just eating.*
Sto guardando la tv. *I'm busy watching television.*
I tempi stanno cambiando. *Times are changing.*

checkpoint 14

1   Write both the present simple and the present continuous of these verbs:

ascoltare	io
scr<u>i</u>vere	voi
arrivare	loro
finire	lei
telefonare	tu
costruire	noi
cercare	lei
chi<u>u</u>dere	loro
sorr<u>i</u>dere	voi
partire*	io
dormire*	lui
l<u>e</u>ggere	noi

*verbs without -isc

2   What's the Italian for these?
   a *We start tomorrow.*   b *Does Gianni understand English?*
   c *Shall we go?*   d *I've been living here for 20 years.*

future tense

	aspettare	vendere	capire
	to wait	*to sell*	*to understand*
io	aspetterò	venderò	capirò
tu	aspetterai	venderai	capirai
lui/lei	aspetterà	venderà	capirà
noi	aspetteremo	venderemo	capiremo
voi	aspetterete	venderete	capirete
loro	aspetteranno	venderanno	capiranno

Verbs ending in **-ciare** and **-giare** drop the **i** in the future tense:
cominciare *to start*: **comincerò, comincerai, comincerà** etc.
mangiare *to eat*: **mangerò, mangerai, mangerà** etc.
whereas verbs ending in **-care** and **-gare** insert **h**:
giocare *to play*: **giocherò, giocherai, giocherà** etc.
pagare *to pay*: **pagherò, pagherai, pagherà** etc.

when to use the future tense

- Future tense endings replace the **-are**, **-ere**, **-ire** of the infinitive when in
  English you say *I will/shall do something* or *I'm going to do something*.
  Comincerò domani. *I'll start tomorrow.*
  Chissà quale sceglierà. *Who knows which one he will choose.*
  Quando tornerà? *When will she/is she going to come back?*
  As in English, you can also use the present tense to talk about events that
  will happen in the future: **Comincio domani.** *I start tomorrow.*

- Both languages also use the future tense to make assumptions:
  La chiave? Sarà nella borsa. *The key? It will be in the bag.*
  Arriveranno fra poco. *They'll be here soon.*

- Unlike English, you use the future tense after **se** *if*, **quando** *when*, **appena**
  as soon as, and with **finché ... non** *until*, when the other verb in the
  sentence is in the future:
  Vi telefonerò appena arriveremo. *I'll ring you as soon as we arrive.*
  Non cambierò niente finché non torneranno. *I won't change anything
  until they come back.*

irregular future tense forms

With the exception of **essere**, irregular verbs differ only slightly from regular ones in the future tense; they remain instantly recognisable.

- The most common are:
  essere *to be* **sarò, sarai, sarà, saremo, sarete, saranno**
  dare *to give* **darò, darai, darà, daremo, darete, daranno**
  fare *to do/make* **farò, farai, farà, faremo, farete, faranno**
  stare *to stay/be* **starò, starai, starà, staremo, starete, staranno**

- The following drop the first vowel of the future ending:
  andare *to go* **andrò, andrai, andrà, andremo, andrete, andranno**
  avere *to have* **avrò, avrai, avrà, avremo, avrete, avranno**
  cadere *to fall* **cadrò, cadrai, cadrà, cadremo, cadrete, cadranno**
  dovere *to have to* **dovrò, dovrai, dovrà, dovremo, dovrete, dovranno**
  potere *to be able to* **potrò, potrai, potrà, potremo, potrete, potranno**
  sapere *to know* **saprò, saprai, saprà, sapremo, saprete, sapranno**
  vedere *to see* **vedrò, vedrai, vedrà, vedremo, vedrete, vedranno**
  vivere *to live* **vivrò, vivrai, vivrà, vivremo, vivrete, vivranno**

- A few verbs end in **-rro, -rrai**, etc.
  bere *to drink* **berrò, berrai, berrà, berremo, berrete, berranno**
  porre *to put* **porrò, porrai, porrà, porremo, porrete, porranno**
  produrre *to produce* **produrrò, produrrai, produrrà, produrremo, produrrete, produrranno**
  rimanere *to stay* **rimarrò, rimarrai, rimarrà, rimarremo, rimarrete rimarranno**
  tenere *to hold* **terrò terrai terrà terremo terrete terranno**
  venire *to come* **verrò verrai verrà verremo verrete verranno**
  volere *to want* **vorrò vorrai vorrà vorremo vorrete vorranno**

conditional

	aspettare	vendere	capire
	to wait	*to sell*	*to understand*
io	aspetterei	venderei	capirei
tu	aspetteresti	venderesti	capiresti
lui/lei	aspetterebbe	venderebbe	capirebbe
noi	aspetteremmo	venderemmo	capiremmo
voi	aspettereste	vendereste	capireste
loro	aspetterebbero	venderebbero	capirebbero

The conditional has a lot in common with the future tense:
- both have the distinctive **r** sound in all the endings.
- they incur the same spelling changes:

	future	conditional
cominciare *to start*	comincerò	comincerei
mangiare *to eat*	mangerò	mangerei
dimenticare *to forget*	dimenticherò	dimenticherei
pagare *to pay*	pagherò	pagherei

- the same verbs are irregular in the future and conditional, and in a similar way: the stem is the same, with only the endings differing:

	future	conditional
essere *to be*	sarò	sarei
dare *to give*	darò	darei
fare *to do/make*	farò	farei
andare *to go*	andrò	andrei
avere *to have*	avrò	avrei
dovere *to have to*	dovrò	dovrei
potere *to be able to*	potrò	potrei
vedere *to see*	vedrò	vedrei
bere *to drink*	berrò	berrei
venire *to come*	verrò	verrei
volere *to want*	vorrò	vorrei

when to use the conditional

- Conditional endings replace the **-are**, **-ere**, **-ire** of the infinitive when in English you say *I would do something*.

  Mi piacerebbe molto … *I would really like to …*
  Andrei io ma sono occupato. *I would go myself but I'm busy.*
  Pagherei volentieri. *I would willingly pay.*
  Non dimenticherebbe mai. *She would never forget.*
  Preferiresti rimanere qui? *Would you prefer to stay here?*
  Quanto costerebbe? *How much would it cost?*
  Quanto costerebbero? *How much would they cost?*

- You can use the conditional to make a request sound more polite:
  Potresti aiutarmi? *Could you help me?*
  Mi darebbe l'indirizzo? *Would you give me the address?*
  Vorresti venire? *Would you like to come?*
  Vorrei due caffè. *I'd like two coffees.*

- It's used by the media to show that they're reporting opinion not fact. English uses speech marks or phrases like *it is alleged that, it was said that*:
  La vittima sarebbe già morta. *It is alleged that the victim is already dead. The victim "is already dead".*
  Sua moglie procederebbe per vie legali. *His wife is said to be resorting to the law.*

When a verb in the conditional is linked to *if* + another verb, the verb in the *if* part of the sentence has to be in the imperfect subjunctive (page 169):
Andrei io se avessi il tempo. *I would go myself if I had the time.*
Se fosse vero, non lo dimenticherebbe mai. *If it were true, she would never forget it.*

---

imperfect tense

	aspettare	vendere	capire
	to wait	*to sell*	*to understand*
io	aspett**avo**	vend**evo**	cap**ivo**
tu	aspett**avi**	vend**evi**	cap**ivi**
lui/lei	aspett**ava**	vend**eva**	cap**iva**
noi	aspett**avamo**	vend**evamo**	cap**ivamo**
voi	aspett**avate**	vend**evate**	cap**ivate**
loro	aspett**avano**	vend**evano**	cap**ivano**

- **Essere** *to be* is irregular in the imperfect:
  ero eri era eravamo eravate e̠rano

- There are very few other verbs that are irregular in this tense, but some
  have irregular stems to which you add regular -**ere** endings:
  bere *to drink* bevevo, bevevi, beveva, bevevamo, bevevate, beve̠vano
  dire *to say* dicevo, dicevi, diceva, dicevamo, dicevate, dice̠vano
  fare *to make* facevo, facevi, faceva, facevamo, facevate, face̠vano
  trarre *to draw* traevo, traevi, traeva, traevamo, traevate, trae̠vano
  porre *to put* ponevo, ponevi, poneva, ponevamo, ponevate, pone̠vano
  produrre *to produce* producevo, producevi, produceva, producevamo,
  producevate, produce̠vano

- Other verbs that end in -**dire**, -**fare**, -**arre**, -**orre** and -**urre** follow the
  same pattern as these.

Just as you use the gerund with the present tense of **stare**
to say you're doing something right at this time (page
135), you can use it with the imperfect of **stare** to say that
something was ongoing when something else happened: **Stavo
mangiando quando ha telefonato Marco.** *I was eating when
Marco rang.*

when to use the imperfect tense

- Imperfect tense endings replace the **-are**, **-ere**, **-ire** of the infinitive when you're saying how things were in the past, or talking about events that happened often or that carried on over a period of time. In English you often use words like *was*, *were* and *used to*.
  Quando avevo vent'anni ... *When I was twenty ...*
  Mentre aspettavamo ... *While we were waiting ...*
  Eravamo stanchi ieri. *We were tired yesterday.*
  Lavoravano in Scozia. *They used to work in Scotland.*
  Andavo spesso a nuotare. *I often used to go swimming.*
  Pioveva molto. *It was raining a lot/It used to rain a lot.*

- English doesn't always use *was/were/used to* when describing things that continued over time. Regardless of the English, it's essential to use the imperfect tense in Italian:
  Da studente *When I was a student*
  ... vivevo con due amici ... *I lived with two friends.*
  ... ci alzavamo tardi ogni giorno ... *we would get up late every day.*
  ... andavamo in vacanza insieme ... *we used to go on holiday together.*

  Look out particularly for this inconsistency with **avere**. English rarely uses *was/were* with *have* but if the sense is that of anything other than a one-off event, you need the imperfect in Italian.
  Avevo un gatto. *I had a cat./I used to have a cat.*
  Non avevamo molti soldi. *We didn't have much money.*

- The imperfect can be used with **da** to say something ***had*** been going on for some time or since a particular time:
  Lavoravo in Scozia da tre anni. *I had been working in Scotland for three years.*
  Pioveva da una settimana. *It had been raining for a week.*
  Aspettavamo da domenica. *We had been waiting since Sunday.*

simple past tense

-ere verbs have alternative io, lui/lei and loro endings.

	aspettare	vendere	capire
	to wait	*to sell*	*to understand*
io	aspettai	vendei/vendetti	capii
tu	aspettasti	vendesti	capisti
lui/lei	aspettò	vendé/vendette	capì
noi	aspettammo	vendemmo	capimmo
voi	aspettaste	vendeste	capiste
loro	aspettarono	venderono/vendettero	capirono

The simple past is used to say that something took place, and was completed, at a specific time in the past.

Nacque nel 1843 e morì nel 1927. *He was born in 1843 and died in 1927.*
Nel 1990 tornarono in Sicilia. *In 1990 they returned to Sicily.*
Venne l'ora della vendetta. *The time for revenge arrived.*
Non capimmo che cominciava una nuova era. *We didn't understand that a new age was beginning.*
Ascoltarono in silenzio, poi partirono. *They listened in silence, then they left.*

Although the simple past appears to be a straight translation for the English *I waited, she sold, we understood*, etc. its use is actually very restricted. While it's used in formal writing, you'll only hear people using it in parts of central and southern Italy.

In most of Italy, the tense used for *I waited, she sold, we understood*, etc. is the perfect tense (page 152):
ho aspettato *I waited*
ha venduto *she sold*
abbiamo capito *we understood*

irregular simple past forms

Most common irregular verbs like **essere**, **avere**, **fare**, **venire**, are irregular in the simple past (pages 191-241).

Many **-ere** verbs which are regular in all the other tenses have irregular **io**, **lui/lei** and **loro** endings in the simple past, and there are patterns to look out for:

- verbs ending in **-dere**, e.g. **chiedere** *to ask*, **chiudere** *to close*, **decidere** *to decide*, **offendere** *to offend*, **perdere** *to lose*
  chiedere: chiesi, chiedesti, chiese, chiedemmo, chiedeste, chiesero

- verbs ending in **-ndere**, e.g. **dipendere** *to depend*, **nascondere** *to hide*, **prendere** *to take*, **scendere** *to go down*, **rispondere** *to reply*
  dipendere: dipesi, dipendesti, dipese, dipendemmo, dipendeste, dipesero

- verbs ending in **-gere**, e.g. **accorgersi** *to realise*, **dipingere** *to paint*, **fingere** *to pretend*, **giungere** *to reach*, **piangere** *to cry*
  giungere: giunsi, giungesti, giunse, giungemmo, giungeste, giunsero

The irregular simple past of some common verbs are very different from the infinitive:

mettere *to put* **misi, mettesti, mise, mettemmo, metteste, misero**

correre *to run* **corsi, corresti, corse, corremmo, correste, corsero**

vincere *to win* **vinsi, vincesti, vinse, vincemmo, vinceste, vinsero**

dirigere *to direct* **diressi, dirigesti, diresse, dirigemmo, dirigeste, diressero**

discutere *to discuss* **discussi, discutesti, discusse, discutemmo, discuteste, discussero**

leggere *to read* **lessi, leggesti, lesse, leggemmo, leggeste, lessero**

scrivere *to write* **scrissi, scrivesti, scrisse, scrivemmo, scriveste, scrissero**

scuotere *to shake* **scossi, scotesti, scosse, scotemmo, scoteste, scossero**

vivere *to live* **vissi, vivesti, visse, vivemmo, viveste, vissero**

cadere *to fall* **caddi, cadesti, cadde, cademmo, cadeste, caddero**

conoscere *to know* **conobbi, conoscesti, conobbe, conoscemmo, conosceste, conobbero**

crescere *to grow* **crebbi, crescesti, crebbe, crescemmo, cresceste, crebbero**

rompere *to break* **ruppi, rompesti, ruppe, rompemmo, rompeste, ruppero**

nascere *to be born* **nacqui, nascesti, nacque, nascemmo, nasceste, nacquero**

word power

-ere verbs

Many **-ere** verbs convert easily from English to Italian, although you need to look out for predictable letter changes in some of them, such as *ex* → **es**.

It's important to remember that the stress on the infinitive of most **-ere** verbs is in a different place from **-are** and **-ire** verbs: **prendere** *to take*, **mettere** *to put*. This doesn't necessarily apply when they have other endings: **prendo** *I take* but **prendiamo** *we take*.

🇬🇧	🇮🇹	
-	-ere	consistere, corrispondere, difendere, dipendere, intendere, offendere, spendere, rispondere
-e	-ere	cedere, decidere, deludere, dividere, escludere, esistere, espellere, ricevere, risolvere

The meaning of many other verbs can be worked out by linking to related English words: **credere** *to believe (credible)*, **leggere** *to write (legible)*, **perdere** *to lose (perdition)*, **scrivere** *to write (scribe, inscribe)*, **sospendere** *to hang (suspend)*

Some irregular **-ere** verbs behave in the same irregular way as other verbs which look similar in structure:

- **accogliere** *to welcome*, **cogliere** *to pick*, **raccogliere** *to gather*, **scegliere** *to choose*, **sciogliere** *to melt*, **togliere** *to remove*
- **tenere** *to hold*, **appartenere** to belong, **contenere** *to contain*, **mantenere** *to maintain*, **ottenere** *to obtain*, **ritenere** *to retain*, **sostenere** *to sustain*

As you might expect, there are false friends among **-ere** verbs too, for example:

intendere *to mean*	*to intend* to **aver intenzione di**
pretendere *to claim, to demand*	*to pretend* **fingere**, **fare finta**

---

word power

-ire verbs

Compared to **-are** and **-ere** verbs, the **-ire** group is relatively small. In the present tense it divides into two sub-groups, with one group inserting **-isc** before all endings except **noi** and **voi**. There's no way of telling which group a verb belongs to; this has to be learnt. On this page, verbs without **-isc** are marked with *.

The stress on the infinitive of all **-ire** verbs is on the **-i** of **-ire**: **aprire*** *to open*, **avvertire*** *to warn*, **seguire*** *to follow*, but this changes when the verb has other endings: **apro** / *open*, **avverto** / *warn*, **seguo** / *follow*.

🇬🇧	🇮🇹	
-	-ire	**convertire*, preferire, partire*** *depart/leave*
-e	-ire	**definire, servire***
-ish	-ire	**abolire, bandire** *banish,* **diminuire, finire, punire, svanire** *vanish*
-ite	-ire	**unire, riunire**

The meaning of other verbs can be worked out by taking predictable letter changes into account (page 21): **ammonire** *to admonish*, **costruire** *to build*, **garantire** *to guarantee*, **proibire** *to prohibit*

... or by linking to related English words: **condire** *to season* *(condiment)*, **dormire*** *to sleep (dormant)*, **divertire*** *to amuse (divert)*, **fornire** *to provide (furnish)*, **nutrire*** *to nourish (nutrition)*, **pulire** *to clean (polish)* **sentire*** *to feel (sentiment)*, **spedire** *to send (expedite)*, **vestire*** *to dress (vestment/vest)*.

Probably the best known verb ending in **-ire** is **dire** *to say/tell*. But, because this is so irregular, it's best to think of it as completely separate from other **-ire** verbs. It includes **c** in several tenses: **dico** / *say*, **dicevo** / *was saying* because it comes from the Latin **dicere**.

checkpoint 15

1   When you come across a new verb, you have to know its
    infinitive before you can look it up in a dictionary. Decide
    whether each of the following is in the present, future,
    conditional, imperfect or simple past, and what person it is, then
    work out what the infinitive is, e.g.
    morì: simple past, lui/lei → morire.

piangeva	urlai	guadagneremmo
sembravano	dipingete	fermerà
cuoceresti	prego	spediremo
ridevamo	ruppero	temeva
otterreste	versano	rifiutò
spiegherei	presterò	salimmo
appoggiavano	scenderà	prometterai

The meanings of the infinitives are given with the answers (page
253) for you to work out the translation of the above words.

2   Replace the ending of these infinitives with the person and tense
    in brackets.

arrivare (io future)	cenare (noi present)
domandare (tu conditional)	comprare (io future)
chiudere (loro imperfect)	credere (lui/lei imperfect)
aprire (io simple past)	scrivere (voi conditional)
pensare (loro imperfect)	organizzare (noi future)
pulire (tu future)	continuare (loro present)
sorridere (lui/lei imperfect)	emigrare (lui/lei simple past)

3   Pair these phrases to make four grammatically correct sentences.

A	B
Quando avevo cinque anni	ma non ho soldi.
Pagherei volentieri	appena finiranno.
Mi piacerebbe molto	abitavamo a Roma.
Ti scriverò	andare a Roma.

Verbs: compound tenses

Compound tenses are those which are made up of two parts:

- an auxiliary verb, e.g. *have*, *had* in English; the simple tenses of **avere** or **e̲ssere*** in Italian.
- the past participle of the main verb. Regular English past participles end in *-ed* while regular Italian past participles end in **-ato**, **-uto** or **-ito**.

In Italian the four main compound tenses are:

- **perfect**, which uses the present tense of **avere**:
  ho lavorato / *have worked, I worked*
- **pluperfect**, which uses the imperfect tense of **avere**:
  avevo lavorato / *had worked*
- **future perfect**, which uses the future tense of **avere**:
  avrò lavorato / *will have worked*
- **past conditional**, which uses the present conditional of **avere**:
  avrei lavorato / *would have worked.*

In all the compound tenses, the only thing that changes is the tense of **avere** or **e̲ssere**. The rules relating to agreement are the same and pronouns and negative words go in the same place.

*While the majority of verbs use **avere** there's a list of verbs that take **e̲ssere** on page 154. The main difference between the two groups is that with verbs using **e̲ssere** the past participle changes to agree with the subject.

the past participle

In English, the past participle is the form of a verb that comes after *has/have* in the perfect tense: *worked, slept, paid, played.*

To form Italian past participles, you change the infinitive like this:

	infinitive	past participle
-are → -ato	**mangiare** *to eat*	**mangiato** *eaten*
-ere → -uto	**vendere** *to sell*	**venduto** *sold*
-ire → -ito	**partire** *to leave*	**partito** *left*

Alongside regular past participles such as *lived, wanted, finished, decided,* there are many English verbs with irregular past participles: *given, thought, spent, eaten.* Many Italian verbs too have irregular past participles – but the irregularities don't necessarily coincide in the two languages.

- **Fare** *to do/make* is the only **-are** verb with an irregular past participle: **fatto** *done, made.*

- **Avere** *to have* has the regular past participle **avuto** *had.* But large numbers of **-ere** verbs have irregular past participles. Most have to be learnt separately, but on the next page there are some patterns that can help you predict what certain past participles might be.

- Most **-ire** verbs have regular past participles. Exceptions include:

apparire *to appear*	→	**apparso** *appeared*
aprire *to open*	→	**aperto** *opened*
coprire *to cover*	→	**coperto** *covered*
dire *to say*	→	**detto** *said*
morire *to die*	→	**morto** *died*
offrire *to offer*	→	**offerto** *offered*
soffrire *to suffer*	→	**sofferto** *suffered*
venire *to come*	→	**venuto** *come*

- Verbs ending in **-arre**, **-orre** and **-urre** form their past participles like these examples:

distrarre *to distract*	→	**distratto** *distracted*
supporre *to suppose*	→	**supposto** *supposed*
tradurre *to translate*	→	**tradotto** *translated*

past participles of -ere verbs

Many **-ere** verbs have past participles which are irregular but which nevertheless fall into clusters based on the letters before **-ere**:

- **-ggere → -tto**
  affliggere *to afflict* → **afflitto**   **friggere** *to fry* → **fritto**
  leggere *to read* → **letto**   **proteggere** *to protect* → **protetto**

- **-gere → -to**
  aggiungere *to add* → **aggiunto**   **fingere** *to pretend* → **finto**
  dipingere *to paint* → **dipinto**   **piangere** *to cry* → **pianto**
  volgere *to turn* → **volto**

  Exceptions include:
  dirigere *to direct* → **diretto**   **stringere** *to squeeze* → **stretto**

- **-gliere → -lto**
  accogliere *to welcome* → **accolto**
  scegliere *to choose* → **scelto**   **togliere** *to take off* → **tolto**

- **-dere/-ndere → -so**
  chiudere *to close* → **chiuso**   **decidere** *to decide* → **deciso**
  mordere *to bite* → **morso**   **offendere** *to offend* → **offeso**
  prendere *to take* → **preso**   **scendere** *to go down* → **sceso**
  spendere *to spend* → **speso**   **uccidere** *to kill* → **ucciso**

  Exceptions include:
  chiedere *to ask* → **chiesto**   **nascondere** *to hide* → **nascosto**
  rispondere to reply → **risposto**   **succedere** *to happen* → **successo**
  and the past participle of **vedere** *to see* can be **visto** or **veduto**.

The following don't fall into clusters but they're such common verbs that it's really worth learning their past participles. Try to think of a related English word that can serve as a memory prompt.

bere *to drink* → **bevuto**   **correre** *to run* → **corso**
discutere *to discuss* → **discusso**   **essere** *to be* → **stato**
mettere *to put* → **messo**   **morire** *to die* → **morto**
muovere *to move* → **mosso**   **nascere** *to be born* → **nato**
riflettere *to reflect* → **riflesso**   **rimanere** *to stay* → **rimasto**
rompere *to break* → **rotto**   **scrivere** *to write* → **scritto**
vincere *to win* → **vinto**   **vivere** *to live* → **vissuto**

when to use past participles

- The main use of the past participle is after **avere** and **essere** in compound tenses, i.e. perfect, pluperfect, future perfect, past conditional (pages 152-159).
  Ti ho telefonato ieri. *I called you yesterday.*
  Avevo già venduto la macchina. *I'd already sold the car.*
  Il treno sarà partito. *The train will have left.*
  Avrei preferito l'altro. *I would have preferred the other one.*

- As in English, many past participles can be used as adjectives – behaving like any other adjectives ending in **-o**:
  Ecco il prodotto finito. *Here's the finished product.*
  Servire con formaggio grattugiato. *Serve with grated cheese.*
  Questo è il mio vino preferito. *This is my favourite/preferred wine.*

- Using the past participle on its own is a simple and useful way of saying *having done something:*
  Tornato a casa, ho trovato il messaggio. *When I got back home* (lit. *returned home), I found the message.*
  Putting **appena** or **non appena** before the past participle adds the sense of *as soon as:*
  Non appena tornato a casa, ho trovato il messaggio. *As soon as I got back home, I found the message.*

- You can use a past participle after the infinitives **avere** and **essere** to mean *to have done something:*
  È un piacere aver fatto la sua conoscenza. *It's a pleasure to have met you.*
  Che sollievo essere arrivati. *What a relief to have arrived.*
  Including **dopo** *after* beforehand changes it to *after having done something,* often translated in English as *after doing something:*
  Dopo aver fatto la sua conoscenza … *After having met you/after meeting you …*

- Past participles are also used with **essere**, **venire** or **andare** for the passive (opposite).

the passive

The passive describes something done **to** the subject, rather than **by** it: *the meat is cooked in the oven, the room was booked by my friend.*

- In Italian, you use the relevant tense of **e̲ssere** with a past participle, which agrees with the subject:
  Il vino bianco è servito fresco. *White wine is served chilled.*
  La torta era fatta da mia nonna. *The cake was made by my grandmother.*
  Le fra̲gole saranno servite con panna. *The strawberries will be served with cream.*
  I tortellini sono stati fatti stamattina. *The tortellini were made this morning.*

- **Venire** can be used instead of **e̲ssere** in the simple tenses only:
  Il vino rosso viene servito a temperatura ambiente. *Red wine is served at room temperature.*
  I tortellini venivano fatti in casa. *The tortellini were home made.*
  Le uova verranno mangiate oggi. *The eggs will be eaten today.*

- When **andare** replaces **e̲ssere** or **venire**, the meaning changes to *should/ must be:*
  Va fatto così. *It should be done this way.*
  La panna va tenuta in frigo. *The cream must be kept in the fridge.*
  I vini bianchi vanno serviti freschi. *White wines should be served chilled.*
  Queste uova vanno mangiate oggi. *These eggs need to be eaten today.*

Very often the English translation of the passive starts with *you*:
È/viene fatto così. *You do it this way. It's done this way.*
Vengono usati d'inverno. *You use them in winter. They're used in winter.*
Viene comprato fresco, congelato, essiccato o salato. *You can buy it fresh, frozen, dried or salted.*
Non vanno mai messi in frigo. *You should never put them in the fridge. They should never be put in the fridge.*

the perfect tense: i) with avere

The perfect tense of the majority of verbs is made up of the present tense of **avere** *to have* plus the past participle of the main verb formed as follows.

	infinitive	past participle
-are → -ato	**lavorare** *to work*	**lavorato** *worked*
-ere → -uto	**vendere** *to sell*	**venduto** *sold*
-ire → -ito	**partire** *to leave*	**partito** *left*

lavorare	io	ho lavorato
	tu	hai lavorato
	lui/lei	ha lavorato
	noi	abbiamo lavorato
	voi	avete lavorato
	loro	hanno lavorato

vendere	io	ho venduto
	tu	hai venduto
	lui/lei	ha venduto
	noi	abbiamo venduto
	voi	avete venduto
	loro	hanno venduto

capire	io	ho capito
	tu	hai capito
	lui/lei	ha capito
	noi	abbiamo capito
	voi	avete capito
	loro	hanno capito

> Most of the time, the past participle doesn't change its ending when used after **avere**. The only exception is explained on page 156.

ii) with essere

Some verbs use <u>e</u>ssere *to be* instead of **avere** for the perfect tense – there's a list on the next page.

Their past participle is formed in exactly the same way as verbs that use **avere**; but with **essere** verbs it has to agree with the subject, behaving just like an adjective ending in **-o**:

		m	f
andare	io	sono andato	sono andata
to go	tu	sei andato	sei andata
	lui/lei	è andato	è andata
	noi	siamo andati	siamo andate
	voi	siete andati	siete andate
	loro	sono andati	sono andate
cadere	io	sono caduto	sono caduta
to fall	tu	sei caduto	sei caduta
	lui/lei	è caduto	è caduta
	noi	siamo caduti	siamo cadute
	voi	siete caduti	siete cadute
	loro	sono caduti	sono cadute
vestirsi	io	mi sono vestito	mi sono vestita
to get dressed	tu	ti sei vestito	ti sei vestita
	lui/lei	si è vestito	si è vestita
	noi	ci siamo vestiti	ci siamo vestite
	voi	vi siete vestiti	vi siete vestite
	loro	si sono vestiti	si sono vestite

Giorgio è arrivato. *Giorgio (has) arrived.*
Anna è arrivata. *Anna (has) arrived.*
Giorgio e Anna sono arrivati. *Giorgio and Anna (have) arrived.*
Anna e Laura sono arrivate. *Anna and Laura (have) arrived.*

verbs that use essere

Some verbs use **essere** in the compound tenses. It's a useful rule of thumb to think of them as belonging in three categories:

- verbs relating to movement, e.g. **andare** *to go*, **cadere** *to fall;*
- verbs relating to existence, e.g. **essere** *to be,* **morire** *to die;*
- reflexive verbs (page 116), e.g. **sposarsi** *to get married,* **accorgersi** *to realise.*

The following are the most common. Only irregular past participles are included here.

andare *to go*	**venire** *to come*
arrivare *to arrive*	**partire** *to leave*
salire *to go up/get into*	**scendere** *to go down/get out of* **sceso**
nascere *to be born* **nato**	**morire** *to die* **morto**
essere *to be* **stato**	**diventare** *to become*
entrare *to enter*	**uscire** *to go out*
sfuggire *to escape*	**rimanere** *to remain* **rimasto**
cadere *to fall*	**succedere** *to happen* **successo**
riuscire *to succeed*	**passare** *to pass by*
(ri)tornare *to return*	**vivere** *to live* **vissuto**

Grammatically speaking, these verbs use **essere** because they're intransitive, i.e. they don't take a direct object. Transitive verbs, which do take a direct object, use **avere** in the compound tenses.

Some verbs can be both transitive and intransitive, and they use **avere** or **essere** in compound tense depending on how they're being used at the time:

transitive:	**Hanno cresciuto due figli.** *They brought up two children.*
	Ho finito il gioco. *I've finished the game.*
	Lo chef ha bruciato la carne. *The chef (has) burnt the meat*
intransitive:	**I figli sono cresciuti.** *The children grew up.*
	Il gioco è finito. *The game is/has finished.*
	La casa è bruciata. *The house burnt down.*

Other verbs that behave in this way are: **aumentare, cambiare, cominciare, diminuire, iniziare, passare.**

when to use the perfect tense

- You use the Italian perfect tense when in English you'd say *I have worked* or *I worked, I have eaten* or *I ate*:
  Ho comprato una macchina. *I (have) bought a car.*
  Mia sorella ha venduto la casa. *My sister (has) sold the house.*

  Abbiamo finito. *We've finished.*
  Abbiamo mangiato frutti di mare. *We ate/we've eaten seafood.*

  Matteo è arrivato. *Matteo (has) arrived.*
  Matteo è caduto stamattina. *Matteo fell this morning.*

  Mi sono divertito molto. *I (have) really enjoyed myself.*
  Si è alzata alle otto. *She got up at eight o'clock.*
  Si sono sposati sabato. *They got married on Saturday.*

- In questions and negatives there's no Italian equivalent of *did*:
  Hai comprato la macchina? *Have you bought the car?/Did you buy the car?*
  Non ha venduto la casa. *She hasn't sold/didn't sell the house.*

  Avete mangiato? *Have you eaten?*
  Avete mangiato il pesce? *Did you eat the fish?*
  Non abbiamo mangiato. *We haven't eaten.*

  Matteo è arrivato? *Has Matteo arrived?/Did Matteo arrive?*
  Matteo non è arrivato. *Matteo hasn't arrived/didn't arrive.*

  Ti sei divertito? *Have you enjoyed yourself?/Did you enjoy yourself?*
  Non si è alzata presto. *She didn't get up early.*

- Some negative words go before the past participle, others after it (pages 122-124):
  Non abbiamo ancora mangiato. *We haven't yet eaten.*
  Non abbiamo mangiato niente. *We haven't eaten anything.*

pronouns with the perfect tense

- Object pronouns, **ci** (page 93) and **ne** (page 94) go before **avere/essere**:
  Vi hanno aspettato. *They waited for you.*
  Me l'hai già detto. *You've already told me.*
  Gliel'ho dato ieri. *I gave it to him/her/them/you yesterday.*
  Ci sono andato ieri. *I went there yesterday.*
  Ne ho comprati due. *I bought two (of them).*

- When **avere** verbs have a direct object pronoun, i.e. **lo, la,** (which both usually shorten to **l'**) **li** or **le**, the past participle agrees with the pronoun:
  Giorgio? L'ho visto oggi. *George? I saw him today.*
  La partita? Non l'ho vista. *The match? I didn't see it.*
  I bambini? Sì, li ho visti. *The children? Yes, I saw them.*
  Le chiavi? Non le ho viste. *The keys? I haven't seen them.*

- Reflexive verbs (page 116) use **essere**, and the reflexive pronoun goes before it:
  Mi sono seduto sulla sabbia. *I sat down on the sand.*
  Guido si è laureato l'anno scorso. *Guido graduated last year.*
  Vi siete sbagliati tutti. *You've all made a mistake.*
  Si sono scusati. *They apologised.*

- When a reflexive verb has the direct object **lo, la, li** or **le**, the past participle agrees with it, not with the subject:
  La password? Te la sei ricordata? *The password? Did you remember it?*
  Le regole – ce le siamo dimenticate. *The rules – we've forgotten them.*

It takes time to get used to Italian personal pronouns - to remember where they go and what they agree with - and most people make mistakes at the beginning. Don't react to this by trying to avoid them. Making a mistake and realising where you've gone wrong is a valuable part of the learning process.

the pluperfect

You use the pluperfect when in English you say *had done something*. The only difference in the way the pluperfect and the perfect tense are formed in Italian is that the pluperfect uses the imperfect of **avere** or **essere** instead of the present. The same verbs use **avere** or **essere**; the rules for agreement are the same; pronouns and negative words go in the same place.

lavorare	io	avevo lavorato	
to work	tu	avevi lavorato	
	lui/lei	aveva lavorato	
	noi	avevamo lavorato	
	voi	avevate lavorato	
	loro	avevano lavorato	

cadere	io	ero caduto	ero caduta
to fall	tu	eri caduto	eri caduta
	lui/lei	era caduto	era caduta
	noi	eravamo caduti	eravamo cadute
	voi	eravate caduti	eravate cadute
	loro	erano caduti	erano cadute

vestirsi	io	mi ero vestito	mi ero vestita
to get dressed	tu	ti eri vestito	ti eri vestita
	lui/lei	si era vestito	si era vestita
	noi	ci eravamo vestiti	ci eravamo vestite
	voi	vi eravate vestiti	vi eravate vestite
	loro	si erano vestiti	si erano vestite

Avevo finito. *I had finished.*
Avevamo telefonato a Luciano. *We had phoned Luciano.*
Avevano già mangiato? *Had they already eaten?*
Non avevi visto quel film? *Had you not seen that film?*
Non si era alzata quando … *She hadn't got up when …*
Matteo era partito prima di me. *Matteo had left before me.*
Non eravamo ancora entrati. *We had not yet gone in.*

the future perfect

The future tense of **avere/essere** + past participle give you the future perfect. The same rules for agreement and position of pronouns apply as for the perfect, the pluperfect and the past conditional.

lavorare	io	avrò lavorato	
to work	tu	avrai lavorato	
	lui/lei	avrà lavorato	
	noi	avremo lavorato	
	voi	avrete lavorato	
	loro	avranno lavorato	

cadere	io	sarò caduto	sarò caduta
to fall	tu	sarai caduto	sarai caduta
	lui/lei	sarà caduto	sarà caduta
	noi	saremo caduti	saremo cadute
	voi	sarete caduti	sarete cadute
	loro	saranno caduti	saranno cadute

vestirsi	io	mi sarò vestito	mi sarò vestita
to get dressed	tu	ti sarai vestito	ti sarai vestita
	lui/lei	si sarà vestito	si sarà vestita
	noi	ci saremo vestiti	ci saremo vestite
	voi	vi sarete vestiti	vi sarete vestite
	loro	si saranno vestiti	si saranno vestite

You use the future perfect when in English you say *will have done something*:
Non avranno visto niente. *They will not have seen anything.*
Sarà arrivato entro le cinque. *He will have arrived by five o'clock.*

Unlike English, you also use it after **se** *if*, **quando** *when*, **appena** *as soon as*, **finché/fino a quando** *until*, when the main verb of the sentence is in the future.

Quando avrò finito, uscirò. *When I've finished* (lit. *will have finished), I'll go out.*
Non lo sapremo finché non sarà tornato Luigi. *We won't know until Luigi comes back* lit. *will have come back.*

the past conditional

The present conditional of **avere/essere** + past participle give you the past conditional. The same rules apply as for the perfect, the pluperfect and the future perfect.

lavorare	**io**	avrei lavorato	
to work	**tu**	avresti lavorato	
	lui/lei	avrebbe lavorato	
	noi	avremmo lavorato	
	voi	avreste lavorato	
	loro	avrebbero lavorato	

cadere	**io**	sarei caduto	sarei caduta
to fall	**tu**	saresti caduto	saresti caduta
	lui/lei	sarebbe caduto	sarebbe caduta
	noi	saremmo caduti	saremmo cadute
	voi	sareste caduti	sareste cadute
	loro	sarebbero caduti	sarebbero cadute

vestirsi	**io**	mi sarei vestito	mi sarei vestita
to get dressed	**tu**	ti saresti vestito	ti saresti vestita
	lui/lei	si sarebbe vestito	si sarebbe vestita
	noi	ci saremmo vestiti	ci saremmo vestite
	voi	vi sareste vestiti	vi sareste vestite
	loro	si sarebbero vestiti	si sarebbero vestite

You use the past conditional when in English you say *would have done something*:
Sarei andato ma ero in ritardo. *I would have gone but I was late.*

When it's followed by *if*, the verb after *if* has to be in the pluperfect subjunctive (page 169):
Sarei andato se avessi saputo. *I would have gone if I'd known.*

After phrases like *he said (that)*, *he thought (that)*, *he hoped (that),* Italian always uses the past conditional *would have* whereas English uses either *would* or *would have*:
Maria ha detto che sarebbe andata. *Maria said she would go.*
Pensavo che avresti aspettato. *I thought you would wait/would have waited.*

checkpoint 16

1   What are the past participles of these verbs? Nine are irregular.

comprare   vendere   garantire   avere
cominciare   morire   trovare   costruire
volere   fare   aprire   credere
ascoltare   venire   tenere   dire
mangiare   spendere   vestire   decidere
bere   chiudere   finire   andare

2   Fill the gaps to create the perfect tense.

a io .... dormito   b noi .... andati
c loro .... capito   d tu non .... telefonato
e lei .... usato   f voi .... arrivati
g io mi .... divertita   h lui non .... organizzato niente

3   Fill in the final letter of the past participle.

a Non avevo parlat_ con Maria.

b Maria? Non l'ho vist_ oggi.

c I ragazzi saranno andat_ in città.

d Hai lavorat_ questa settimana, Carla?

e Si sono sposat_ sabato.

f Anna e sua sorella sono partit_ verso mezzanotte.

4   Change these from the present tense to the tense indicated.

a Non capisco. .... pluperfect

b Andiamo via. .... past conditional

c Paolo arriva alle otto. .... perfect

d Quando mangiamo? .... future perfect

e Mi alzo (f) presto. .... pluperfect

f Che cosa compri? .... perfect

g Lei organizza un pranzo. .... past conditional

h Invitano tutti gli amici. .... future perfect

i Lucia finisce la scuola quest'anno. .... perfect

j Lui si veste in fretta. .... pluperfect

Gerund, imperative, subjunctive

Italian verb endings not only provide information about tense, i.e. whether things are happening in the past, present or future, they indicate other functions of the verb too.

These functions include:

- the **gerund**, the equivalent of the *-ing* ending in English, although in Italian it's used much less and not always in the same way.

- the **imperative**, used to tell somebody what to do. In English there's only one version but there are three in Italian because of the three different words for *you*: **tu**, **lei**, **voi**:

  There's also a **noi** imperative, used to say *Let's* .... This is identical to the present indicative.

- the **subjunctive**, no longer used much in English but used extensively in Italian. A verb in the subjunctive doesn't convey hard fact but is usually the second verb of a sentence, following another verb which expresses someone's attitude or opinion, doubt or uncertainty.

  The sort of phrase that triggers a subjunctive is made up of words like *hope, wish, doubt, suppose, fear, advise, suggest* followed by **che** *that*.

the gerund

The gerund is the equivalent of the *-ing* ending in English, formed by changing the infinitive to **-ando** or **-endo**:

	infinitive	gerund
-are → -ando	**lavorare** *to work*	**lavorando** *working*
-ere → -endo	**v̲endere** *to sell*	**vendendo** *selling*
-ire → -endo	**partire** *to leave*	**partendo** *leaving*

- A common use of the gerund is with the present tense of **stare** to emphasise that something is happening right now:
  Cosa stai cercando? *What are you looking for?*
  Sto scherzando! *I'm only joking!*
  or with the imperfect of **stare** to say what was going on at the moment something else happened:
  Stavo leggendo quando è venuto. *I was reading when he came.*
  Stavo aspettando Francesca quando … *I was waiting for Francesca when …*

  Pronouns go before **stare**:
  La stavo aspettando quando … *I was waiting for her when …*

- It can also be the equivalent of *while/on doing something*:
  Seguendo il tuo esempio, sono partito. *Following your example, I left.*
  Leggendo la sua l̲ettera, capisco il problema. *Reading his letter, I understand the problem.*

  In sentences like the above, pronouns follow the gerund and combine with it:
  Rileg̲gendola, ho imparato che … *Re-reading it, I learnt that …*

- **Pur**, short for **pure**, is used with the gerund to mean *even though*:
  Pur essendo bravo, non è il migliore. *Even though he's good, he's not the best.*
  Pur avendo paura, è tornata. *Even though she's afraid, she has come back.*

... and when *not* to use it

The thing to remember about the gerund is that it's used far less in Italian. It's not used:

- after any other verb except **stare** (page 232). You use the infinitive instead:

  Mi piace cantare. *I like singing.*
  Preferisco rimanere qui. *I prefer staying here.*

- or after prepositions like **prima di** *before*, **invece di** *instead*, **oltre a** *as well as*, **senza** *without* or **dopo** *after*:

  prima di pagare *before paying*; **invece di uscire** *instead of going out*
  senza parlare *without speaking*

Only a few verbs have an irregular gerund, adding **-endo** to irregular stems:

bere *to drink* → **bevendo**	**attrarre** *to attract* → **attraendo**
dire *to say* → **dicendo**	**opporre** *to oppose* → **opponendo**
fare *to make* → **facendo**	**produrre** *to produce* → **producendo**

Other verbs ending in **-dire**, **-fare**, **-arre**, **-orre** and **-urre** follow the same patterns.

checkpoint 17

1 Write the gerund of the following verbs – keeping an eye open for verbs similar to the above – and work out what they all mean.

a aiutare .... b introdurre ....

c finire .... d decidere ....

e supporre .... f contraddire ....

g bere .... h distrarre ....

i sedurre .... j dormire ....

2 Gerund or infinitive?

a [cercare] Stavo .... un sito web.

b [pagare] È partito senza ....

c [nuotare] Non mi piace ....

d [sapere] Sono andata pur .... la verità.

e [andare] Dove stiamo .... ?

f [continuare] Preferirei tornare a casa invece di ....

the imperative

The imperative, used to give instructions, has four forms: **tu**, **lei**, **noi** and **voi**.

	-are	-ere	-ire*	-ire
	lavorare *to work*	vendere *to sell*	partire *to leave*	capire *to understand*
tu	lavora	vendi	parti	capisci
lei	lavori	venda	parta	capisca
noi	lavoriamo	vendiamo	partiamo	capiamo
voi	lavorate	vendete	partite	capite

* verbs without -isc

The following verbs have irregular **tu** imperatives:

andare	avere	dare	dire	essere	fare	sapere	stare
to go	*to have*	*to give*	*to say*	*to be*	*to do*	*to know*	*to stay*
vai/va'	abbi	dai/da'	di'	sii	fai/fa'	sappi	stai/sta'

- **lei** imperatives are identical to the **lei** present subjunctive (page 166):

  andare *to go* → **vada**   **dire** *to say* → **dica**
  essere *to be* → **sia**   **fare** *to do* → **faccia**
  porre *to put* → **ponga**   **venire** *to come* → **venga**

- **noi** imperatives are identical to the **noi** present tense endings (page 132).

- most **voi** imperatives are identical to the **voi** present tense endings (page 132). Only **avere**, **essere** and **sapere** are irregular, and they're identical to the present subjunctive:

  avere *to have* → **abbiate**   **essere** *to be* → **siate**
  sapere *to know* → **sappiate**

For negatives:
- you put **non** in front of **lei**, **noi** and **voi** imperatives:

lei	**Non aspetti.** *Don't wait.*
noi	**Non mangiamo qui.** *Let's not eat here.*
voi	**Non dimenticate!** *Don't forget!*

- when using **tu**, you put **non** in front of the infinitive of the verb, ***not*** the imperative:

  Non aspettare. *Don't wait.*
  Non aprire quello lì. *Don't open that one.*
  Non fare lo scemo. *Don't be an idiot.*

... and how to use it

You use the **tu**, **lei** and **voi** imperatives to tell someone what to do and give advice, and the **noi** imperative to make suggestions:

tu	**Aspetta qui.** *Wait here.*
lei	**Vada fino alla stazione.** *Go as far as the station.*
noi	**Andiamo.** *Let's go.*
voi	**Guardate il conto.** *Look at the bill.*

Object pronouns, reflexive pronouns, **ci** *there* and **ne**:

- go before the **lei** imperative:
  Lo prenda. *Take it*
  Si accomodi. *Make yourself comfortable.*
  Non si preoccupi. *Don't worry.*
  Ci torni domani. *Go back there tomorrow.*
  Ne assaggi un po'. *Taste a bit of it.*

- go after the other imperatives and combine with them:

tu	**Prendilo.**
	Accomodati.
	Non preoccuparti.
	Tornaci domani.
	Assaggiane un po'.

voi	**Prendetelo.**
	Accomodatevi.
	Non preoccupatevi.
	Tornateci domani.
	Assaggiatene un po'.

noi	**Prendiamolo.** *Let's take it.*
	Accomodiamoci. *Let's make ourselves at home.*
	Non preoccupiamoci. *Let's not worry.*
	Torniamoci domani. *Let's go back there tomorrow.*
	Assaggiamone un po'. *Let's taste some.*

The initial letter of pronouns (except **gli**) is doubled with the irregular **tu** imperative of **dare**, **dire** and **fare**: **da'**, **di'** and **fa'**:
Dammi una bottiglia. *Give me a bottle.*
Dimmi la verità. *Tell me the truth.*
Facci un favore. *Do us a favour.*

the subjunctive: regular verbs

In the **present subjunctive**, -ire verbs separate into two groups, one of which adds -isc in all forms except noi and voi (page 145).

	-are	-ere	-ire (no -isc)	-ire (-isc)
io	lavori	venda	parta	capisca
tu	lavori	venda	parta	capisca
lui/lei	lavori	venda	parta	capisca
noi	lavoriamo	vendiamo	partiamo	capiamo
voi	lavoriate	vendiate	partiate	capiate
loro	lavorino	vendano	partano	capiscano

In the **imperfect subjunctive**, no -ire verbs add -isc.

	-are	-ere	-ire
io	lavorassi	vendessi	capissi
tu	lavorassi	vendessi	capissi
lui/lei	lavorasse	vendesse	capisse
noi	lavorassimo	vendessimo	capissimo
voi	lavoraste	vendeste	capiste
loro	lavorassero	vendessero	capissero

The **perfect subjunctive** is the present subjunctive of avere or essere followed by the past participle*:

io	abbia lavorato	sia partito/a
tu	abbia lavorato	sia partito/a
lui/lei	abbia lavorato	sia partito/a
noi	abbiamo lavorato	siamo partiti/e
voi	abbiate lavorato	siate partiti/e
loro	abbiano lavorato	siano partiti/e

The **pluperfect subjunctive** is the imperfect subjunctive of avere or essere followed by the past participle*:

io	avessi lavorato	fossi partito/a
tu	avessi lavorato	fossi partito/a
lui/lei	avesse lavorato	fosse partito/a
noi	avessimo lavorato	fossimo partiti/e
voi	aveste lavorato	foste partiti/e
loro	avessero lavorato	fossero partiti/e

*The rules for agreement of the past participle are the same as for the other compound tenses (pages 152-153).

... and irregular verbs

Most common irregular verbs are also irregular in the present subjunctive:

andare *to go* vada, vada, vada, andiamo, andiate, vadano

avere *to have* abbia, abbia, abbia, abbiamo, abbiate, abbiano

dare *to give* dia, dia, dia, diamo, diate, diano

dire *to say* dica, dica, dica, diciamo, diciate, dicano

dovere *to have to* debba, debba, debba, dobbiamo, dobbiate, debbano

essere *to be* sia, sia, sia, siamo, siate, siano

fare *to do* faccia, faccia, faccia, facciamo, facciate, facciano

potere *to be able to* possa, possa, possa, possiamo, possiate, possano

sapere *to know* sappia, sappia, sappia, sappiamo, sappiate, sappiano

stare *to be* stia, stia, stia, stiamo, stiate, stiano

venire *to come* venga, venga, venga, veniamo, veniate, vengano

volere *to want* voglia, voglia, voglia, vogliamo, vogliate, vogliano

A useful reminder of how to form the subjunctive is to think of the first person singular of the present indicative (page 132), remove the -o ending, and add subjunctive endings:
capire → capisco → capisca

This even works for many irregular verbs:
andare → vado → vada   potere → posso → possa

In the imperfect subjunctive:

- essere is irregular:
  fossi, fossi, fosse, fossimo, foste, fossero

- many verbs which are irregular in the imperfect indicative (page 140) use the same irregular stem for the imperfect subjunctive, then add regular subjunctive -ere endings to it:
  bere *to drink* → bevevo → bev → bevessi
  porre *to put* → ponevo → pon → ponessi

when to use the subjunctive

In English, the subjunctive is no longer widely used and appears most often in expressions like these: *if only it were true; be that as it may; until death do us part; perish the thought.*

In Italian, it's used much more widely; it's needed whenever opinions and attitudes are involved, whenever you're talking about things that aren't actual fact. Generally introduced by **che**, it's used after another verb expressing:

- opinion:

  Penso che sia importante. *I think it's important.*
  Suppongo che debba andare io. *I suppose I'll have to go.*
  È strano che non ci sia nessuno. *It's odd there's nobody here.*
  È preferibile che l'acqua sia tiepida. *It's preferable for the water to be lukewarm.*

- hope, doubt, wishing, fear:

  Spero che non ci sia traffico. *I hope there's no traffic.*
  Dubito che vengano. *I doubt they'll come.*
  Preferisco che tu non vada. *I prefer you not to go.*
  Vorrei che fossi qui. *I wish you were here.*
  Vogliono che aspettiamo. *They want us to wait.*
  Ha paura che finisca male. *He's afraid it might end badly.*

- possibility or probability:

  È probabile che io arrivi tardi. *It's likely that I'll arrive late.*
  Non è possibile che sia legale. *It can't possibly be legal.*
  Può darsi che abbia dimenticato. *It may be that he's forgotten.*

The subjunctive is also needed after

- superlatives:

  Il migliore film che abbia mai visto. *The best film I've ever seen.*

- conjunctions like **benché** *although*, **perché/affinché** *in order to*, **a condizione che** *on condition that*, **prima che** *before*, **purché** *provided that*, **a meno che non** *unless*:

  benché non mi piaccia molto *even though I don't like it much*
  perché tu possa partire domani *so that you can leave tomorrow*
  prima che sia troppo tardi *before it's too late*
  a meno che non piova *unless it rains*

... and which tense to choose

- When the verb before **che** is in the present tense, you use the present or the perfect subjunctive:
  Penso che capiscano. *I think they understand.*
  Penso che abbiano capito. *I think they've understood.*
  Credo che Luca parta oggi. *I believe Luca's leaving today.*
  È possibile che sia già partito. *He might already have left.*

- When the verb before **che** is in a past tense, you use the imperfect or the pluperfect subjunctive:
  Pensavo che capissero. *I thought they understood.*
  Credevo che avessero capito. *I believed they had understood.*
  Era probabile che Luca fosse già partito. *Luca had probably left already.*
  Ho immaginato che tu fossi contenta. *I imagined you were happy.*
  Avrei preferito che tu fossi andato. *I would have preferred you to go/to have gone.*

- With the present conditional (page 139) + *if*, you use the imperfect subjunctive:
  Andrei se volessi andare. *I would go if I wanted to go.*
  Lo comprerei se costasse meno. *I'd buy it if it cost less.*

- With the past conditional (page 159) + *if*, you use the pluperfect subjunctive:
  Sarei andata se non avessi dimenticato. *I would have gone if I hadn't forgotten.*
  L'avrei comprato se fosse costato meno. *I would have bought it if it had cost less.*

Because there's only one form for all three singular persons in the present and the perfect subjunctive, you'll find that you often need to use subject pronouns to avoid ambiguity.
È meglio che io vada. *It's better that I go.*
È meglio che tu/lei vada. *It's better that you go.*

checkpoint 18

1   Identify the imperatives in this set of directions.

"Allora ... non prenda la prima a sinistra ma vada
sempre dritto fino al semaforo. Giri a sinistra,
attraversi la piazza poi prenda la seconda a destra.
Non si preoccupi – non è lontano."

2   If you followed the
directions on this
map, would you end
up at A, B, C or D?

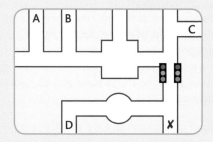

3   Is the person giving the directions using **tu** or **lei**? How would
he/she give them using the other one?

4   Find the correct ending from list B for the phrases in list A.

A	B
Questo è il migliore libro che io	sia egoista.
Credevo che voi	sia già partita.
È molto probabile che lei	non abbiate dimenticato.
Vai adesso, prima che	avessero telefonato.
Aspetterei se tu	foste partiti.
Amo Luciano benché	abbia mai letto.
Avrei aspettato se loro	l'ultimo treno parta.
Spero che voi	fossi con me.

In everyday spoken Italian you often hear the present
indicative used instead of the present subjunctive.
So don't be surprised to hear **Penso che è importante**
instead of **Penso che sia importante** for *I think it's
important.*

Key verbs

In Italian, as in most languages, some verbs are used more frequently than others. These include verbs like **andare** *to go*, **dare** *to give*, **dire** *to say*, **mangiare** *to eat*, **pensare** *to think*, which relate to basic human activity. *Liking* falls into the category of basic human activity, but Italian expresses likes and dislikes very differently from English, using **piacere** *to be pleasing*.

Some verbs are used very frequently because their grammatical uses extend beyond their fundamental meaning:

- **dovere** *to have to*, **potere** *to be able to* and **volere** *to want to*, known as modal verbs, are used with the infinitive of a second verb
- **stare** *to be*, *to stay* can be used with the gerund (page 162) and can also be followed by **per** + infinitive to mean *to be about to*
- **essere** *to be* and **avere** *to have* are used with a past participle to form past tenses (pages 152-159)
- **avere** also features in many expressions that don't use the word *have* in English
- **fare** *to do/make* is used in a whole range of situations when it's not translated as *do* or *make*.

These are all irregular and written out in full in the verb tables.

Some common Italian verbs don't have a direct equivalent in English. Both **sapere** and **conoscere** translate *to know*, but they're not at all interchangeable. **Sapere** means to know information and facts, and to know how to do something, whereas you use **conoscere** when you're talking about knowing or being acquainted with a person or a place.

modal verbs

Dovere *to have to*, **potere** *to be able to* and **volere** *to want to*, are known as modal verbs. Used in this way, they're always followed by another verb and they all behave in a similar way.

All three verbs are irregular (pages 209, 221, 241).

- Verbs which follow a modal verb are always in the infinitive:
  Devo cambiare? *Do I have to change?*
  Puoi scegliere tu. *You can choose.*
  Vogliamo uscire. *We want to go out.*

- In the perfect tense, the modal verbs use **avere** or **essere**, according to which one the infinitive that follows the modal normally uses:
  Abbiamo dovuto aspettare. *We had to wait.*
  Siamo dovuti partire. *We had to leave.*
  Non ho potuto invitarli. *I couldn't invite them.*
  Non sono potuto andare. *I couldn't go.*
  However, in everyday Italian you'll often hear **avere** used instead of **essere**:
  Ho dovuto partire.
  Non ho potuto andare.

- There are two possible positions for pronouns with modal verbs – they can either go before **dovere**, **potere**, **volere** or after the infinitive, which drops its final **-e** and combines with the pronouns:
  Gli devo telefonare. *I have to phone him.*
  Devo telefonargli.
  Come ve lo posso spiegare? *How can I explain it to you?*
  Come posso spiegarvelo?
  Ne vorrei comprare una. *I'd like to buy one of them.*
  Vorrei comprarne una.

  The same applies when **dovere**, **potere** or **volere** are used with reflexive verbs (page 116):
  Dovrei alzarmi./Mi dovrei alzare. *I ought to get up.*

modal verbs with reflexive verbs

When reflexive verbs are used after **dovere**, **potere** or **volere**, there are two possible positions for reflexive pronouns.

They can go:
- after the infinitive, which drops the final **-e** and combines with the pronoun to form one word:
  Devo sedermi. *I have to sit down*
  Vogliamo sederci. *We want to sit down.*
  Dovrebbe alzarsi. *She ought to get up.*
  Potresti abituarti. *You could get used to it*
  Non volevano annoiarsi. *They didn't want to be bored.*

- or before **dovere, potere, volere**:
  Mi devo sedere.
  Ci vogliamo sedere.
  Si dovrebbe alzare.
  Ti potresti abituare.
  Non si volevano annoiare.

In the perfect tense, the combination of reflexive verbs and modal verbs can take **avere** or **essere**.

- With **avere**, the reflexive pronoun goes after the infinitive and combines with it. The past participle doesn't have to agree.
  Abbiamo dovuto alzarci presto. *We had to get up early.*
  Mia moglie non ha potuto addormentarsi. *My wife couldn't get to sleep.*
  Avevo voluto presentarmi. *I had wanted to introduce myself.*

- With **essere**, the reflexive pronoun comes before **dovere, potere** and **volere**, and the past participle agrees with the subject.
  Ci siamo dovuti alzare presto.
  Mia moglie non si è potuta addormentare.
  Mi ero voluto presentare.

dovere

Dovere can mean *to owe*:
Quanto le devo? *How much do I owe you?*
Mi deve cento euro. *He owes me 100 euro.*

This meaning is entirely separate from its use as a modal verb (page 172), when it has the following range of English translations:

- *have to, must, should* – present tense:
  Devo tornare a casa. *I have to go back home.*
  A che ora devi partire? *What time do you have to leave?*
  Non dobbiamo dimenticare. *We must not forget.*
  Le chiavi devono essere in camera. *The keys must be in the room.*
  Deve arrivare fra poco. *He should arrive soon.*

- *had to* – perfect, imperfect and imperfect subjunctive, all with slight differences in meaning:
  Sono dovuto tornare a casa. *I had to go back home.*
  Dovevo lavorare tanto. *I had to (used to have to) work so much.*
  Perché dovevi andare? *Why did you have to go?*
  Doveva partire a mezzogiorno. *He had to leave at midday.*
  Se dovessero scegliere …. *If they had to choose …*

- *ought to, should* – conditional:
  Dovrebbe abbassare il prezzo. *He ought to reduce the price.*
  Non dovrei lamentarmi. *I ought not to/shouldn't complain.*
  Dovreste andare a vedere Roma. *You should go to see Rome.*

- *should have, was supposed to* – past conditional:
  Sarei dovuto andare in ufficio. *I should have gone to the office.*
  Avrei dovuto telefonare alla banca. *I was supposed to ring the bank.*
  Avresti dovuto riposarti. *You should have rested.*

potere

Potere *to be able to* is a modal verb (page 172) with a range of English translations:

- *can, may* – present tense:
  Può spiegare? *Can you explain?*
  Non possiamo venire oggi. *We can't come today.*
  Posso pagare con la carta di credito? *May I pay by credit card?*
  But when *can* means *know how to*, you use **sapere** not **potere**:
  Sai nuotare? *Can you swim?*
  Non sa cucinare. *He can't cook.*

- *could* – imperfect, perfect, conditional and subjunctive:
  Potevo aiutare. *I could help (was able to help).*
  Ho potuto aiutare. *I could help (managed to help).*
  Potrei aiutare. *I could help (would be able to help).*
  Mi potrebbe aiutare? *Could you (would you be able to) help me?*
  Se potessi aiutare, aiuterei. *If I could (were able to) help, I would help.*

- *could have, might have* – past conditional:
  Avrei potuto aiutarti. *I could have helped you.*
  Sarebbe potuto essere stupendo. *It could have been superb.*
  Avresti potuto almeno chiederglielo. *You might at least have asked him.*

Si può is very often used instead of **posso** or **possiamo** to ask if you can do something, if something can be done:
Si può prenotare adesso? *Can we/one book now?*

If the following verb has a plural direct object, **si può** becomes **si possono:**
Si può comprare un biglietto? *Can I buy a ticket?*
Si possono comprare i biglietti qui? *Can you buy tickets here?*

volere

Volere *to want* can be followed by a noun:
Voglio un caffè. *I want a coffee.*
Vorrei una camera doppia. *I'd like a double room.*
Volevo una camera più grande. *I wanted a bigger room.*

It can also be followed by another verb. Used in this way, it's a modal verb (page 172) and it has a range of English translations:

- *want, will* – present:
  Non voglio rimanere qui. *I don't want to stay here.*
  Vogliamo vedere il museo. *We want to see the museum.*
  Cosa vuoi fare? *What do you want to do?*
  Vuole firmare qui? *Will you/would you like to sign here?*

- *wanted* – imperfect and perfect, with different meanings:
  Volevo uscire. *I wanted to go out (and this might or might not have happened).*
  Ho voluto uscire. *I wanted to go out (and this is what happened).*

- *would like, would have liked* – conditional and past conditional:
  Vorrei vedere la camera. *I'd like to see the room.*
  Avrei voluto vedere la camera. *I would have liked to see the room.*

Volere occurs in some useful phrases:
Quanto ci vuole? *How much is needed? How long does it take?*
Ci vogliono cinque minuti. *It takes five minutes.*
Ci vuole pazienza. *It takes patience.*
Cosa vuol dire? *What does it mean?*
Volere è potere. *Where there's a will there's a way.*
Ti voglio bene. *I love you.*

---

piacere

In English, *to like*, which is one of the most commonly used words, is a regular verb which takes a direct object:
I like cheese.   *I like walking.*   *I like mushrooms.*

Saying what you like and don't like in Italian is different. The verb to use is **piacere**, which literally means *to be pleasing*, so that to translate the above examples, what you literally say is:
Cheese is pleasing to me. **Il formaggio mi piace/Mi piace il formaggio.**
Walking is pleasing to me. **Camminare mi piace/Mi piace camminare.**
Mushrooms are pleasing to me. **I funghi mi piacciono/Mi piacciono i funghi.**
I like mushrooms.

In grammatical terms, the object of the English sentence is the subject in Italian.

Saying what somebody else likes is the equivalent of, e.g. *cheese is pleasing to us, mushrooms are pleasing to Sonia.* All you do is replace **mi** with the relevant indirect object pronoun (page 80) or with **a** + noun:
Il formaggio ci piace/Ci piace il formaggio. *We like cheese.*
I funghi piacciono a Sonia. *Sonia likes mushrooms.*
Camminare non piace a mio figlio. *My son doesn't like walking.*

To talk about liking something in the past, you use the imperfect or the perfect tense of **piacere**.

- The imperfect is for saying *used to like* or *liked* over a period of time rather than a one-off:
  Mi piaceva la casa dove abitavamo. *I liked the house where we lived/used to live.*
  Camminare non piaceva a mio figlio. *My son didn't (use to) like walking.*

- The perfect is for saying you liked/enjoyed something on a particular occasion. **Piacere** uses <u>essere</u> in the perfect so the past participle has to agree with what you like, because this is the subject of the sentence:
  Mi è piaciuto il film. *I liked the film.*
  Gli è piaciuta la maratona. *He enjoyed the marathon.*
  I fiori sono piaciuti a Sonia. *Sonia liked the flowers.*
  Non ti sono piaciute le foto? *Didn't you like the photos?*

essere

Essere to be is the most used and the most irregular verb in English and Italian (page 210).

- As well as its basic use, **essere** is used with a past participle to form the past tenses of certain verbs (pages 153-154):
  Sono arrivata in ritardo. *I (have) arrived late.*
  È morto. *He died.*
  Eravamo partiti prima delle nove. *We had left before nine o'clock.*
  Sarà andato in vacanza. *He will have gone on holiday.*
  Loro sarebbero tornati. *They would have come back.*

- **È** with an adjective creates an impersonal expression:
  È necessario/essenziale. *It's necessary/essential.*
  È consigliabile. *It's advisable.*
  È facile/difficile. *It's easy/difficult.*
  È possibile/impossibile. *It's possible/impossible.*
  È probabile. *It's probable.*
  È utile/inutile. *It's useful/useless.*

  These can be followed by an infinitive:
  È essenziale sapere. *It's essential to know.*
  È consigliabile partire adesso. *It's advisable to leave now.*
  È inutile aspettare. *It's useless to wait.*

  But if the following verb has its own subject, you need **che** *that* and a subjunctive (pages 166-169), even when English doesn't use *that*:
  È essenziale che lui sappia. *It's essential (that) he knows.*
  È consigliabile che Sandro parta adesso. *It's advisable for Sandro to leave now.*
  È inutile che voi aspettiate. *It's useless for you to wait.*

  When you're using an impersonal phrase to talk about a one-off event in the past, è becomes **è stato**:
  È stato facile parcheggiare. *It was easy to park.*

stare

Stare is closely related to **essere** *to be*. They share the same past participle **stato** *been*, and **stare** is often translated as *to be*, for example:

- when talking about health:
  Come stai? *How are you?*
  Stai bene? *Are you well?*
  Sto un po' meglio oggi. *I'm a bit better today.*

- when it's followed by the gerund (page 162):
  Sto lavorando. *I'm working.*
  Stanno giocando a tennis. *They're playing tennis.*
  Stava dormendo quando è arrivata Maria. *He was sleeping when Maria arrived.*

But **stare** has other meanings too.

- Followed by **per** + infinitive, it means *to be (just) about to*:
  Sta per diventare mamma. *She's about to become a mother.*
  Stiamo per uscire. *We're just about to go out.*

- It can mean *to stay, to remain, to live*:
  Sto in un albergo magnifico. *I'm staying in a superb hotel.*
  Mi piace stare a letto. *I like to stay in bed.*
  Dovresti stare all'ombra. *You ought to remain in the shade.*
  Stai fermo! *Keep still!*
  State calmi. *Stay calm.*
  Stiamo in via Verdi. *We live in via Verdi.*

Stare forms part of many expressions:
Preferisco stare in piedi. *I prefer to stand.*
Ti stanno bene queste scarpe. *These shoes suit you.*
Stai attento a non perderlo. *Be careful not to lose it.*
Sta sulle sue. *He keeps himself to himself.*
Lascia stare! *Leave it alone!*

avere

Avere, often shortened to **aver**, translates the English *to have*:
Abbiamo un cane pastore. *We have a sheepdog.*
Non ho molto tempo. *I don't have much time.*
Ha mal di testa. *She has a headache*
Matteo ha attitudine per la musica. *Matteo has a flair for music.*
Nina ha una cotta per Matteo. *Nina has a crush on Matteo.*

It's used with a past participle to form past tenses:
Ho capito. *I (have) understood.*
Avevano finito? *Had they finished?*

It also features in many expressions that don't use the word *have* in English. For example, **aver luogo** means *to take place* while **avere intenzione di ...** means *to intend to ....* The following are some of the uses of **avere**:

- talking about age:
  Quanti anni ha il bambino? *How old is the child?*
  Ha otto anni. *He's eight years old.*

- saying what you feel like physically:
  avere sonno *to feel sleepy*
  avere fame/sete *to be hungry/thirsty*
  avere caldo/freddo *to be hot/cold*
  avere la nausea/le vertigini *to feel sick/dizzy*
  avere il mal di mare/mal d'aereo *to be seasick/airsick*

- saying what you feel like mentally:
  avere paura/vergogna *to be afraid/ ashamed*
  avere voglia *to feel like*
  avere ragione/torto *to be right/wrong*
  avere compassione per *to sympathise with, to feel for*
  avere del riguardo per *to respect*

Avere appears in some everyday phrases:
aver fortuna *to be lucky*
avere buone intenzioni *to mean well*
avere pazienza con *to bear with*
avere fiducia in *to put one's trust in*

---

fare

The basic translations of **fare** are *to do* and *to make*:

Non ho niente da fare. *I've got nothing to do.*

Che cosa fai? *What are you doing?*

Hanno fatto l'amore. *They made love.*

Abbiamo fatto un errore. *We made a mistake.*

It's also used in many other ways that don't use *do* or *have:*

- it's used to talk about the weather:

    fa bel/brutto tempo *it's fine/awful weather*

    fa caldo/freddo *it's hot/cold*

    fanno quaranta gradi all'ombra *it's 40 degrees in the shade*

- it can translate *take*:

    fare una pausa *to take a break*

    fare una gita *to take a trip*

    fare una foto *to take a photo*

    fare il bagno *to take a bath*

    fare un sonnellino *to take a nap*

- it can translate *go*:

    fare una passeggiata *to go for a walk*

    fare arrampicata/fare scalate *to go climbing*

    fare il trekking *to go rambling*

    fare una crociera *to go on a cruise*

    fare sciopero *to go on strike*

    fare un viaggio *to go on a journey*

    fare la spesa *to go food shopping*

    fare alla romana *to go dutch*

    fare da solo *to go it alone*

- it has many other translations:

    fare una domanda *to ask a question*

    fare il tifo *to support (a team)*

    fare colazione *to have breakfast*

    fare lo straordinario *to work overtime*

    fare bella figura *to project a good image, to be cool*

    fare brutta figura *to look silly, to lose face*

    fare finta *to pretend*

    fare la valigia *to pack*

    Non fa niente. *It doesn't matter.*

    Ce la fai? *Can you manage?*

checkpoint 19

1   Choose the correct ending.

Il pesce non è piaciuto a	i frutti di mare.
Non ci piacciono	da bambino.
Mi piace molto	sabato sera.
Mi piaceva andare in bicicletta	alla mia amica.
Gli è piaciuta la musica	Marcello.
Sciare non piace	sciare sulle Alpi.

2   Fill each gap with one of the words from the box.

a   Mi piacerebbe .... una crociera.

b   .... inutile piangere.

c   Il treno .... per partire.

d   Ti ho .... una domanda.

e   .... la nausea.

f   È necessario .... in piedi.

g   È .... necessario ritornare.

h   .... mangiando.

> stanno
> stato
> ho
> è
> sta
> fatto
> fare
> stare

3   Fill in the missing words:

a   .... partire. *I'd like to leave.*

b   .... aspettare. *You (voi) ought to wait.*

c   .... cominciare? *Do they want to start?*

d   .... telefonare. *I should have phoned.*

e   .... parcheggiare qui? *Can one park here?*

f   .... vedere. *I want to see.*

g   .... nuotare? *Can you (lei) swim?*

h   .... pagare. *We could have paid.*

i   .... aiutare? *Can you (tu) help?*

j   .... andare via. *She must go away.*

4   When you're tired, which of these are you most likely to feel like doing: fare lo straordinario, fare alla romana, fare scalate, fare un sonnellino?

Verbs followed by prepositions

Italian verbs are linked to other words in a sentence in various ways.

They can be:

- followed directly by another verb. This second verb is always in the infinitive in Italian, even though in English it can be an infinitive, e.g. *to think*, *to work* or a gerund e.g. *thinking*, *working*:
  voglio viaggiare *I want to travel*
  mi piace viaggiare *I like travelling*

- followed by **a** or **di** before the second verb. More often than not, the preposition has no equivalent in English:
  continuare a viaggiare *to continue travelling*
  decidere di viaggiare *to decide to travel*

- followed by **a** + person + **di** + verb:
  dire a qualcuno di entrare *to tell (to) somebody to come in*

- followed directly by a noun:
  invitare qualcuno *to invite somebody*
  mangiare qualcosa *to eat something*

- followed by **a** or **di** before the noun. There are also a few verbs that are followed by other prepositions:
  parlare a qualcuno *to talk to somebody*
  parlare di qualcuno *to talk of/about somebody*
  entrare in una casa *to enter (into) a house*

  It's not always this straightforward because the preposition often has no equivalent in English or has an unexpected translation:
  giocare a calcio *to play football*
  riempire di acqua *to fill with water*

verbs followed by a

Some Italian verbs are always linked to the rest of their sentence by **a**, which often becomes **ad** before a vowel. The most common are listed opposite.

- When these verbs are followed by another verb, this is always in the infinitive in Italian, even though in English it can be an infinitive, e.g. *to think*, *to work* or a gerund e.g. *thinking*, *working*.

  Although there's no English equivalent for **a** with most verbs, it has a translation with a few:
  Non rinuncio a sperare. *I'm not giving up hoping.*
  Sei riuscito a trovarlo? *Did you manage to find it?*
  Insistono a sposarsi. *They insist on getting married.*
  Proverò ad aprirlo. *I'll try to open it.*
  Si sono divertiti a partecipare alla gara. *They enjoyed taking part in the competition.*

- When these verbs are followed by a noun, **a** often has no equivalent in English or has an unexpected translation. If there's a definite article with the noun, it combines with **a** to become **al**, **alla**, etc. (page 48):
  Vuoi giocare a tennis? *Do you want to play tennis?*
  Si è avvicinato alla casa. *He approached the house.*
  Assomiglia tanto al nonno. *He looks so much like his grandfather.*
  Mi sto abituando all'idea. *I'm getting used to the idea.*

- When the object of these verbs is a pronoun rather than a noun, it's an indirect object pronoun (page 80) if it refers to a person and **ci** when it refers to anything else:
  Ho telefonato a Piero. *I've phoned Piero.*
  Gli ho telefonato. *I've phoned him.*
  Dà fastidio a mia moglie. *It bothers my wife.*
  Le dà fastidio. *It bothers her.*
  Penso molto al futuro. *I think a lot about the future.*
  Ci penso molto. *I think a lot about it.*

abituarsi a *to get used to*
affrettarsi a *to hurry to*
aiutare a *to help to*
andare a *to go and*
annoiarsi a *to be bored with*
assistere *to attend, participate in*
assomigliare a *to look like*
avere ragione a *to be right to*
avere torto a *to be wrong to*
avvicinarsi a *to approach*
cominciare a *to start to*
condannare a *to condemn to*
continuare a *to continue to*
convenire a *to suit*
convincere *to persuade to*
costringere a *to compel to*
dare fastidio a *to bother, annoy*
decidersi a *to decide to*
dedicarsi a *to devote oneself to*
divertirsi a *to enjoy*
esitare a *to hesitate to*
essere deciso a *to be determined to*
essere disposto a *to be prepared to*
essere pronto a *to be ready to*
fermarsi a *to stop*
forzare a *to force to*
giocare a *to play*
imparare a *to learn to*
impegnarsi a *to undertake to*

incoraggiare a *to encourage to*
indugiare a *to delay in*
insegnare a *to teach*
insistere a *to insist on*
invitare a *to invite to*
mandare a *to send to*
mettersi a *to get down to, get on with*
obbligare a *to oblige to*
parlare a *to talk to*
pensare a *to think of/about*
persuadere a *to persuade*
piacere a *to please*
prepararsi a *to get ready to*
provare a *to try to*
rassegnarsi a *to resign oneself to*
rinunciare a *to give up*
risalire a *to date from*
rispondere a *to reply to*
riuscire a *to succeed in/ to manage to*
rivolgersi a *to address oneself to*
servire a *to be good for*
sopravvivere a *to survive, to outlive*
sparare a *to shoot at*
telefonare a *to telephone*
tornare a *to go back and*
ubbidire a *to obey*
venire a *to come and*
voler bene a *to be fond of, to love*

verbs followed by di

Some Italian verbs are always linked to the rest of their sentence by **di**. The most common are listed opposite.

- When these verbs are followed by another verb, this is always in the infinitive in Italian, even though in English it can be an infinitive, e.g. *to think*, *to work* or a gerund e.g. *thinking*, *working*.
  Although there's no English equivalent for **di** with most verbs, it has a translation with a few:
  Ho dimenticato di chiuderla. *I've forgotten to lock it.*
  Non mi sento di andare. *I don't feel like going.*
  Non vedo l'ora di rivederti. *I can't wait to see you again.*
  Sogno di ritornare. *I dream of coming back.*
  Mi sembra di conoscerla. *I seem to know her.*

- When these verbs are followed by a noun, **di** is translated in a variety of ways or sometimes not translated at all. If there's a definite article with the noun, it combines with **di** to become **del, della**, etc. (page 48):
  Non parla mai della famiglia. *She never talks about her family.*
  Hai bisogno del computer? *Do you need the computer?*
  Si è accorto del problema. *He has noticed the problem.*
  L'ho riempito d' acqua. *I filled it with water.*

  With some verbs you can replace **di** + noun with **ne** (page 94):
  Non ne parla mai. *She never talks about it/them.*
  Ne hai bisogno? *Do you need it?*
  Se n'è accorto. *He has noticed it.*

Avere bisogno di *to need* literally means *to have need of*. Don't confuse it with the impersonal **bisogna** *it's necessary to*, *you need to* which is followed directly by an infinitive: **non bisogna aspettare** *you needn't wait*.

accettare di *to accept*
accorgersi di *to notice*
ammettere di *to admit to*
aspettarsi di *to expect to*
aver bisogno di *to need*
avere fretta di *to be in a hurry to*
avere intenzione di *to intend to*
avere paura di *to be afraid of*
avere tempo di *to have time to*
avere vergogna di *to be ashamed of*
avere voglia di *to feel like …ing*
avvisare di *to inform, to advise of*
cercare di *to try to*
cessare di *to stop …ing*
chiedere di *to ask to*
consigliare di *to advise to*
credere di *to believe in*
decidere di *to decide to*
dimenticare di *to forget to*
domandare di *to ask to*
dubitare di *to doubt*
evitare di *to avoid …ing*
fare a meno di *to do without*
fidarsi di *to trust in*
fingere di/fare finta di *to pretend to*
finire di *to finish …ing*
innamorarsi di *to fall in love with*
lagnarsi/lamentarsi di *to complain about*
meravigliarsi di *to be surprised at*
meritare di *to deserve to*
minacciare di *to threaten to*

non vedere l'ora di *to look forward to*
offrirsi di *to offer to*
parlare di *to talk about*
pensare di *to think of*
pentirsi di *to regret …ing*
pregare di *to beg to*
proibire di *to ban from*
promettere di *to promise to*
proporre di *to propose to*
raccomandare di *to recommend to*
ricordare di *to remember to*
ricordarsi di *to remember to*
ridere di *to laugh at*
riempire di *to fill with*
rifiutare di *to refuse to*
ringraziare di *to thank for*
scegliere di *to choose to*
sembrare di *to seem to*
sentirsi di *to feel like*
sforzarsi di *to make an effort to*
smettere di *to give up …ing*
sognare di *to dream about*
sperare di *to hope to*
stancarsi di *to get tired of*
stufarsi di *to be fed up with*
temere di *to be afraid of*
tentare di *to try to*
trattarsi di *to be about to*
vantarsi di *to boast about*
vietare di *to forbid to*
vivere di *to live on*

verb + a + person + di + infinitive

Whereas in English you *ask someone to do something*, in Italian you *ask **to** them to do something*:

chiedere a qualcuno di fare qualcosa

There are several other verbs which behave in the same way:

comandare a ... di *to order ... to*
consentir a ... di *to allow ... to*
consigliare a ... di *to advise ... to*
dire a ... di *to tell ... to*
domandare a ... di *to ask ... to*
impedire a ... di *to prevent ... from*
ordinare a ... di *to order ... to*
permettere a .. di *to allow ... to*
proibire a ... di *to ban ... from*
promettere a ... di *to promise ... to*
proporre a ... di *to propose to ... to*
ricordare a ... di *to remind ... to*
sconsigliare a ... di *to advise ... not to*
suggerire a ... di *to suggest to ... to*
vietare a ... di *to forbid ... to*

Puoi chiedere a Lucia di aspettare? *Can you ask Lucia to wait?*
Devo ricordare al mio amico di pagare. *I must remind my friend to pay.*
Consiglierei agli studenti di rispondere. *I'd advise the students to reply.*
Dica a sua sorella di venire domani. *Tell your sister to come tomorrow.*

To replace a + person with a pronoun, you use an indirect object pronoun (page 80):

Puoi chiederle di aspettare? *Can you ask her to wait?*
Devo ricordargli di pagare. *I must remind him to pay.*
Gli consiglierei di rispondere. *I'd advise them to reply.*
Le dica di venire domani. *Tell her to come tomorrow.*

verb + da, per, con, in

A few verbs are followed by **da**, **per**, **con** or **in**.

- Some are followed by a verb in the infinitive:
  avere da *to have … to*
  Ho da fare. *I have a lot to do.*
  stare per *to be just about to*
  Sta per uscire. *She's just about to go out.*

- Others are followed by a noun, e.g. **dipendere da** *to depend on*, **congratularsi con** *to congratulate*, **entrare in** *to enter*, **credere in** *to believe in*, **scommettere su** *to bet on*:
  Dipende dal meteo. *It depends on the weather forecast.*
  Mi sono congratulato con Michele. *I congratulated Michele.*
  Siamo entrati nel duomo. *We entered the cathedral.*
  Tu credi in Dio? *Do you believe in God?*
  Ho scommesso sulle elezioni. *I bet on the elections.*

verbs with no preposition in Italian

Although these verbs have a preposition before a noun in English, they don't need one in Italian – they have a direct object:

ascoltare *to listen **to***
aspettare *to wait **for***
chiedere *to ask **for***
domandare *to ask **for***
cercare *to look **for***
guardare *to look **at***
pagare *to pay **for***

Aspetto un mio amico. *I'm waiting for one of my friends.*
Ho chiesto una birra. *I've asked for a beer.*
Sto cercando il passaporto. *I'm looking for my passport.*
Vuoi guardare le foto? *Would you like to look at the photos?*
Pago io le pizze. *I'll pay for the pizzas.*

checkpoint 20

1   Does a or di belong in the gap?

a   **Ho promesso** .... **andare.** *I've promised to go.*

b   **Puoi aiutare Luca** .... **portarli?** *Can you help Luca to carry them?*

c   **Hanno deciso** .... **partire.** *They've decided to leave.*

d   **Fa finta** .... **non capire.** *She's pretending not to understand.*

e   **Mi piacerebbe imparare** .... **sciare.** *I'd like to learn to ski.*

f   **Si è stancato** .... **aspettare.** *He got tired of waiting.*

g   **Avete paura** .... **uscire?** *Are you afraid of going out?*

h   **Avete ragione** .... **non uscire.** *You're right not to go out.*

2   To fill these gaps, you need the combination of preposition + *the*. Check with page 48 if you need to.

a   **Vorrei parlare** .... **direttore.** *I'd like to talk to the manager.*

b   **Dipende** .... **orario.** *It depends on the timetable.*

c   **Dovresti rispondere** .... **lettera.** *You ought to reply to the letter.*

d   **Ci siamo stufati** .... **spettacolo.** *We got fed up of the show.*

e   **Roberto è entrato** .... **esercito.** *Roberto went into the army.*

f   **Non posso fare a meno** .... **caffè.** *I can't do without coffee.*

g   **Hai bisogno** .... **forbici.** *Do you need the scissors?*

h   **Mi sono abituato** .... **caldo.** *I've got used to the heat.*

3   Translate these into Italian.

a   *They're waiting for the train.*

b   *I like playing tennis.*

c   *She forgot to go.*

d   *We're about to eat.*

e   *I intend to visit Rome.*

f   *Can you (tu) ask Maria to phone?*

g   *She needs the phone number.*

h   *We hope to come back next year.*

Verb tables

The following pages present 50 key verbs, which are listed on page 242 for easy reference. They include:

- **aspettare** *to wait*, **vendere** *to sell*, **dormire** *to sleep* and **capire** *to understand*, which provide the regular patterns for **-are** verbs, **-ere** verbs, **-ire** verbs without **isc** and **-ire** verbs with **isc**

- the reflexive verbs **abituarsi** *to get used to*, which is regular, and **accorgersi** *to realise*, which is regular except in the simple past and the past participle

- **cercare** *to look for*, **cominciare** *to start*, **mangiare** *to eat*, **leggere** *to read*, **pagare** *to pay*, which illustrate the spelling changes that verbs with **c** or **g** before **-are/-ere** undergo in some tenses

- key irregular verbs such as **essere** *to be*, **avere** *to have*, **andare** *to go* and the modal verbs **dovere** *to have to*, **potere** *to be able to* and **volere** *to want to*

- other irregular verbs such as **dire** *to say* and **porre** *to put*, which provide the pattern for verbs that behave in the same way. These are listed underneath.

All 50 verbs are written out in all persons in the present, future, conditional, imperfect, simple past, perfect, present subjunctive and imperfect subjunctive.

The perfect tense shows you whether the verb takes **avere** or **essere** in the compound tenses. All you need then do to form the pluperfect (page 157), future perfect (page 158), past conditional (page 159), perfect and pluperfect subjunctive (page 166) is to change the tense of **avere/essere**.

A few verbs have alternative forms in some tenses. The more commonly used version is listed first.

1 abituarsi *to get used to*

	present	future	conditional
io	mi abituo	mi abituerò	mi abituerei
tu	ti abitui	ti abituerai	ti abitueresti
lui/lei	si abitua	si abituerà	si abituerebbe
noi	ci abituiamo	ci abitueremo	ci abitueremmo
voi	vi abituate	vi abituerete	vi abituereste
loro	si abituano	si abitueranno	si abituerebbero

	imperfect	simple past	perfect
io	mi abituavo	mi abituai	mi sono abituato/a
tu	ti abituavi	ti abituasti	ti sei abituato/a
lui/lei	si abituava	si abituò	si è abituato/a
noi	ci abituavamo	ci abituammo	ci siamo abituati/e
voi	vi abituavate	vi abituaste	vi siete abituati/e
loro	si abituavano	si abituarono	si sono abituati/e

	present subjunctive	imperfect subjunctive
io	mi abitui	mi abituassi
tu	ti abitui	ti abituassi
lui/lei	si abitui	si abituasse
noi	ci abituiamo	ci abituassimo
voi	vi abituiate	vi abituaste
loro	si abituino	si abituassero

past participle **abituato**

gerund **abituandosi**

imperative **abituati, si abitui, abituiamoci, abituatevi**

2 accorgersi *to realise*

	present	future	conditional
io	mi accorgo	mi accorgerò	mi accorgerei
tu	ti accorgi	ti accorgerai	ti accorgeresti
lui/lei	si accorge	si accorgerà	si accorgerebbe
noi	ci accorgiamo	ci accorgeremo	ci accorgeremmo
voi	vi accorgete	vi accorgerete	vi accorgereste
loro	si accorgono	si accorgeranno	si accorgerebbero

	imperfect	simple past	perfect
io	mi accorgevo	mi accorsi	mi sono accorto/a
tu	ti accorgevi	ti accorgesti	ti sei accorto/a
lui/lei	si accorgeva	si accorse	si è accorto/a
noi	ci accorgevamo	ci accorgemmo	ci siamo accorti/e
voi	vi accorgevate	vi accorgeste	vi siete accorti/e
loro	si accorgevano	si accorsero	si sono accorti/e

	present subjunctive	imperfect subjunctive
io	mi accorga	mi accorgessi
tu	ti accorga	ti accorgessi
lui/lei	si accorga	si accorgesse
noi	ci accorgiamo	ci accorgessimo
voi	vi accorgiate	vi accorgeste
loro	si accorgano	si accorgessero

past participle **accorto**

gerund **accorgendosi**

imperative **accorgiti, accorgiamoci, accorgetevi**

3 andare *to go*

	present	future	conditional
io	vado	andrò	andrei
tu	vai	andrai	andresti
lui/lei	va	andrà	andrebbe
noi	andiamo	andremo	andremmo
voi	andate	andrete	andreste
loro	vanno	andranno	andrebbero

	imperfect	simple past	perfect
io	andavo	andai	sono andato/a
tu	andavi	andasti	sei andato/a
lui/lei	andava	andò	è andato/a
noi	andavamo	andammo	siamo andati/e
voi	andavate	andaste	siete andati/e
loro	andavano	andarono	sono andati/e

	present subjunctive	imperfect subjunctive
io	vada	andassi
tu	vada	andassi
lui/lei	vada	andasse
noi	andiamo	andassimo
voi	andiate	andaste
loro	vadano	andassero

past participle **andato**

gerund **andando**

imperative **vai/va', vada, andiamo, andate**

4   **apparire** *to appear*

	present	future	conditional
io	appaio	apparirò	apparirei
tu	appari	apparirai	appariresti
lui/lei	appare	apparirà	apparirebbe
noi	appariamo	appariremo	appariremmo
voi	apparite	apparirete	apparireste
loro	appaiono	appariranno	apparirebbero

	imperfect	simple past	perfect
io	apparivo	apparvi	sono apparso/a
tu	apparivi	apparisti	sei apparso/a
lui/lei	appariva	apparve	è apparso/a
noi	apparivamo	apparimmo	siamo apparsi/e
voi	apparivate	appariste	siete apparsi/e
loro	apparivano	apparvero	sono apparsi/e

	present subjunctive	imperfect subjunctive
io	appaia	apparissi
tu	appaia	apparissi
lui/lei	appaia	apparisse
noi	appariamo	apparissimo
voi	appariate	appariste
loro	appaiano	apparissero

past participle **apparso**

gerund **apparendo**

imperative **appari**, **appaia**, **appariamo**, **apparite**

5 aprire *to open*

	present	future	conditional
io	apro	aprirò	aprirei
tu	apri	aprirai	apriresti
lui/lei	apre	aprirà	aprirebbe
noi	apriamo	apriremo	apriremmo
voi	aprite	aprirete	aprireste
loro	aprono	apriranno	aprirebbero

	imperfect	simple past	perfect
io	aprivo	aprii/apersi	ho aperto
tu	aprivi	apristi	hai aperto
lui/lei	apriva	aprì/aperse	ha aperto
noi	aprivamo	aprimmo	abbiamo aperto
voi	aprivate	apriste	avete aperto
loro	aprivano	aprirono/ apersero	hanno aperto

	present subjunctive	imperfect subjunctive
io	apra	aprissi
tu	apra	aprissi
lui/lei	apra	aprisse
noi	apriamo	aprissimo
voi	apriate	apriste
loro	aprano	aprissero

past participle **aperto**

gerund **aprendo**

imperative **apri, apra, apriamo, aprite**

6   aspettare *to wait*

	present	future	conditional
io	aspetto	aspetterò	aspetterei
tu	aspetti	aspetterai	aspetteresti
lui/lei	aspetta	aspetterà	aspetterebbe
noi	aspettiamo	aspetteremo	aspetteremmo
voi	aspettate	aspetterete	aspettereste
loro	aspettano	aspetteranno	aspetterebbero

	imperfect	simple past	perfect
io	aspettavo	aspettai	ho aspettato
tu	aspettavi	aspettasti	hai aspettato
lui/lei	aspettava	aspettò	ha aspettato
noi	aspettavamo	aspettammo	abbiamo aspettato
voi	aspettavate	aspettaste	avete aspettato
loro	aspettavano	aspettarono	hanno aspettato

	present subjunctive	imperfect subjunctive
io	aspetti	aspettassi
tu	aspetti	aspettassi
lui/lei	aspetti	aspettasse
noi	aspettiamo	aspettassimo
voi	aspettiate	aspettaste
loro	aspettino	aspettassero

past participle **aspettato**

gerund **aspettando**

imperative **aspetta**, **aspetti**, **aspettiamo**, **aspettate**

7 avere *to have*

	present	future	conditional
io	ho	avrò	avrei
tu	hai	avrai	avresti
lui/lei	ha	avrà	avrebbe
noi	abbiamo	avremo	avremmo
voi	avete	avrete	avreste
loro	hanno	avranno	avrebbero

	imperfect	simple past	perfect
io	avevo	ebbi	ho avuto
tu	avevi	avesti	hai avuto
lui/lei	aveva	ebbe	ha avuto
noi	avevamo	avemmo	abbiamo avuto
voi	avevate	aveste	avete avuto
loro	avevano	ebbero	hanno avuto

	present subjunctive	imperfect subjunctive
io	abbia	avessi
tu	abbia	avessi
lui/lei	abbia	avesse
noi	abbiamo	avessimo
voi	abbiate	aveste
loro	abbiano	avessero

past participle **avuto**

gerund **avendo**

imperative **abbi, abbia, abbiamo, abbiate**

8 bere *to drink*

	present	future	conditional
io	bevo	berrò	berrei
tu	bevi	berrai	berresti
lui/lei	beve	berrà	berrebbe
noi	beviamo	berremo	berremmo
voi	bevete	berrete	berreste
loro	bevono	berranno	berrebbero

	imperfect	simple past	perfect
io	bevevo	bevvi/bevetti	ho bevuto
tu	bevevi	bevesti	hai bevuto
lui/lei	beveva	bevve/bevette	ha bevuto
noi	bevevamo	bevemmo	abbiamo bevuto
voi	bevevate	beveste	avete bevuto
loro	bevevano	bevvero/bevettero	hanno bevuto

	present subjunctive	imperfect subjunctive
io	beva	bevessi
tu	beva	bevessi
lui/lei	beva	bevesse
noi	beviamo	bevessimo
voi	beviate	beveste
loro	bevano	bevessero

past participle **bevuto**

gerund **bevendo**

imperative **bevi, beva, beviamo, bevete**

9 capire *to understand*

	present	future	conditional
io	capisco	capirò	capirei
tu	capisci	capirai	capiresti
lui/lei	capisce	capirà	capirebbe
noi	capiamo	capiremo	capiremmo
voi	capite	capirete	capireste
loro	capiscono	capiranno	capirebbero

	imperfect	simple past	perfect
io	capivo	capii	ho capito
tu	capivi	capisti	hai capito
lui/lei	capiva	capì	ha capito
noi	capivamo	capimmo	abbiamo capito
voi	capivate	capiste	avete capito
loro	capivano	capirono	hanno capito

	present subjunctive	imperfect subjunctive
io	capisca	capissi
tu	capisca	capissi
lui/lei	capisca	capisse
noi	capiamo	capimmo
voi	capiate	capiste
loro	capiscano	capissero

past participle **capito**

gerund **capendo**

imperative **capisci, capisca, capiamo, capite**

10 cercare *to look for*

	present	future	conditional
io	cerco	cercherò	cercherei
tu	cerchi	cercherai	cercheresti
lui/lei	cerca	cercherà	cercherebbe
noi	cerchiamo	cercheremo	cercheremmo
voi	cercate	cercherete	cerchereste
loro	cercano	cercheranno	cercherebbero

	imperfect	simple past	perfect
io	cercavo	cercai	ho cercato
tu	cercavi	cercasti	hai cercato
lui/lei	cercava	cercò	ha cercato
noi	cercavamo	cercammo	abbiamo cercato
voi	cercavate	cercaste	avete cercato
loro	cercavano	cercarono	hanno cercato

	present subjunctive	imperfect subjunctive
io	cerchi	cercassi
tu	cerchi	cercassi
lui/lei	cerchi	cercasse
noi	cerchiamo	cercassimo
voi	cerchiate	cercaste
loro	cerchino	cercassero

past participle **cercato**

gerund **cercando**

imperative **cerca, cerchi, cerchiamo, cercate**

11 chiudere *to close*

	present	future	conditional
io	chiudo	chiuderò	chiuderei
tu	chiudi	chiuderai	chiuderesti
lui/lei	chiude	chiuderà	chiuderebbe
noi	chiudiamo	chiuderemo	chiuderemmo
voi	chiudete	chiuderete	chiudereste
loro	chiudono	chiuderanno	chiuderebbero

	imperfect	simple past	perfect
io	chiudevo	chiusi	ho chiuso
tu	chiudevi	chiudesti	hai chiuso
lui/lei	chiudeva	chiuse	ha chiuso
noi	chiudevamo	chiudemmo	abbiamo chiuso
voi	chiudevate	chiudeste	avete chiuso
loro	chiudevano	chiusero	hanno chiuso

	present subjunctive	imperfect subjunctive
io	chiuda	chiudessi
tu	chiuda	chiudessi
lui/lei	chiuda	chiudesse
noi	chiudiamo	chiudessimo
voi	chiudiate	chiudeste
loro	chiudano	chiudessero

past participle **chiuso**

gerund **chiudendo**

imperative **chiudi, chiuda, chiudiamo, chiudete**

12   cogliere *to pick*

	present	future	conditional
io	colgo	coglierò	coglierei
tu	cogli	coglierai	coglieresti
lui/lei	coglie	coglierà	coglierebbe
noi	cogliamo	coglieremo	coglieremmo
voi	cogliete	coglierete	cogliereste
loro	colgono	coglieranno	coglierebbero

	imperfect	simple past	perfect
io	coglievo	colsi	ho colto
tu	coglievi	cogliesti	hai colto
lui/lei	coglieva	colse	ha colto
noi	coglievamo	cogliemmo	abbiamo colto
voi	coglievate	coglieste	avete colto
loro	coglievano	colsero	hanno colto

	present subjunctive	imperfect subjunctive
io	colga	cogliessi
tu	colga	cogliessi
lui/lei	colga	cogliesse
noi	cogliamo	cogliessimo
voi	cogliate	coglieste
loro	colgano	cogliessero

past participle **colto**

gerund **cogliendo**

imperative **cogli, colga, cogliamo, cogliete**

Verbs that follow the same pattern as **cogliere** include **accogliere** *to welcome*, **raccogliere** *to pick/gather*, **sciogliere** *to melt/dissolve*, **togliere** *to remove*.

13 conoscere *to know*

	present	future	conditional
io	conosco	conoscerò	conoscerei
tu	conosci	conoscerai	conosceresti
lui/lei	conosce	conoscerà	conoscerebbe
noi	conosciamo	conosceremo	conosceremmo
voi	conoscete	conoscerete	conoscereste
loro	conoscono	conosceranno	conoscerebbero

	imperfect	simple past	perfect
io	conoscevo	conobbi	ho conosciuto
tu	conoscevi	conoscesti	hai conosciuto
lui/lei	conosceva	conobbe	ha conosciuto
noi	conoscevamo	conoscemmo	abbiamo conosciuto
voi	conoscevate	conosceste	avete conosciuto
loro	conoscevano	conobbero	hanno conosciuto

	present subjunctive	imperfect subjunctive
io	conosca	conoscessi
tu	conosca	conoscessi
lui/lei	conosca	conoscesse
noi	conosciamo	conoscessimo
voi	conosciate	conosceste
loro	conoscano	conoscessero

past participle conosciuto

gerund conoscendo

imperative conosci, conosca, conosciamo, conoscete

14 correre to run

	present	future	conditional
io	corro	correrò	correrei
tu	corri	correrai	correresti
lui/lei	corre	correrà	correrebbe
noi	corriamo	correremo	correremmo
voi	correte	correrete	correreste
loro	corrono	correranno	correrebbero

	imperfect	simple past	perfect
io	correvo	corsi	ho corso
tu	correvi	corresti	hai corso
lui/lei	correva	corse	ha corso
noi	correvamo	corremmo	abbiamo corso
voi	correvate	correste	avete corso
loro	correvano	corsero	hanno corso

	present subjunctive	imperfect subjunctive
io	corra	corressi
tu	corra	corressi
lui/lei	corra	corresse
noi	corriamo	corressimo
voi	corriate	correste
loro	corrano	corressero

past participle **corso**

gerund **correndo**

imperative **corri, corra, corriamo, correte**

15 crescere *to grow*

	present	future	conditional
io	cresco	crescerò	crescerei
tu	cresci	crescerai	cresceresti
lui/lei	cresce	crescerà	crescerebbe
noi	cresciamo	cresceremo	cresceremmo
voi	crescete	crescerete	crescereste
loro	crescono	cresceranno	crescerebbero

	imperfect	simple past	perfect
io	crescevo	crebbi	sono cresciuto/a
tu	crescevi	crescesti	sei cresciuto/a
lui/lei	cresceva	crebbe	è cresciuto/a
noi	crescevamo	crescemmo	siamo cresciuti/e
voi	crescevate	cresceste	siete cresciuti/e
loro	crescevano	crebbero	sono cresciuti/e

	present subjunctive	imperfect subjunctive
io	cresca	crescessi
tu	cresca	crescessi
lui/lei	cresca	crescesse
noi	cresciamo	crescessimo
voi	cresciate	cresceste
loro	crescano	crescessero

past participle **cresciuto**

gerund **crescendo**

imperative **cresci, cresca, cresciamo, crescete**

16 dare *to give*

	present	future	conditional
io	do	darò	darei
tu	dai	darai	daresti
lui/lei	dà	darà	darebbe
noi	diamo	daremo	daremmo
voi	date	darete	dareste
loro	danno	daranno	darebbero

	imperfect	simple past	perfect
io	davo	diedi/detti	ho dato
tu	davi	desti	hai dato
lui/lei	dava	diede/dette	ha dato
noi	davamo	demmo	abbiamo dato
voi	davate	deste	avete dato
loro	davano	diedero/ dettero	hanno dato

	present subjunctive	imperfect subjunctive
io	dia	dessi
tu	dia	dessi
lui/lei	dia	desse
noi	diamo	dessimo
voi	diate	deste
loro	diano	dessero

past participle **dato**

gerund **dando**

imperative **dai/da', dia, diamo, date**

17 dire *to say*

	present	future	conditional
io	dico	dirò	direi
tu	dici	dirai	diresti
lui/lei	dice	dirà	direbbe
noi	diciamo	diremo	diremmo
voi	dite	direte	direste
loro	dicono	diranno	direbbero

	imperfect	simple past	perfect
io	dicevo	dissi	ho detto
tu	dicevi	dicesti	hai detto
lui/lei	diceva	disse	ha detto
noi	dicevamo	dicemmo	abbiamo detto
voi	dicevate	diceste	avete detto
loro	dicevano	dissero	hanno detto

	present subjunctive	imperfect subjunctive
io	dica	dicessi
tu	dica	dicessi
lui/lei	dica	dicesse
noi	diciamo	dicessimo
voi	diciate	diceste
loro	dicano	dicessero

past participle **detto**

gerund **dicendo**

imperative **di'**, **dica**, **diciamo**, **dite**

Verbs that follow the same pattern as **dire** include **benedire** *to bless,* **contraddire** *to contradict,* **disdire** *to cancel,* **maledire** *to curse,* **predire** *to predict.*

18 dormire *to sleep*

	present	future	conditional
io	dormo	dormirò	dormirei
tu	dormi	dormirai	dormiresti
lui/lei	dorme	dormirà	dormirebbe
noi	dormiamo	dormiremo	dormiremmo
voi	dormite	dormirete	dormireste
loro	dormono	dormiranno	dormirebbero

	imperfect	simple past	perfect
io	dormivo	dormii	ho dormito
tu	dormivi	dormisti	hai dormito
lui/lei	dormiva	dormì	ha dormito
noi	dormivamo	dormimmo	abbiamo dormito
voi	dormivate	dormiste	avete dormito
loro	dormivano	dormirono	hanno dormito

	present subjunctive	imperfect subjunctive
io	dorma	dormissi
tu	dorma	dormissi
lui/lei	dorma	dormisse
noi	dormiamo	dormimmo
voi	dormiate	dormiste
loro	dormano	dormissero

past participle **dormito**

gerund **dormendo**

imperative **dormi, dorma, dormiamo, dormite**

19 dovere *to have to*

	present	future	conditional
io	devo	dovrò	dovrei
tu	devi	dovrai	dovresti
lui/lei	deve	dovrà	dovrebbe
noi	dobbiamo	dovremo	dovremmo
voi	dovete	dovrete	dovreste
loro	devono	dovranno	dovrebbero

	imperfect	simple past	perfect
io	dovevo	dovei/dovetti	ho dovuto
tu	dovevi	dovesti	hai dovuto
lui/lei	doveva	dové/dovette	ha dovuto
noi	dovevamo	dovemmo	abbiamo dovuto
voi	dovevate	doveste	avete dovuto
loro	dovevano	doverono/ dovettero	hanno dovuto

	present subjunctive	imperfect subjunctive
io	deva/debba	dovessi
tu	deva/debba	dovessi
lui/lei	deva/debba	dovesse
noi	dobbiamo	dovessimo
voi	dobbiate	doveste
loro	devano/ debbano	dovessero

past participle **dovuto**

gerund **dovendo**

Dovere can take **essere** in the compound tenses if the infinitive following it normally takes **essere**. It has no imperative.

20 essere *to be*

	present	future	conditional
io	sono	sarò	sarei
tu	sei	sarai	saresti
lui/lei	è	sarà	sarebbe
noi	siamo	saremo	saremmo
voi	siete	sarete	sareste
loro	sono	saranno	sarebbero

	imperfect	simple past	perfect
io	ero	fui	sono stato/a
tu	eri	fosti	sei stato/a
lui/lei	era	fu	è stato/a
noi	eravamo	fummo	siamo stati/e
voi	eravate	foste	siete stati/e
loro	erano	furono	sono stati/e

	present subjunctive	imperfect subjunctive
io	sia	fossi
tu	sia	fossi
lui/lei	sia	fosse
noi	siamo	fossimo
voi	siate	foste
loro	siano	fossero

past participle **stato**

gerund **essendo**

imperative **sii, sia, siamo, siate**

21 fare *to do, to make*

	present	future	conditional
io	faccio	farò	farei
tu	fai	farai	faresti
lui/lei	fa	farà	farebbe
noi	facciamo	faremo	faremmo
voi	fate	farete	fareste
loro	fanno	faranno	farebbero

	imperfect	simple past	perfect
io	facevo	feci	ho fatto
tu	facevi	facesti	hai fatto
lui/lei	faceva	fece	ha fatto
noi	facevamo	facemmo	abbiamo fatto
voi	facevate	faceste	avete fatto
loro	facevano	fecero	hanno fatto

	present subjunctive	imperfect subjunctive
io	faccia	facessi
tu	faccia	facessi
lui/lei	faccia	facesse
noi	facciamo	facessimo
voi	facciate	faceste
loro	facciano	facessero

past participle **fatto**

gerund **facendo**

imperative **fai/fa', faccia, facciamo, fate**

Verbs that follow the same pattern as **fare** include **soddisfare** *to satisfy*, **sopraffare** *to overcome*, **stupefare** *to amaze*.

22 fuggire *to run away*

	present	future	conditional
io	fuggo	fuggirò	fuggirei
tu	fuggi	fuggirai	fuggiresti
lui/lei	fugge	fuggirà	fuggirebbe
noi	fuggiamo	fuggiremo	fuggiremmo
voi	fuggite	fuggirete	fuggireste
loro	fuggono	fuggiranno	fuggirebbero

	imperfect	simple past	perfect
io	fuggivo	fuggii	sono fuggito/a
tu	fuggivi	fuggisti	sei fuggito/a
lui/lei	fuggiva	fuggì	è fuggito/a
noi	fuggivamo	fuggimmo	siamo fuggiti/e
voi	fuggivate	fuggiste	siete fuggiti/e
loro	fuggivano	fuggirono	sono fuggiti/e

	present subjunctive	imperfect subjunctive
io	fugga	fuggissi
tu	fugga	fuggissi
lui/lei	fugga	fuggisse
noi	fuggiamo	fuggissimo
voi	fuggiate	fuggiste
loro	fuggano	fuggissero

past participle **fuggito**

gerund **fuggendo**

imperative **fuggi, fugga, fuggiamo, fuggite**

23 leggere to read

	present	future	conditional
io	leggo	leggerò	leggerei
tu	leggi	leggerai	leggeresti
lui/lei	legge	leggerà	leggerebbe
noi	leggiamo	leggeremo	leggeremmo
voi	leggete	leggerete	leggereste
loro	leggono	leggeranno	leggerebbero

	imperfect	simple past	perfect
io	leggevo	lessi	ho letto
tu	leggevi	leggesti	hai letto
lui/lei	leggeva	lesse	ha letto
noi	leggevamo	leggemmo	abbiamo letto
voi	leggevate	leggeste	avete letto
loro	leggevano	lessero	hanno letto

	present subjunctive	imperfect subjunctive
io	legga	leggessi
tu	legga	leggessi
lui/lei	legga	leggesse
noi	leggiamo	leggessimo
voi	leggiate	leggeste
loro	leggano	leggessero

past participle **letto**

gerund **leggendo**

imperative **leggi, legga, leggiamo, leggete**

24 mangiare *to eat*

	present	future	conditional
io	mangio	mangerò	mangerei
tu	mangi	mangerai	mangeresti
lui/lei	mangia	mangerà	mangerebbe
noi	mangiamo	mangeremo	mangeremmo
voi	mangiate	mangerete	mangereste
loro	mangiano	mangeranno	mangerebbero

	imperfect	simple past	perfect
io	mangiavo	mangiai	ho mangiato
tu	mangiavi	mangiasti	hai mangiato
lui/lei	mangiava	mangiò	ha mangiato
noi	mangiavamo	mangiammo	abbiamo mangiato
voi	mangiavate	mangiaste	avete mangiato
loro	mangiavano	mangiarono	hanno mangiato

	present subjunctive	imperfect subjunctive
io	mangi	mangiassi
tu	mangi	mangiassi
lui/lei	mangi	mangiasse
noi	mangiamo	mangiassimo
voi	mangiate	mangiaste
loro	mangino	mangiassero

past participle **mangiato**

gerund **mangiando**

imperative **mangia, mangi, mangiamo, mangiate**

25 morire *to die*

	present	future	conditional
io	muoio	morirò	morirei
tu	muori	morirai	moriresti
lui/lei	muore	morirà	morirebbe
noi	moriamo	moriremo	moriremmo
voi	morite	morirete	morireste
loro	muoiono	moriranno	morirebbero

	imperfect	simple past	perfect
io	morivo	morii	sono morto/a
tu	morivi	moristi	sei morto/a
lui/lei	moriva	morì	è morto/a
noi	morivamo	morimmo	siamo morti/e
voi	morivate	moriste	siete morti/e
loro	morivano	morirono	sono morti/e

	present subjunctive	imperfect subjunctive
io	muoia	morissi
tu	muoia	morissi
lui/lei	muoia	morisse
noi	moriamo	morissimo
voi	moriate	moriste
loro	muoiano	morissero

past participle **morto**

gerund **morendo**

imperative **muori, muoia, moriamo, morite**

26 mu<u>o</u>vere *to move*

	present	future	conditional
io	muovo	muoverò	muoverei
tu	muovi	muoverai	muoveresti
lui/lei	muove	muoverà	muoverebbe
noi	m(u)oviamo	muoveremo	muoveremmo
voi	m(u)ovete	muoverete	muovereste
loro	mu<u>o</u>vono	muoveranno	muoverebbero

	imperfect	simple past	perfect
io	muovevo	mossi	ho mosso
tu	muovevi	movesti	hai mosso
lui/lei	muoveva	mosse	ha mosso
noi	muovevamo	movemmo	abbiamo mosso
voi	muovevate	moveste	avete mosso
loro	muov<u>e</u>vano	mossero	hanno mosso

	present subjunctive	imperfect subjunctive
io	muova	m(u)ovessi
tu	muova	m(u)ovessi
lui/lei	muova	m(u)ovesse
noi	m(u)oviamo	m(u)ov<u>e</u>ssimo
voi	m(u)oviate	m(u)oveste
loro	mu<u>o</u>vano	m(u)ov<u>e</u>ssero

past participle **mosso**

gerund **muovendo**

imperative **muovi, muova, muoviamo, muovete**

27 pagare *to pay*

	present	future	conditional
io	pago	pagherò	pagherei
tu	paghi	pagherai	pagheresti
lui/lei	paga	pagherà	pagherebbe
noi	paghiamo	pagheremo	pagheremmo
voi	pagate	pagherete	paghereste
loro	pagano	pagheranno	pagherebbero

	imperfect	simple past	perfect
io	pagavo	pagai	ho pagato
tu	pagavi	pagasti	hai pagato
lui/lei	pagava	pagò	ha pagato
noi	pagavamo	pagammo	abbiamo pagato
voi	pagavate	pagaste	avete pagato
loro	pagavano	pagarono	hanno pagato

	present subjunctive	imperfect subjunctive
io	paghi	pagassi
tu	paghi	pagassi
lui/lei	paghi	pagasse
noi	paghiamo	pagassimo
voi	paghiate	pagaste
loro	paghino	pagassero

past participle **pagato**

gerund **pagando**

imperative **paga, paghi, paghiamo, pagate**

28 parere *to seem*

	present	future	conditional
io	paio	parrò	parrei
tu	pari	parrai	parresti
lui/lei	pare	parrà	parrebbe
noi	paiamo	parremo	parremmo
voi	parete	parrete	parreste
loro	paiono	parranno	parrebbero

	imperfect	simple past	perfect
io	parevo	parvi	sono parso/a
tu	parevi	paresti	sei parso/a
lui/lei	pareva	parve	è parso/a
noi	parevamo	paremmo	siamo parsi/e
voi	parevate	pareste	siete parsi/e
loro	parevano	parvero	sono parsi/e

	present subjunctive	imperfect subjunctive
io	paia	paressi
tu	paia	paressi
lui/lei	paia	paresse
noi	pariamo	paressimo
voi	pariate	pareste
loro	paiano	paressero

past participle **parso**

gerund **parendo**

imperative **pari, paia, pariamo, parete**

29 piacere *to please*

	present	future	conditional
io	piaccio	piacerò	piacerei
tu	piaci	piacerai	piaceresti
lui/lei	piace	piacerà	piacerebbe
noi	piacciamo	piaceremo	piaceremmo
voi	piacete	piacerete	piacereste
loro	piacciono	piaceranno	piacerebbero

	imperfect	simple past	perfect
io	piacevo	piacqui	sono piaciuto/a
tu	piacevi	piacesti	sei piaciuto/a
lui/lei	piaceva	piacque	è piaciuto/a
noi	piacevamo	piacemmo	siamo piaciuti/e
voi	piacevate	piaceste	siete piaciuti/e
loro	piacevano	piacquero	sono piaciuti/e

	present subjunctive	imperfect subjunctive
io	piaccia	piacessi
tu	piaccia	piacessi
lui/lei	piaccia	piacesse
noi	piacciamo	piacessimo
voi	piacciate	piaceste
loro	piacciano	piacessero

past participle **piaciuto**

gerund **piacendo**

imperative **piaci, piaccia, piacciamo, piacciate**

30 porre *to put, to place*

	present	future	conditional
io	pongo	porrò	porrei
tu	poni	porrai	porresti
lui/lei	pone	porrà	porrebbe
noi	poniamo	porremo	porremmo
voi	ponete	porrete	porreste
loro	pongono	porranno	porrebbero

	imperfect	simple past	perfect
io	ponevo	posi	ho posto
tu	ponevi	ponesti	hai posto
lui/lei	poneva	pose	ha posto
noi	ponevano	ponemmo	abbiamo posto
voi	ponevate	poneste	avete posto
loro	ponevano	posero	hanno posto

	present subjunctive	imperfect subjunctive
io	ponga	ponessi
tu	ponga	ponessi
lui/lei	ponga	ponesse
noi	poniamo	ponessimo
voi	poniate	poneste
loro	pongano	ponessero

past participle **posto**

gerund **ponendo**

imperative **poni, ponga, poniamo, ponete**

Verbs that follow the same pattern as **porre** include **comporre** *to compose*, **disporre** *to dispose*, **esporre** *to expose*, **imporre** *to impose*, **opporre** *to oppose*, **proporre** *to propose*, **supporre** *to suppose*.

31 potere *to be able to*

	present	future	conditional
io	posso	potrò	potrei
tu	puoi	potrai	potresti
lui/lei	può	potrà	potrebbe
noi	possiamo	potremo	potremmo
voi	potete	potrete	potreste
loro	possono	potranno	potrebbero

	imperfect	simple past	perfect
io	potevo	potei/potetti	ho potuto
tu	potevi	potesti	hai potuto
lui/lei	poteva	poté/potette	ha potuto
noi	potevamo	potemmo	abbiamo potuto
voi	potevate	poteste	avete potuto
loro	potevano	poterono/ potettero	hanno potuto

	present subjunctive	imperfect subjunctive
io	possa	potessi
tu	possa	potessi
lui/lei	possa	potesse
noi	possiamo	potessimo
voi	possiate	poteste
loro	possano	potessero

past participle **potuto**

gerund **potendo**

Potere can take **essere** in the compound tenses if the infinitive following it normally takes **essere**. It has no imperative.

32 prendere *to take*

	present	future	conditional
io	prendo	prenderò	prenderei
tu	prendi	prenderai	prenderesti
lui/lei	prende	prenderà	prenderebbe
noi	prendiamo	prenderemo	prenderemmo
voi	prendete	prenderete	prendereste
loro	prendono	prenderanno	prenderebbero

	imperfect	simple past	perfect
io	prendevo	presi	ho preso
tu	prendevi	prendesti	hai preso
lui/lei	prendeva	prese	ha preso
noi	prendevamo	prendemmo	abbiamo preso
voi	prendevate	prendeste	avete preso
loro	prendevano	presero	hanno preso

	present subjunctive	imperfect subjunctive
io	prenda	prendessi
tu	prenda	prendessi
lui/lei	prenda	prendesse
noi	prendiamo	prendessimo
voi	prendiate	prendeste
loro	prendano	prendessero

past participle **preso**

gerund **prendendo**

imperative **prendi, prenda, prendiamo, prendete**

33 produrre *to produce*

	present	future	conditional
io	produco	produrrò	produrrei
tu	produci	produrrai	produrresti
lui/lei	produce	produrrà	produrrebbe
noi	produciamo	produrremo	produrremmo
voi	producete	produrrete	produrreste
loro	producono	produrranno	produrrebbero

	imperfect	simple past	perfect
io	producevo	produssi	ho prodotto
tu	producevi	producesti	hai prodotto
lui/lei	produceva	produssi	ha prodotto
noi	producevamo	producemmo	abbiamo prodotto
voi	producevate	produceste	avete prodotto
loro	producevano	produssero	hanno prodotto

	present subjunctive	imperfect subjunctive
io	produca	producessi
tu	produca	producessi
lui/lei	produca	producesse
noi	produciamo	producessimo
voi	produciate	produceste
loro	producano	producessero

past participle **prodotto**

gerund **producendo**

imperative **produci, produca, produciamo, producete**

Verbs that follow the same pattern as **produrre** include **condurre** *to conduct*, **dedurre** *to deduce*, **introdurre** *to introduce*, **ridurre** *to reduce*, **sedurre** *to seduce*, **tradurre** *to translate*.

34 rimanere *to stay, to remain*

	present	future	confitional
io	rimango	rimarrò	rimarrei
tu	rimani	rimarrai	rimarresti
lui/lei	rimane	rimarrà	rimarrebbe
noi	rimaniamo	rimarremo	rimarremmo
voi	rimanete	rimarrete	rimarreste
loro	rimangano	rimarranno	rimarrebbero

	imperfect	simple past	perfect
io	rimanevo	rimasi	sono rimasto/a
tu	rimanevi	rimanesti	sei rimasto/a
lui/lei	rimaneva	rimase	è rimasto/a
noi	rimanevamo	rimanemmo	siamo rimasti/e
voi	rimanevate	rimaneste	siete rimasti/e
loro	rimanevano	rimasero	sono rimasti/e

	present subjunctive	imperfect subjunctive
io	rimanga	rimanessi
tu	rimanga	rimanessi
lui/lei	rimanga	rimanesse
noi	rimaniamo	rimanessimo
voi	rimaniate	rimaneste
loro	rimangano	rimanessero

past participle **rimasto**

gerund **rimanendo**

imperative **rimani, rimanga, rimaniamo, rimanete**

35 rispondere *to answer*

	present	future	conditional
io	rispondo	risponderò	risponderei
tu	rispondi	risponderai	risponderesti
lui/lei	risponde	risponderà	risponderebbe
noi	rispondiamo	risponderemo	risponderemmo
voi	rispondete	risponderete	rispondereste
loro	rispondono	risponderanno	risponderebbero

	imperfect	simple past	perfect
io	rispondevo	risposi	ho risposto
tu	rispondevi	rispondesti	hai risposto
lui/lei	rispondeva	rispose	ha risposto
noi	rispondevamo	rispondemmo	abbiamo risposto
voi	rispondevate	rispondeste	avete risposto
loro	rispondevano	risposero	hanno risposto

	present subjunctive	imperfect subjunctive
io	risponda	rispondessi
tu	risponda	rispondessi
lui/lei	risponda	rispondesse
noi	rispondiamo	rispondessimo
voi	rispondiate	rispondeste
loro	rispondano	rispondessero

past participle **risposto**

gerund **rispondendo**

imperative **rispondi, risponda, rispondiamo, rispondete**

36 r<u>o</u>mpere *to break*

	present	future	conditional
io	rompo	romperò	romperei
tu	rompi	romperai	romperesti
lui/lei	rompe	romperà	romperebbe
noi	rompiamo	romperemo	romperemmo
voi	rompete	romperete	rompereste
loro	r<u>o</u>mpono	romperanno	romperebbero

	imperfect	simple past	perfect
io	rompevo	ruppi	ho rotto
tu	rompevi	rompesti	hai rotto
lui/lei	rompeva	ruppe	ha rotto
noi	rompevamo	rompemmo	abbiamo rotto
voi	rompevate	rompeste	avete rotto
loro	romp<u>e</u>vano	r<u>u</u>ppero	hanno rotto

	present subjunctive	imperfect subjunctive
io	rompa	rompessi
tu	rompa	rompessi
lui/lei	rompa	rompesse
noi	rompiamo	romp<u>e</u>ssimo
voi	rompiate	rompeste
loro	r<u>o</u>mpano	romp<u>e</u>ssero

past participle **rotto**

gerund **rompendo**

imperative **rompi, rompa, rompiamo, rompete**

37 salire *to go up*

	present	future	conditional
io	salgo	salirò	salirei
tu	sali	salirai	saliresti
lui/lei	sale	salirà	salirebbe
noi	saliamo	saliremo	saliremmo
voi	salite	salirete	salireste
loro	salgono	saliranno	salirebbero

	imperfect	simple past	perfect
io	salivo	salii	sono salito/a
tu	salivi	salisti	sei salito/a
lui/lei	saliva	salì	è salito/a
noi	salivamo	salimmo	siamo saliti/e
voi	salivate	saliste	siete saliti/e
loro	salivano	salirono	sono saliti/e

	present subjunctive	imperfect subjunctive
io	salga	salissi
tu	salga	salissi
lui/lei	salga	salisse
noi	saliamo	salissimo
voi	saliate	saliste
loro	salgano	salissero

past participle **salito**

gerund **salendo**

imperative **sali, salga, saliamo, salite**

38 sapere *to know*

	present	future	conditional
io	so	saprò	saprei
tu	sai	saprai	sapresti
lui/lei	sa	saprà	saprebbe
noi	sappiamo	sapremo	sapremmo
voi	sapete	saprete	sapreste
loro	sanno	sapranno	saprebbero

	imperfect	simple past	perfect
io	sapevo	seppi	ho saputo
tu	sapevi	sapesti	hai saputo
lui/lei	sapeva	seppe	ha saputo
noi	sapevamo	sapemmo	abbiamo saputo
voi	sapevate	sapeste	avete saputo
loro	sapevano	seppero	hanno saputo

	present subjunctive	imperfect subjunctive
io	sappia	sapessi
tu	sappia	sapessi
ui/lei	sappia	sapesse
noi	sappiamo	sapessimo
voi	sappiate	sapeste
loro	sappiano	sapessero

past participle **saputo**

gerund **sapendo**

imperative **sappi, sappia, sappiamo, sappiate**

39 scegliere *to choose*

	present	future	conditional
io	scelgo	sceglierò	sceglierei
tu	scegli	sceglierai	sceglieresti
lui/lei	sceglie	sceglierà	sceglierebbe
noi	scegliamo	sceglieremo	sceglieremmo
voi	scegliete	sceglierete	scegliereste
loro	scelgono	sceglieranno	sceglierebbero

	imperfect	simple past	perfect
io	sceglievo	scelsi	ho scelto
tu	sceglievi	scegliesti	hai scelto
lui/lei	sceglieva	scelse	ha scelto
noi	sceglievamo	scegliemmo	abbiamo scelto
voi	sceglievate	sceglieste	avete scelto
loro	sceglievano	scelsero	hanno scelto

	present subjunctive	imperfect subjunctive
io	scelga	scegliessi
tu	scelga	scegliessi
lui/lei	scelga	scegliesse
noi	scegliamo	scegliessimo
voi	scegliate	sceglieste
loro	scelgano	scegliessero

past participle **scelto**

gerund **scegliendo**

imperative **scegli, scelga, scegliamo, scegliete**

40 sedere *to sit*

	present	future	conditional
io	siedo/seggo	s(i)ederò	s(i)ederei
tu	siedi	s(i)ederai	s(i)ederesti
lui/lei	siede	s(i)ederà	s(i)ederebbe
noi	sediamo	s(i)ederemo	s(i)ederemmo
voi	sedete	s(i)ederete	s(i)edereste
loro	siedono/seggono	s(i)ederanno	s(i)ederebbero

	imperfect	simple past	perfect
io	sedevo	sedetti/sedei	sono seduto/a
tu	sedevi	sedesti	sei seduto/a
lui/lei	sedeva	sedette/sedé	è seduto/a
noi	sedevamo	sedemmo	siamo seduti/e
voi	sedevate	sedeste	siete seduti/e
loro	sedevano	sedettero/sederono	sono seduti/e

	present subjunctive	imperfect subjunctive
io	sieda/segga	sedessi
tu	sieda/segga	sedessi
lui/lei	sieda/segga	sedesse
noi	sediamo	sedessimo
voi	sediate	sedeste
loro	siedano/seggano	sedessero

past participle **seduto**

gerund **sedendo**

imperative **siedi, sieda, sediamo, sedete**

41 spegnere *to switch off*

	present	future	conditional
io	spengo	spegnerò	spegnerei
tu	spegni	spegnerai	spegneresti
lui/lei	spegne	spegnerà	spegnerebbe
noi	spegniamo	spegneremo	spegneremmo
voi	spegnete	spegnerete	spegnereste
loro	spengono	spegneranno	spegnerebbero

	imperfect	simple past	perfect
io	spegnevo	spensi	ho spento
tu	spegnevi	spegnesti	hai spento
lui/lei	spegneva	spense	ha spento
noi	spegnevamo	spegnemmo	abbiamo spento
voi	spegnevate	spegneste	avete spento
loro	spegnevano	spensero	hanno spento

	present subjunctive	imperfect subjunctive
io	spenga	spegnessi
tu	spenga	spegnessi
lui/lei	spenga	spegnesse
noi	spegniamo	spegnessimo
voi	spegniate	spegneste
loro	spengano	spegnessero

past participle **spento**

gerund **spegnendo**

imperative **spegni, spenga, spegniamo, spegnete**

42 stare *to stay, to be*

	present	future	conditional
io	sto	starò	starei
tu	stai	starai	staresti
lui/lei	sta	starà	starebbe
noi	stiamo	staremo	staremmo
voi	state	starete	stareste
loro	stanno	staranno	starebbero

	imperfect	simple past	perfect
io	stavo	stetti	sono stato/a
tu	stavi	stesti	sei stato/a
lui/lei	stava	stette	è stato/a
noi	stavamo	stemmo	siamo stati/e
voi	stavate	steste	siete stati/e
loro	stavano	stettero	sono stati/e

	present subjunctive	imperfect subjunctive
io	stia	stessi
tu	stia	stessi
lui/lei	stia	stesse
noi	stiamo	stessimo
voi	stiate	steste
loro	stiano	stessero

past participle **stato**

gerund **stando**

imperative **stai/sta', stia, stiamo, state**

43 tenere *to hold*

	present	future	conditional
io	tengo	terrò	terrei
tu	tieni	terrai	terresti
lui/lei	tiene	terrà	terrebbe
noi	teniamo	terremo	terremmo
voi	tenete	terrete	terreste
loro	tengono	terranno	terrebbero

	imperfect	simple past	perfect
io	tenevo	tenni	ho tenuto
tu	tenevi	tenesti	hai tenuto
lui/lei	teneva	tenne	ha tenuto
noi	tenevamo	tenemmo	abbiamo tenuto
voi	tenevate	teneste	avete tenuto
loro	tenevano	tennero	hanno tenuto

	present subjunctive	imperfect subjunctive
io	tenga	tenessi
tu	tenga	tenessi
lui/lei	tenga	tenesse
noi	teniamo	tenessimo
voi	teniate	teneste
loro	tengano	tenessero

past participle **tenuto**

gerund **tenendo**

imperative **tieni, tenga, teniamo, tenete**

Verbs that follow the same pattern as **tenere** include **appartenere** *to belong*, **contenere** *to contain*, **mantenere** *to maintain*, **ottenere** *to obtain*, **ritenere** *to retain*, **sostenere** *to sustain*, **trattenersi** *to stay*.

44 **trarre** *to pull, to draw*

	present	future	conditional
io	traggo	trarrò	trarrei
tu	trai	trarrai	trarresti
lui/lei	trae	trarrà	trarrebbe
noi	traiamo	trarremo	trarremmo
voi	traete	trarrete	trarreste
loro	traggono	trarranno	trarrebbero

	imperfect	simple past	perfect
io	traevo	trassi	ho tratto
tu	traevi	traesti	hai tratto
lui/lei	traeva	trasse	ha tratto
noi	traevamo	traemmo	abbiamo tratto
voi	traevate	traeste	avete tratto
loro	traevano	trassero	hanno tratto

	present subjunctive	imperfect subjunctive
io	tragga	traessi
tu	tragga	traessi
lui/lei	tragga	traesse
noi	traiamo	traessimo
oi	traiate	traeste
loro	traggano	traessero

past participle **tratto**

gerund **traendo**

imperative **trai**, **tragga**, **traiamo**, **traete**

Verbs that follow the same pattern as **trarre** include **attrarre** *to attract*, **contrarre** *to contract*, **distrarre** *to distract*, **estrarre** *to extract*, **sottrarre** *to subtract*.

45 uscire *to go out*

	present	future	conditional
io	esco	uscirò	uscirei
tu	esci	uscirai	usciresti
lui/lei	esce	uscirà	uscirebbe
noi	usciamo	usciremo	usciremmo
voi	uscite	uscirete	uscireste
loro	escono	usciranno	uscirebbero

	imperfect	simple past	perfect
io	uscivo	uscii	sono uscito/a
tu	uscivi	uscisti	sei uscito/a
lui/lei	usciva	uscì	è uscito/a
noi	uscivamo	uscimmo	siamo usciti/e
voi	uscivate	usciste	siete usciti/e
loro	uscivano	uscirono	sono usciti/e

	present subjunctive	imperfect subjunctive
io	esca	uscissi
tu	esca	uscissi
lui/lei	esca	uscisse
noi	usciamo	uscissimo
voi	usciate	usciste
loro	escano	uscissero

past participle **uscito**

gerund **uscendo**

imperative **esci, esca, usciamo, uscite**

Riuscire *to manage to/succeed in* follows the same pattern as **uscire**.

46 valere *to be worth*

	present	future	conditional
io	valgo	varrò	varrei
tu	vali	varrai	varresti
lui/lei	vale	varrà	varrebbe
noi	valiamo	varremo	varremmo
voi	valete	varrete	varreste
loro	valgono	varranno	varrebbero

	imperfect	simple past	perfect
io	valevo	valsi	sono valso/a
tu	valevi	valesti	sei valso/a
lui/lei	valeva	valse	è valso/a
noi	valevamo	valemmo	siamo valsi/e
voi	valevate	valeste	siete valsi/e
loro	valevano	valsero	sono valsi/e

	present subjunctive	imperfect subjunctive
io	valga	valessi
tu	valga	valessi
lui/lei	valga	valesse
noi	valiamo	valessimo
voi	valiate	valeste
loro	valgano	valessero

past participle **valso**

gerund **valendo**

imperative **vali**, **valga**, **valiamo**, **valete**

47 ve̱ndere *to sell*

	present	future	conditional
io	vendo	venderò	venderei
tu	vendi	venderai	venderesti
lui/lei	vende	venderà	venderebbe
noi	vendiamo	venderemo	venderemmo
voi	vendete	venderete	vendereste
loro	ve̱ndono	venderanno	venderebbero

	imperfect	simple past	perfect
io	vendevo	vendei/ vendetti	ho venduto
tu	vendevi	vendesti	hai venduto
lui/lei	vendeva	vendé/ vendette	ha venduto
noi	vendevamo	vendemmo	abbiamo venduto
voi	vendevate	vendeste	avete venduto
loro	vende̱vano	vende̱rono/ vende̱ttero	hanno venduto

	present subjunctive	imperfect subjunctive
io	venda	vendessi
tu	venda	vendessi
lui/lei	venda	vendesse
noi	vendiamo	vende̱ssimo
voi	vendiate	vendeste
loro	ve̱ndano	vende̱ssero

past participle **venduto**

gerund **vendendo**

imperative **vendi, venda, vendiamo, vendete**

48 venire *to come*

	present	future	conditional
io	vengo	verrò	verrei
tu	vieni	verrai	verresti
lui/lei	viene	verrà	verrebbe
noi	veniamo	verremo	verremmo
voi	venite	verrete	verreste
loro	vengono	verranno	verrebbero

	imperfect	simple past	perfect
io	venivo	venni	sono venuto/a
tu	venivi	venisti	sei venuto/a
lui/lei	veniva	venne	è venuto/a
noi	venivamo	venimmo	siamo venuti/e
voi	venivate	veniste	siete venuti/e
loro	venivano	vennero	sono venuti/e

	present subjunctive	imperfect subjunctive
io	venga	venissi
tu	venga	venissi
lui/lei	venga	venisse
noi	veniamo	venissimo
voi	veniate	veniste
loro	vengano	venissero

past participle **venuto**

gerund **venendo**

imperative **vieni, venga, veniamo, venite**

Verbs that follow the same pattern as **venire** include **avvenire** *to happen,*
divenire *to become,* **intervenire** *to intervene,* **svenire** *to faint.*

49 vincere *to win, to defeat*

	present	future	conditional
io	vinco	vincerò	vincerei
tu	vinci	vincerai	vinceresti
lui/lei	vince	vincerà	vincerebbe
noi	vinciamo	vinceremo	vinceremmo
voi	vincete	vincerete	vincereste
loro	vincono	vinceranno	vincerebbero

	imperfect	simple past	perfect
io	vincevo	vinsi	ho vinto
tu	vincevi	vincesti	hai vinto
lui/lei	vinceva	vinse	ha vinto
noi	vincevamo	vincemmo	abbiamo vinto
voi	vincevate	vinceste	avete vinto
loro	vincevano	vinsero	hanno vinto

	present subjunctive	imperfect subjunctive
io	vinca	vincessi
tu	vinca	vincessi
lui/lei	vinca	vincesse
noi	vinciamo	vincessimo
voi	vinciate	vinceste
loro	vincano	vincessero

past participle **vinto**

gerund **vincendo**

imperative **vinci, vinca, vinciamo, vincete**

50 volere *to want to*

	present	future	conditional
io	voglio	vorrò	vorrei
tu	vuoi	vorrai	vorresti
lui/lei	vuole	vorrà	vorrebbe
noi	vogliamo	vorremo	vorremmo
voi	volete	vorrete	vorreste
loro	vogliono	vorranno	vorrebbero

	imperfect	simple past	perfect
io	volevo	volli	ho voluto
tu	volevi	volesti	hai voluto
lui/lei	voleva	volle	ha voluto
noi	volevamo	volemmo	abbiamo voluto
voi	volevate	voleste	avete voluto
loro	volevano	vollero	hanno voluto

	present subjunctive	imperfect subjunctive
io	voglia	volessi
tu	voglia	volessi
lui/lei	voglia	volesse
noi	vogliamo	volessimo
voi	vogliate	voleste
loro	vogliano	volessero

past participle **voluto**

gerund **volendo**

Volere can take **essere** in the compound tenses if the infinitive following it normally takes **essere**. It has no imperative.

Verb index

Pages 192-241

Grammar terms

Abstract nouns are the words for intangible things like *liberty, silence, poverty, fear, happiness*. They're the opposite of concrete nouns such as *table, dog, water*.

Adjectives are words that describe or add information to nouns and pronouns: *small* car, It was *superb*, *Italian* wine, *first* class, *my* name, *which* hotel?, *those* people.

Adverbs add information to adjectives, verbs and other adverbs: *very* small car, She speaks *clearly*, She speaks *really* clearly.

Agreement Unlike English, adjectives and articles in Italian change according to the noun/pronoun they relate to, needing to agree, i.e. match, in terms of gender (masculine/feminine) and number (singular/plural).

Articles are **the** (definite article), *a/an* (indefinite article) and *some* (partitive article). Italian has more than English.

Auxiliary verbs are verbs that support the main verb: *We **have** eaten, **Has** she gone?* In English, but not Italian, *do/does* is used as an auxiliary verb in questions like *Do you understand?*

Cardinal numbers are *one, two, three, four, etc.*

Comparatives are used when making comparisons. English has two ways of comparing with adjectives: adding -er as in *bigger*, *cheaper*, and using the word *more* as in *more expensive*. Italian always uses the second alternative, with più *more* or meno *less*.

Compound tenses are two-word tenses. Most English tenses are compound whereas most Italian tenses are simple one-word tenses, except for past tenses, e.g. the **perfect** *I have waited*, the **pluperfect** *I had waited*.

The **conditional** is a verb form used to say what would or could happen: *I would like to go, Would/Could you help me?* The **past conditional** translates *would have*: *I would have liked to go*.

Conjunctions are linking words like *and, but, while, because*.

Consonants and **vowels** make up the alphabet. The vowels are **a**, **e**, **i**, **o**, **u**; the rest: **b**, **c**, **d**, **f**, etc. are consonants.

Continuous tenses are used to say *I am/was doing* something. Italian uses stare where English uses *to be*.

The **definite article** is the word *the*, which has several Italian translations.

Demonstrative words are used to point things out. *This, these, that, those* are demonstrative adjectives; *this one, that one, these (ones), those (ones)* are demonstrative pronouns.

A **direct object** is directly at the receiving end of a verb. In the sentence *We saw John, we* is the subject, *saw* is the verb and *John* is the direct object. Compare with **indirect object**.

Direct object pronouns are *me, us, you, him, her, it, them.*

Feminine See **gender**.

Formal is used to describe **lei**, the word for *you* when talking to someone you don't know well. The informal word for *you* is **tu**.

The **future tense** of a verb translates the English *will*: *We will be there, I'll go later, She'll be at work.*

The **future perfect** translates *will have*: *She will have gone to work.*

Gender Every Italian noun is either masculine or feminine, as are any articles and adjectives that relate to that noun.

A **gerund** in English ends in *-ing*: *reading, driving, knowing.*

Imperative is the verb form used to give instructions or commands: ***Wait** for me, **Don't do** that, **Turn** the top clockwise.*

The **imperfect tense** of a verb is used to describe how things were and to talk about things that happened over a period of time or repeatedly: *She **was** furious, We **were watching** the match, We **used to go** there often.*

An **impersonal verb** is a verb form that doesn't relate to people or things and generally starts with *it*: *It's raining, It's possible.*

The **indefinite article** is *a/an* in English; **un/un'/uno/una** in Italian.

The **indicative mood** is used for factual statements: *He **goes** to school.* See also **mood**.

An **indirect object** is usually separated from its verb by *to*. In the sentence *We talked to John, we* is the subject, *talked* is the verb and *John* is the indirect object. Compare with **direct object**.

Indirect object pronouns usually have *to* or *for* in front of **direct object pronouns**, e.g. *to/for me, to/for them* in English. In Italian they're a single word.

Infinitive Italian verbs are listed in a dictionary in the infinitive form, ending in **-are**, **-ere** or **-ire**. The English equivalent uses *to*: **mangiare** *to eat*, **avere** *to have*, **capire** *to understand*.

Informal is used to describe **tu**, the word for *you* when talking to someone you call by their first name. The formal word for *you* is **lei**.

Interrogative words are used in questions, e.g. *who, what, when, where, how, why, how much/many*.

Intransitive verbs need only a subject to make sense: *go, laugh*; unlike **transitive verbs** which need a subject and a direct object.

Invariable words don't change to agree with/match anything else.

Irregular nouns, verbs or adjectives don't behave in a predictable way like regular ones, and have to be learnt separately.

Masculine See **gender**.

Modal verbs are verbs like *want, be able to, must,* which are followed by other verbs: *I **want** to stay here, I **can** swim, You **ought** to leave.*

The **mood** of a verb defines how it's used, e.g. the **indicative mood** is used for factual statements: *He **goes** to school*; while the **subjunctive mood** indicates that hard facts are not involved: *If he **were to go** to school …*

Negatives are words like *not, never, nothing, nobody*; and *not … ever, not … anybody, not … anything.*

Nouns are the words for living beings, things, places and concepts: *son, doctor, dog, table, house, Scotland, time, freedom.* See also **proper nouns**.

Number refers to the difference between singular (one) and plural (more than one).

Numbers See **cardinal numbers** and **ordinal numbers**.

The **object** of a sentence is at the receiving end of the verb. It can be direct: *They have **two children***; or indirect: *Anna talks **to the children.***

Object pronoun. See **direct/indirect object pronouns**.

Ordinal numbers are *first, second, third, fourth,* etc.

Parts of speech are the grammatical building blocks of a sentence: *adjective, article, noun, pronoun, verb,* etc.

The **passive** describes something done ***to*** the subject rather than ***by*** it: *The meat is cooked in the oven, The room was booked by my friend.*

The **past participle** of a verb is used with *have* when talking about the past: *I have **finished**, He has **eaten**, They had **gone***. Some past participles can also be used as adjectives: *the **finished** product.*

The **perfect tense** of a verb is used in Italian to talk about the past; equivalent to the English *I worked* and *I have worked.*

The **person** of a verb indicates who or what is doing something:

first person = the speaker: *I* (singular), *we* (plural)

second person = the person(s) being addressed: *you*

third person = who/what is being talked about: *he/she/it/they*

Personal pronouns are words like *I, you, we, she, her, them.*

The **pluperfect tense** translates *had* done something: *She had worked hard all day.*

Plural means more than one.

Possessive relates to ownership: the **possessive adjectives** are *my, our, your, his/her/its, their*; the **possessive pronouns** are *mine, ours, yours, his/hers, theirs.*

Prepositions are words like *by, in, on, with, for, through, next to*. They relate a noun/pronoun to another part of the sentence by e.g. place, time, purpose: *It's **on** the back seat, We're here **until** Friday, I've got a letter **for** Tom.*

The **present** tense of a verb is used to talk about things being done now: *I work, I'm working.*

Present participles end in *-ing* in English. In Italian they end in **-ante** or **-ente**, and they're used only as adjectives.

Pronouns replace nouns to avoid the need to repeat them. They can be personal: *we, she, us*; demonstrative: *this one, those*; possessive: *mine, theirs*. They can also involve *one/ones: the big one, the red ones.*

Proper nouns are the names of specific people, places or organisations. They're written with a capital letter: *Sally, Cambridge, European Union.*

Reflexive pronouns are **mi**, **ti**, **si**, **ci**, **vi**, used as an integral part of **reflexive verbs** in Italian.

Reflexive verbs have **-si** at the end of the infinitive in Italian. There's no consistent English equivalent, although many reflexive verbs include *get* or *oneself* in the translation: **sposarsi** *to get married,* **divertirsi** *to enjoy oneself.*

Regular nouns, adjectives, verbs etc. behave in a predictable way, conforming to the pattern for that particular part of speech.

Relative pronouns are words like *which*, *who*, *that*, used to join together parts of a sentence without repeating the noun.

The **simple past tense** in English is, for example, *I worked, We ate, They spoke*. There's also a simple past tense in Italian but it's used rarely when speaking – the **perfect tense** is used instead.

Simple tenses are one-word tenses like *I play, I played*. Italian has more simple tenses than English.

Singular means one.

The **stem** of an Italian verb is what's left when you remove the **-are**, **-ere** or **-ire** ending of the infinitive. You can then add other endings to this stem.

Stressed pronouns are the pronouns used in Italian after prepositions: **me**, **te**, **lui**, **lei**, **noi**, **voi**, **loro**.

The **subject** of a sentence is whoever or whatever is carrying out the verb: ***They*** have two children, ***Anna*** reads the paper, ***This house*** cost a lot of money, ***Peace*** is possible.

Subject pronouns are *I, we, you, he, she, it, they*.

Subjunctive is a form of a verb that's much more widely used in Italian than English. It equates to the English *may* or *were*: ***May*** *all your dreams come true, if I **were** rich*, but it's also used in a range of well-defined grammatical circumstances. See also **mood**.

Superlative is *the most/least* … when comparing several things. In English you can add *-est* to many adjectives: *biggest, cheapest,* or you can use *most*: *most expensive*. There's no Italian equivalent of *-est*.

A **syllable** is a unit that contains a vowel and consists of a single sound: *can* has one syllable, *can-ter* has two, while *Can-ter-bu-ry* has four.

The **tense** of a verb indicates when something is done:

in the past	perfect tense: *I (have) worked*
	imperfect tense: *I was working, I used to work*
now	present tense: *I work, I'm working*
in the future	future tense: *I will work*

Transitive verbs need both a **subject** and a **direct object**: *use, give, throw*, unlike **intransitive verbs** which need only a subject: *sleep*, *sit*, *sneeze*. Some verbs can be used both transitively and intransitively: *The pilot flew the plane* (transitive), *I flew at eight o'clock this morning* (intransitive).

Verbs are words like *to go, to sleep, to eat, to like, to have, to be, to think*; they refer to doing and being.

Vowels and **consonants** make up the alphabet. Vowels are the sounds made by the letters **a**, **e**, **i**, **o**, **u**; the rest: **b**, **c**, **d**, **f**, etc. are consonants.

Answers

Getting started Page 9

1   *a* Sofia N; glossy ADJ; magazine
    N; organises V; interviews N;
    hires V; professional ADJ; models
    N; photographers N; travels V;
    world N; boyfriend N; well-known
    ADJ; actor N; *b* my ADJ; father N;
    comes V; Naples N; lives V; Rome
    N; works V; central ADJ; office N;
    large ADJ; company N; *c* prepared
    V; fantastic ADJ; meal N; ate
    V; grilled ADJ; fish N; fresh ADJ;
    asparagus N; new ADJ; potatoes
    N; drank V; superb ADJ; Italian
    ADJ; white ADJ; wine N; dessert N;
    incredible ADJ

2   *a* very ADV; reasonable ADJ;
    rather ADV; dilapidated ADJ; really
    ADV; small ADJ; overgrown ADJ;
    b superbly ADV; terribly ADV;
    uneven ADJ; deliberately ADV;
    unfair ADJ

Checkpoint 1 Page 22

1   Men: Victor; Matthew; Hugo;
    Hector; Philip; Henry
    Women: Julia; Jade; Helen; Hilary;
    Alexandra; Josephine
    Countries: Chile; Turkey; Jamaica;
    The Philippines; China
2   adventure; obsessive; perfect;
    phosphorous; obscure;
    photocopy; tractor; admiration;
    admiral; extravagant; horrendous
3   Bologna; Firenze; Napoli; Roma
4   vu vu vu
5   chiocciolina
6   Tanzania
7   last syllable but one
8   Papa
9   te; da

10 Finlandia; Francia; Galles;
    Germania; Inghilterra; Irlanda;
    Irlanda del Nord; Italia; Regno
    Unito; Scozia; Spagna; Svezia;
    Svizzera

Checkpoint 2 Page 30

1   *a* zero; *b* tre zeri
2   smaller
3   otto; diciotto; ventotto;
    ottantotto
4   2 400 000; 2.400.000
5   *a* it's five o'clock; *b* at seven
    o'clock in the evening; *c* after
    midnight; *d* at seven o'clock
    yesterday evening; *e* at half past
    three; *f* before 11 in the morning;
    g it's quarter past one; *h* one
    o'clock in the afternoon; *i* on
    Saturday at seven o'clock exactly;
    j on Monday at 18:00
6   *a* sono le undici; *b* alle nove di
    mattina; c a mezzogiorno; *d* dopo
    le diciotto; *e* alle nove in punto;
    f domani alle dieci; *g* ieri alle
    dieci; *h* domenica alle sedici; *i* alle
    sette ogni giorno; *j* prima delle tre
    di pomeriggio
7   trenta
8   una quarantina
9   il primo gennaio; il venticinque
    dicembre; il trentuno dicembre
10 for the umpteenth time
11 16:43
12 diciassettesimo
13 19th
14 primavera
15 il settantacinque per cento

Checkpoint 3 Page 42

1   from left to right: m; m/f; m; m;
    m; f; f; f; m/f; f; f; m

2 ragazze; conversazioni; caffè; cappuccini; sistemi; sport; ciclisti/cicliste; amiche; difficoltà; analisi; figli; filglie; serie; sci; uomini; luoghi; foto; braccia

3 feminine

4 brothers; brothers and sisters

5 leone, because it has a feminine form

6 several female colleagues

7 guida; persona; spia; vittima

8 *a* biologia *b* scienza *c* probabilità *d* differenza e nazione *f* situazione *g* femminismo

9 oysters; crickets

10 librone

11 capigruppo; capireparto

12 redattrice

Checkpoint 4 Page 50

1 from left to right: una; un; una; uno; un'; un; un; un; una; un'; uno; una; un; una; un

2 from left to right: la; il; la; lo; l'; l'; l'; il; la; l'; lo; la; il; la; il

3 from left to right: i; le; gli; le; gli; le; i; le; i; gli; i; le; le; le; i

4 from left to right: alla; dello; dall'; nella; sulle; sullo; degli; ai; nel; dalle

Checkpoint 5 Page 60

1 *a* primo: the prime minister; *b* Bianca: the White House; *c* alpini: mountain paths; *d* popolare: popular/folk music; *e* verde: eco/green-tourism; *f* italiane: the big Italian cities; *g* Azzurra: the Cote d'Azur; *h* maschio: a male panther; *i* seconda: in second class; *j* rosso scuro: dark red stripes; *k* moderna: modern dance; *l* materialista: a materialistic man

2 *a* educato; *b* simpatico;

c ordinario, comune; *d* facile, semplice; *e* interessante; *f* importante; *g* formale; *h* stupido

3 *a* professionale; *b* evidente; *c* terribile; *d* romantico; *e* generoso; *f* assoluto; *g* neutrale; *h* indifferente; *i* elettrico; *j* possibile

4 extra large; very old; extraordinary

5 *a* il/quello bianco; le/quelle grandi; il/quello vecchio; la/quella verde scuro; *b* qualcosa di impossibile; qualcosa di differente; niente di nuovo; niente di speciale

Checkpoint 6 Page 68

1 *a* assoluto; *b* veloce; *c* tipico; *d* raro; *e* normale; *f* simbolico; *g* abituale; *h* misterioso; *i* dolce

2 *a* pazientemente; *b* incidentalmente; *c* logicamente; *d* scientificamente; *e* diversamente; *f* regolarmente; *g* relativamente; *h* estremamente; *i* indifferentemente

3 *a* fortunatamente; *b* meglio; *c* facilmente; *d* lontano; *e* spesso; *f* giustamente

4 *a* L'aereo è più rapido. *b* Però, il treno è meno caro. Costa meno di 20 euro. *c* Secondo me, quei film sono i più interessanti. *d* Gianfranco è più alto di Enrico. *e* Questo menù è migliore/più buono. *f* Loro hanno giocato meglio di noi. *g* Preferirei giocare a tennis che nuotare. *h* Questa chiesa è la più grande della città. *i* Mia figlia è stanchissima oggi.

j Questa è la più importante biblioteca del mondo.

5 onestamente – sinceramente; ovviamente – evidentemente; crudelmente – brutalmente; s<u>u</u>bito – immediatamente; drammaticamente = dramatically

Checkpoint 7 **Page 76**

1 *a* molti; *b* tanto; *c* molto; *d* poco; *e* troppo

2 c

3 di

4 *a* questa; *b* questi; *c* questo; *d* questo; *e* questa; *f* queste

5 *a* quello; *b* quella; *c* quelle; *d* quegli; *e* quell'; *f* quel; *g* quei; *h* quel

6 qui/qua; lì/là

7 to say this or that when referring to a whole idea or situation

8 *a* mia; *b* i miei; *c* il mio; *d* mio; *e* mia; *f* le mie

9 their family

10 la tua m<u>a</u>cchina, la sua m<u>a</u>cchina, la vostra m<u>a</u>cchina; la tua, la sua, la vostra

11 la loro; È la loro.

12 la mia nuova m<u>a</u>cchina

Checkpoint 8 **Page 86**

1 Ciao, sono io.

2 *a* tu; *b* lei; *c* voi; *d* lei; *e* tu; *f* lei

3 *a* Did you see it yourself?; *b* Them too. *c* I don't know him/ it well. *d* I have spoken to him/ them. *e* We have eaten them. *f* Didn't you see her/it? *g* I explain it to you/him/them. *h* Excuse us.

4 *a* gli; *b* mi; *c* loro; *d* vi; *e* l'; *f* ci; *g* le; *h* le

5 Lo volete assaggiare/Volete assaggiarlo? Li devo comprare/ Devo comprarli.

6 *a* con loro; *b* per me; *c* secondo

lei; *d* da lui; *e* La conosci?; *f* Vi ho telefonato. *g* L'ho visto. *h* L'ho vista. *i* Gliel'ho mandato/L'ho mandato a lui. *j* Anna me l'ha mandato/L'ha mandato a me.

7 English is spoken here.

8 stesso – L'ho fatto io stesso.

9 They all contain the word *for* and take a direct object.

10 gli, loro

Checkpoint 9 **Page 91**

1 che

2 cui

3 che

4 il che

5 quale

6 che

7 cui

8 cui

Checkpoint 10 **Page 96**

1 *a* da una parte; *b* Cosa ne pensi? *c* Boh! *d* Secondo me; *e* Sono d'accordo. Allora (so, well) is left over.

2 *a* which; *b* who; *c* who/whom; *d* which; *e* who/whom; *f* how; *g* whom; *h* which

3 i cui

4 *a* ci; *b* ne; *c* ne; *d* c'; *e* ci; *f* ne

5 perciò

6 Me ne vado. (You could also say Vado via.)

7 comunque, ma

Checkpoint 11 **Page 108**

1 *a* nel; *b* dai; *c* sul; *d* per; *e* da; *f* alle; *g* in; *h* a, fra

2 *a* by the seaside; *b* my uncle's; *c* holiday home; *d* made of wood; *e* in the mountains; *f* in the Azores; *g* at the foot of Mt Etna; *h* made to measure/ bespoke; *i* my grandparents';

j on three floors; *k* worth 35 million euro; *l* between two roads

3 *a* la macchina di Stefano; *b* un numero di telefono; *c* la buccia d'arancia; *d* ciascuno di noi; *e* la fine del film; *f* il cugino della mamma/di mia madre; *g* l'indirizzo del medico; *h* il treno delle dieci meno cinque/delle nove e cinquantacinque

4 un bicchiere da champagne

5 in the

6 trainers (gym shoes); leather shoes; men's shoes

7 È dietro di te/di lei/di voi.

8 in; per; da

Checkpoint 12 Page 120

1 arrival, deep
2 dream
3 are (largest), ere, ire (smallest)
4 tense
5 I, they
6 third person singular
7 four: andare, dare, fare, stare
8 pull
9 irregular verb, reflexive verb
10 to greet
11 accelerare, illustrare, separare, navigare; to commercialise, to utilise, to monopolise
12 unblock, unbutton, disqualify, to re-start/start again, to re-think/think again, to recycle, to recreate

Checkpoint 13 Page 130

1 *a* Non lavorano con noi.
b Giovanni non è andato via.
c Non mi piace il tè. *d* Non sono stato in Perù. *e* Non abbiamo figli.
f Non so dove abitano.

2 niente: nothing/not … anything; nessuno: nobody/not … anybody; mai: never/not … ever; nulla: nothing/not … anything; non

… affatto: not at all; non … per niente: not at all; non … mica: not in the least, not as if; non … più: no longer, not any more

3 nessuno

4 di or d'

5 *a* Non mi piacciono né le cipolle né i pomodori. *b* Salvatore non ha mangiato mai le ostriche.

6 quale and quanto

7 che, che cosa, cosa

8 *a* Quando parte il treno per Roma? *b* Perché vuoi parlare con mia sorella?

9 vero?

10 *a* Quale studente è inglese?
b Cosa facciamo questa sera?
c Di dove siete voi? *d* Di chi sono questi giornali? *e* Perché vuoi partire subito? *f* Quante camere desiderate?

Checkpoint 14 Page 135

1 io ascolto, sto ascoltando
voi scrivete, state scrivendo
loro arrivano, stanno arrivando
lei finisce, sta finendo
tu telefoni, stai telefonando
noi costruiamo, stiamo costruendo
lei cerca, sta cercando
loro chiudono, stanno chiudendo
voi sorridete, state sorridendo
io parto, sto partendo
lui dorme, sta dormendo
noi leggiamo, stiamo leggendo

2 *a* Cominciamo domani. *b* Gianni capisce l'inglese? *c* Andiamo?
d Abito qui da venti anni.

Checkpoint 15 Page 146

1 piangeva: imperfect, lui/lei → piangere to cry
urlai: simple past, io → urlare to shout

guadagneremmo: conditional, noi → guadagnare to earn

sembravano: imperfect, loro → sembrare to seem

dipingete: present, voi → dipingere to paint

fermerà: future, lui/lei → fermare to stop

cuoceresti: conditional, tu → cuocere to cook

prego: present, io → pregare to pray

spediremo: future, noi → spedire to send

ridevamo: imperfect, noi → ridere to laugh

ruppero: simple past, loro → rompere to break

temeva: imperfect, lui/lei → temere to fear

otterreste: conditional, voi → ottenere to obtain

versano: present, loro, → versare to pour

rifiutò: simple past, lui/lei → rifiutare to refuse

spiegherei: conditional, io → spiegare to explain

presterò: future, io → prestare to lend

salimmo: simple past, noi → salire to go/come up

appoggiavano: imperfect, loro → appoggiare to lean

scenderà: future, lui/lei → scendere to go/come down

prometterai: future, tu → promettere to promise

2 arriverò; ceniamo; domanderesti; comprerò; chiudevano; credeva; aprii; scrivereste; pensavano; organizzeremo; pulirai; continuano; sorrideva; emigrò

3 Quando avevo cinque anni abitavamo a Roma. Pagherei volentieri ma non ho soldi. Mi piacerebbe molto andare a Roma. Ti scriverò appena finiranno.

Checkpoint 16 Page 160

1 from left to right: comprato; venduto; garantito; avuto; cominciato; morto; trovato; costruito; voluto; fatto; aperto; creduto; ascoltato; venuto; tenuto; detto; mangiato; speso; vestito; deciso; bevuto; chiuso; finito; andato

2 *a* io ho dormito; *b* noi siamo andati; *c* loro hanno capito; *d* tu non hai telefonato; *e* lei ha usato; *f* voi siete arrivati; *g* io mi sono divertita; *h* lui non ha organizzato niente

3 *a* Non avevo parlato con Maria. *b* Maria? Non l'ho vista oggi. *c* I ragazzi saranno andati in città. *d* Hai lavorato questa settimana, Carla? *e* Si sono sposati sabato. *f* Anna e sua sorella sono partite verso mezzanotte.

4 *a* Non avevo capito. *b* Saremmo andati via. *c* Paolo è arrivato alle otto. *d* Quando avremo mangiato? *e* Mi ero alzata presto. *f* Che cosa hai comprato? *g* Lei avrebbe organizzato un pranzo. *h* Avranno invitato tutti gli amici. *i* Lucia ha finito la scuola quest'anno. *j* Lui si era vestito in fretta.

Checkpoint 17 Page 163

1 *a* aiutando; *b* introducendo; *c* finendo; *d* decidendo; *e* supponendo; *f* contraddicendo; *g* bevendo; *h* distraendo; *i* seducendo; *j* dormendo

2 *a* Stavo cercando un sito web.
b È partito senza pagare.
c Non mi piace nuotare. *d* Sono
andata pur sapendo la verità.
e Dove stiamo andando?
f Preferirei tornare a casa invece
di continuare.

Checkpoint 18 Page 170

1 "Allora … non <u>prenda</u> la prima
a sinistra ma <u>vada</u> sempre dritto
fino al semaforo. <u>Giri</u> a sinistra,
<u>attraversi</u> la piazza poi <u>prenda</u>
la seconda a destra. <u>Non si
preoccupi</u> – non è lontano."

2 A

3 lei; tu would be: "Allora … non
<u>prendere</u> la prima a sinistra
ma <u>vai/va</u>' sempre dritto fino
al semaforo. <u>Gira</u> a sinistra,
<u>attraversa</u> la piazza poi <u>prendi</u>
la seconda a destra. <u>Non
preoccuparti</u> – non è lontano."

4 Questo è il migliore libro che io
abbia mai letto.
Credevo che voi foste partiti.
È molto probabile che lei sia già
partita.
Vai adesso, prima che l'ultimo
treno parta.
Aspetterei se tu fossi con me.
Amo Luciano benché sia egoista.
Avrei aspettato se loro avessero
telefonato.
Spero che voi non abbiate
dimenticato.

Checkpoint 19 Page 182

1 Il pesce non è piaciuto a Marcello.
Non ci piacciono i frutti di mare.
Mi piace molto sciare sulle Alpi.
Mi piaceva andare in bicicletta da
bambino.
Gli è piaciuta la musica sabato
sera.

Sciare non piace alla mia amica.

2 *a* Mi piacerebbe fare una crociera.
b È inutile piangere. *c* Il treno
sta per partire. *d* Ti ho fatto una
domanda. *e* Ho la nausea. *f* È
necessario stare in piedi. *g* È stato
necessario ritornare. *h* Stanno
mangiando.

3 *a* Vorrei partire. *b* Dovreste
aspettare. *c* Vogliono cominciare?
d Avrei dovuto telefonare. *e* Si
può parcheggiare qui? *f* Voglio
vedere. *g* Sa nuotare?;
h Avremmo potuto pagare.
i Puoi aiutare? *j* Deve andare via.

4 fare un sonnellino

Checkpoint 20 Page 190

1 *a* Ho promesso di andare.
b Puoi aiutare Luca a portarli?
c Hanno deciso di partire.
d Fa finta di non capire. *e* Mi
piacerebbe imparare a sciare.
f Si è stancato di aspettare.
g Avete paura di uscire?.
h Avete ragione a non uscire.

2 *a* Vorrei parlare al direttore.
b Dipende dall'orario. *c* Dovresti
rispondere alla lettera. *d* Ci siamo
stufati dello spettacolo.
e Roberto è entrato nell'esercito.
f Non posso fare a meno del
caffè. *g* Hai bisogno delle forbici.
h Mi sono abituato al caldo.

3 *a* Aspettano il treno. *b* Mi piace
giocare a tennis. *c* Ha dimenticato
di andare. *d* Stiamo per mangiare.
e Ho intenzione di visitare
Roma. *f* Puoi chiedere a Maria
di telefonare? *g* Ha bisogno del
numero di telefono. *h* Speriamo di
(ri)tornare l'anno prossimo.

Index